D0501035

VOICES IN THE STREET

Born in Dundee in 1938, Maureen Reynolds grew up in wartime Scotland, a young girl surrounded by adult concerns. There was the endless queuing for rations that never seemed to stretch quite far enough, the blackouts and the air raids, but if times were hard, they were also simpler. Maureen remembers with great fondness her early years with her wise old grandad, the enjoyment of riding on tram cars, and the weekly wash house gossip. Leaving school at fifteen, she came of age in the era of Teddy Boys and rock 'n' roll, but she would never forget her childhood in Dundee.

VOICES IN THE STREET

VOICES IN THE STREET

by

Maureen Reynolds

Magna Large Print Books
Long Preston, North Yorkshire,
BD23 4ND, England.

British Library Cataloguing in Publication Data.

Reynolds, Maureen
    Voices in the street.

    A catalogue record of this book is
    available from the British Library

    ISBN   978-0-7505-2890-0

First published in Great Britain 2006
by Black & White Publishing Ltd.

Copyright © Maureen Reynolds 2006

Cover illustration © Gordon Crabb by arrangement with
Alison Eldred

The right of Maureen Reynolds to be identified as the author of this work has been asserted by her in accordance with the Copyright, Designs and Patents Act, 1988

Published in Large Print 2008 by arrangement with
Black & White Publishing Ltd.

All Rights reserved. No part of this publication may be reproduced, stored in a retrieval system, or transmitted in any form or by any means, electronic, mechanical, photocopying, recording or otherwise without the prior permission of the Copyright owner.

Magna Large Print is an imprint of Library Magna Books Ltd.

Printed and bound in Great Britain by
T.J. (International) Ltd., Cornwall, PL28 8RW

PART ONE

VOICES IN THE STREET

CHAPTER 1

Memories, like fingerprints, are such a personal thing. Those fleeting and intangible yet tantalisingly elusive fragments of a bygone age can suddenly fall into place like a piece from a giant jigsaw, sometimes with nothing more than a smell or a sound.

I was almost four years old at the time of my first clear memory of Grandad Dwyer. The vivid clarity I'm convinced was imprinted on my brain by the excited anticipation of a night-time walk in the pitch-black darkness. It was the blackout conditions of wartime.

Grandad had tied my pixie hood close to my ears, leaving the long knitted ends in a bow under my chin and he was now trying to manoeuvre my tiny fingers into the enormous depths of a pair of gloves that were obviously too large for my podgy hands. I danced around in excitement while he patiently tried to place each finger in its proper knitted socket and I could see by his face that my fidgeting was making his job more difficult. In fact it was becoming increasingly futile.

'Now lass, we'll no get anywhere if you don't stand still.'

'Where are we going, Grandad?' I asked, my voice shrill with the thought of the unknown and wonderful delights of this unexpected excursion.

His face was patient in spite of all the hassle.

'We're going out for a wee walk because your mum is no feeling awfy well. After we've gone it'll give her a bit of peace and quiet tae settle your new brother tae sleep.'

I glanced over at my mother. She was sitting at the fireside, beside the old wooden cradle. She bent over and tucked the well-patched but still serviceable blanket around the tiny newcomer – my brother George. I had been full of delight the previous day when she had appeared home with this newcomer but the novelty for me had soon worn off when I realised he wasn't the dolly I was expecting. Suddenly, as if he realised all eyes in this tiny audience were on him, he began to cry, with sharp screeching wails that echoed loudly in the small kitchen.

In an effort to pacify him, Mum rocked the cradle but this made matters worse. We now had the groaning and protesting squeaks from the old wood mingling with the rapidly rising loud howls from this tiny scrap of humanity. It all merged into a deafening crescendo.

She rocked the cradle even harder but the rhythmic motions failed to stop his fractious cries. While this noisy scene was taking place, Grandad had succeeded with the gloves. Raising my hands in the air with a loud whoop of delight I ran over to Mum. Grandad stopped me and placed a finger to his lips. 'Wheesht now. Don't make a din because your brother is trying to get tae sleep.'

This stern warning stopped me in my tracks but I was puzzled. Surely my noise wasn't as loud as the horrendous racket that rose from the cradle? I soon forgot about it when Grandad

10

approached with my coat.

'Where are we going?' I asked again in a whisper that would have done justice to a crowded theatre.

'Will you just hold your horses and wheesht?' he warned.

He wrapped a long scarf around his neck before placing the ends into his thick, shapeless, sludge-coloured coat. Meanwhile I did a silent war dance by his side, almost bursting with excitement yet desperate to keep quiet lest I jeopardised this wonderful forthcoming adventure.

We descended the nineteen wooden stairs and stepped out on to the pavement of McDonald Street, the baby's cries echoing behind us in a cacophony of sound, rising and falling in a multitude of strident sharps and flats. The cold December air smacked painfully against our faces as we were enveloped by the darkness. I could barely contain my joy and elation at the thought of the journey ahead.

When we reached the Hilltown I was surprised to hear voices in the street. In spite of the darkness the entire street appeared to be busy and full of people. Vague ghostly shapes flitted past us, their footsteps tapping noisily against the stone slabs. Snatches from a dozen or more conversations lingered tantalisingly in the cold night air while misty, crystallised breath vapours from the passing pedestrians floated upwards like phoney ectoplasm in a séance scene from a low-budget film. I was mystified by all this activity, especially in the middle of the night. I mentioned this to Grandad and he roared with laughter. 'It's no the middle of the night, you daft gowk. It's just six o'clock.'

He had brought his little torch with him. In compliance with the blackout regulations this torch had a paper collar around its neck in order to mask the light. This wartime restriction meant that the pale yellow circle of light at our feet was barely visible.

'Eh thought we would go tae the Dudhope Park,' he said, 'if that's no too far for you to walk.'

His words sounded muffled and distorted in the velvet black darkness and the thickness of his muffler. I had no idea how far the park was so it was fine by me. But I could now feel the cold night air seep insidiously between my collar and pixie hood and my fingers were tingling inside the huge gloves. Still, this discomfort was a mere triviality compared to the adventure. When we reached the park we found the stone wall covered with a glittery white coating of frost that sparkled in the pale watery circle of torchlight. I peered at the wall, my nose barely an inch away from the stone surface.

'Everything is sparkly!' I shouted.

Grandad drew his finger along the white stone. 'Jackie Frost does that,' he explained. 'On cold days he paints glitter dust over everything.'

By now my eyes had become accustomed to the darkness and I was astonished that it wasn't as black as I had first imagined. I gazed up at the clear starry sky. I was quite overawed by the cold crystal beauty of the night and would have loved to remain for hours under the canopy of glittering stars. But Grandad said it was time to go home. We marched briskly past the sprawling dark mass of the infirmary then down the steep hill towards Garland Place. This street, unlike the Hilltown, was silently deserted and full of deep, scary shadows cast by the tall tenements with their blacked-out windows glinting darkly in the pallid starlight. We were almost home when Grandad issued a warning.

'Mind now, when we get home you've to be as quiet as a wee mouse and let your brother sleep. If you do that then we can have another treat.'

There was no doubt in my mind what I wanted. 'Can we go for another walk in the dark and hear the voices in the street and see the stars?'

He smiled in the darkness. 'Whatever you like but only if you're awfy good.'

We were climbing the stairs when it suddenly struck me. Surely Grandad was warning the wrong person to be quiet. Judging from the earlier howls from the baby, I was silence personified. So much for sisterly love. All was peaceful in the kitchen apart from the spluttering and hissing noises from the wet coal on the banked up fire. Even the gas-lamp was turned down low. Mum and George were both asleep so we crept around on tiptoe. When I pulled the gloves off my fingers were really cold and tingling. Grandad began to rub them with a rough towel.

'Aye, that's Jackie Frost again. Every winter he comes along and paints pictures on folk's windows with his long nails. He also nips wee lassies' fingers and toes when they've been out in the cold.'

To be honest I didn't like the sound of this guy

at all. I turned my terrified face towards him. 'Eh didn't see him when we were out, Grandad. He must have crept up behind me when Eh wasn't looking!' I wailed, quite forgetting in my panic my promise to stay quiet.

This unholy racket rebounded noisily around the kitchen but fortunately the baby didn't stir. Mum, however, sat up in the bed, propping herself up on her elbow, her slim body encased in a pink winceyette nightgown and her pale face tired-looking under a circle of dark hair.

'Did you have a good walk?' Her voice was weary

Grandad glared at me. 'Just you lie still, Molly. Eh'll make the supper then put Maureen tae her bed.'

He busied himself at the stove while I kept a wary eye on the window, determined to keep an eye out for this horrible Jackie Frost. This was the first I had heard of this invisible creature who crept around nipping you with his sharp teeth and long nails. But I could see nothing of the window because of the blackout blind and for that I was grateful. Grandad filled the tin kettle and I heard the distinctive plop of gas as he lit the grill. Within minutes a wonderful aroma of toast wafted over, a smell that completely erased any thoughts of long-nailed, icy men with nippy teeth. To my dismay I watched as he spread a thick white layer of beef dripping over the hot toast. I hated this dripping but Grandad was shocked by this dislike.

'The world is full of starving bairns. You don't know how lucky you are to get enough to eat –

what with the war shortages and rationing.'

I'm afraid this homespun philosophy fell on deaf ears and as far as I was concerned the world's starving children were more than welcome to the dreaded dripping. I also detested margarine; the butter I loved was a luxury we hardly ever saw.

The house at 5 McDonald Street belonged to Grandad but he had put us all up while my father worked in some far-off boatyard. Dad was a painter and decorator to trade but he had found a job at the Caledon shipyard before moving to England a few months before the outbreak of war. Because this was a wartime job he wasn't called up to the armed forces like thousands of other men but remained at his original job. A 'reserved job' it was called.

Dad was a vague unknown presence to me – not like Grandad with his kindly ways and his deeply lined face – merely a blurred image on a photograph which sat in its dark wooden frame on the well-polished sideboard. It showed him frozen in time, smiling against a backdrop of the Glasgow Empire Exhibition of 1938, dressed smartly in a bright check sports jacket and a pair of wide-legged flannel Oxford bags which, according to Mum, were the trouser fashion of the time.

Still, Mum often said it was a blessing he was away from home because there wouldn't have been room for him in this tiny flat. The kitchen, measuring twelve feet by ten, was enormous when compared to the minuscule bedroom which resembled a redundant cupboard. This tiny bedroom was Grandad's domain and was so small that the only piece of furniture in it was his narrow iron-framed bed with its wafer-thin mattress which he loved.

'There's nothing like a hard bed for your back,' he would constantly say.

This spartan metal affair was in sharp contrast to the big double bed that I shared with Mum. This took up almost an entire corner of the kitchen and had a thick, lumpy feather mattress with a multitude of mounds and hollows. In fact, it was so squashy and deep that I often thought I could disappear forever amongst its downy depths.

The kitchen was lit by a single gas-lamp above the mantelpiece, a long slender brass fitting that could be turned in a half circle but which was normally kept in one position in order to preserve the fragile grey mantle. Usually a soft hissing sound came from this burner but occasionally, in spite of our careful handling, a small hole would develop. When this happened the blue flame would erupt and push relentlessly through the grey filament, a long streaming flame that popped and pulsated in an annoying manner – not to mention the patch of blistered paint on the wooden mantelpiece. But gas mantles were as scarce as gold dust, so we had to endure this distraction until the ironmonger received his allocated quota.

Once, when I asked Grandad how long he had lived in the house, he just smiled and said it was so long that he had forgotten. His grandparents had emigrated from Ireland around 1840. It was actually his grandmother, Mary McManus, who had arrived first, along with hundreds of young girls and women, all seeking work in the rapidly expanding jute mills. Having secured a job in Cox's mill and lodgings in Lochee she promptly sent for her fiancé Andrew Dwyer, married him and they settled in to bring up a family.

One of their sons, John, married Mary Redichen, a blacksmith's daughter, in 1865. The wedding took place on 2 January in St Mary's Catholic chapel in Lochee and was interesting because the bride was illiterate and signed the register with a cross. Still, it didn't stop her having a large family. When Grandad was born in 1881 and christened Charles, he already had six brothers and sisters.

At the outbreak of the Great War, Grandad, now married with two children, enlisted in the Black Watch. Before the war's end in 1918 he was to witness the trauma, death and carnage of trench warfare, an experience which left a deep and sad impression on him – so much so that he was never able to speak about the terrible sights he had witnessed. It was in the trenches that he suffered, along with thousands of other soldiers, the terrible effects of chlorine gas, or mustard gas as it was called. It left him with a health problem he never really recovered from, at least not fully.

In spite of this he felt it was his duty to do his bit in this new war and he joined the Black Watch reserves in 1939. However, due to his age and indifferent health, he was discharged in 1941, much to his chagrin. Mum had a quiet chuckle every time she recalled his outrage at being told he was unfit for duty.

'Imagine telling an old soldier that he's over the

hill,' he fumed.

Mum tried to console him.

'Well, Dad, you're sixty-one. Surely there's other work you can do for the war effort without rushing into a uniform again.'

As a result of this conversation he joined the Home Guard and was soon on duty patrolling the Tay Bridge.

'Eh never thought Eh would see the day when Eh would be reduced to guarding a pile of metal girders,' he said angrily.

Personally, I thought guarding the bridge was a wonderful honour and such was my confidence in him that I just knew the German army would be frightened to come anywhere near Dundee. After all, he had fought them once before and he had the medals to prove it. These medals were in a tatty, imitation-leather case in the sideboard drawer. Often on a wet day I would sit with this drawer on my lap and rummage through the myriad contents, a jumble of old wool, pieces of string and a hundred other delights. The medals nestled together, their striped ribbons still bright after twenty-three years of dark imprisonment. I thought they were beautiful but one day, when I tried to pin one on to his threadbare khaki shirt, he just shook his head.

'Put them back in the box, that's a good lass. After all, they're nothing but bits of brass and no worth a maik. When Eh think back tae the last war when we were told it would be a better world for everybody ... now here we are, in the middle of more strife, and Eh'm reduced to looking after a heap of metal.'

His eyes held such a deep sadness that I was alarmed. I gazed at this wonderful man who, in my opinion, was the wisest person alive. I looked at his grey hair and moustache, trying hard but failing miserably to visualise the vibrant deep auburn-coloured hair that he often told me he sported in his youth.

'You're not old, Grandad,' I said, gazing at his sad, kind face with its wrinkles and deep lines grooved no doubt by years of hard work and ill health. I added, 'Well, you're no awfy old.'

Although Mum sympathised and understood his deep desire to feel he was still a useful member of wartime society, she was still bitterly angry by the offhand and uncaring treatment he had suffered, along with thousands of others, after the end of the Great War.

'Don't worry about not being in the army, Dad,' she said firmly. 'Eh mean, where did it get you after you were demobbed in 1918? No work and no dole money unless you swept the snow off the streets.'

She was referring to that bleak period in the country's history after the war. Instead of returning home to a promised 'land fit for heroes', thousands of men found themselves unemployed and entire families starving or living on the breadline. This sad state of affairs exploded into a three-day riot in Dundee in 1921 when a large crowd of jobless people, many of whom had been cut off from their dole money and were now relying on the Parish pittance, gathered outside the Parish office in Bell Street. On receiving no reply to their complaints of distressing poverty, the crowd grew restless and missiles were thrown through the office window. Three days and hundreds of broken windows later, the riot was over, at least for the time being.

The Parish council decided to make immediate payments to the destitute families, but this small gesture failed to calm down the inflamed workless people who had the bleak prospect of having to exist on the meagre allowance of under a pound a week. Such was the unhappy lot of the average unemployed family. To make matters worse, in 1923 the owners of Cox's mill installed new spinning frames which replaced at a single stroke the jobs of one third of the female spinners. Another injustice was that unemployed men were sent out with a shovel to clear snow from the High Street or else forfeit their dole money. The riot was duly calmed down with promises which were merely a thin panacea, and the 1920s and 1930s were two decades marred by the bleak prospects of the jobless masses. Hopelessness eroded the hearts and minds of countless families and spawned the brave but futile protests of the Hunger Marches.

Grandad had managed to find the odd casual job during this time but by 1929 he was jobless once again. This brave soldier who had spent four years in the appalling conditions of the French and Belgian trenches, fighting for King and Country, was now on unemployment benefit which was a pittance. Mum wouldn't let him forget it.

'As Eh said, Dad, you fought for King and bloody Country and where did it get you? Living on a pittance from the Parish then having your dole money cut off unless you shovelled snow.'

Grandad, being the gentleman he was, was prepared as usual to be more charitable. 'Och well, Molly, it's all water under the bridge now.'

CHAPTER 2

It was eight o'clock on Hogmanay, the last night of 1941, and we were all busy cleaning the house. This annual tradition seemingly had to be tackled before the start of a new year. As usual, Grandad was in charge.

'Eh must say, Molly, that it's a great feeling tae have the house cleaned up before the Bells,' he said, stopping briefly in his task of scrubbing the wooden kitchen table.

While Mum nodded in agreement he threw the soapy water down the sink. Then, after a great deal of rummaging around in the kitchen cupboard, he approached with a tin of Mansion polish and a piece of old flannelette sheet. As he handed me the tin I noticed it was almost empty. There was just a residual ring of dried-up yellow polish clinging coyly to the contours of the tin.

'Now, just put a wee smear of polish on the sideboard, Maureen, and give it plenty of elbow grease,' he told me.

I gazed dubiously at the ring of cracked yellow pieces. 'Is the elbow grease in the tin, Grandad?'

He laughed, 'No, no, this is elbow grease.' He took the cloth from me and rubbed it briskly against the wooden surface. 'You see? It's your elbow moving back and forward that's doing the hard work.'

He stood for a moment and watched until I got the hang of it then he said, 'When you've finished polishing the sideboard you can start on the chairs, and mind you do the legs as well as the seats.'

Earlier that morning, before setting the fire, he had set about black-leading the grate with Zebrite. Now the metal frame gleamed brightly under the soft glow from the gaslight, the flickering flames from the fire reflecting against the shiny iron. Meanwhile Mum was scraping a piece of emery paper around the gas jets on the cooker. Grandad poured some pungent San Izal into a bucket of water and padded along the lobby to the small toilet at the top of the stairs.

'After Eh've washed the floor, Molly, Eh'll leave the doorstep for you. Make sure it gets washed just before midnight.'

Mum was now attacking the oven but she poked her head from its dark depths and promised she wouldn't forget this important chore. As usual, being nosy, I had to hear the reason for this strange ritual.

'Well it's like this,' said Grandad. 'It's supposed tae bring lots of luck into a house when the doorstep gets scrubbed just before the Bells. Then, of course, the first-foot should be tall and dark and that brings more good luck.'

By half past ten, we had finished all our chores, apart from the doorstep. We sat down to admire our efforts. The kitchen glowed with all the hard work and there was a cleanly scrubbed smell in

22

the air, which was a mixture of carbolic soap, polish and disinfectant. The pungent aroma of San Izal also invaded our nostrils. Grandad surveyed his small kingdom for a moment before putting on his coat. On seeing this I immediately ran for mine but he stopped me.

'No, lass, it's too cold and dark for you but maybe when you're older Eh'll take you to see the auld year out.'

I was peeved and demanded to know where he was going.

'Eh'm going to the City Square to bring the New Year in but maybe your mum will let you stay up till Eh get back to first-foot you.'

Mum switched the wireless on and laughed. 'Och, she'll be sound asleep by then.'

Oh no I won't, I thought. I sat beside the fire, too full of excitement to ever contemplate going to bed. I felt sorry for George. He had slept through all the earlier frenzied activity and he was now missing out on all this magical anticipation of welcoming in a new year.

At five minutes to twelve Mum dutifully washed the doorstep then brought out six tiny glasses that resembled thimbles, a small bottle of sherry and a larger bottle of raspberry cordial. She had also changed into a soft green woollen dress with long sleeves and a row of buttons down the front – shiny mother-of-pearl buttons that gleamed in the light. She still looked pale and tired in spite of brushing some rouge across her cheeks. This rouge was in a small round box with a minute powder puff and of course I had to have some on my face as well. The effect was

23

comical. While Mum looked fetching with her rosy circles I merely resembled a clown.

I watched the hands of the clock tick slowly round, impatient for this wonderful New Year to start. Suddenly the quietness of the street below was broken by the noisy clatter of feet and the muffled voices of the revellers as they hurried up the Hilltown. Snatches of songs floated up to the window and one lovely baritone voice rose above the disjointed babble. 'It's a long way to Tipperary,' he sang, the notes becoming louder as the unknown singer passed under the window before slowly fading away.

Mum was cynical. 'Aye, it's a long way right enough. Still, by the end of the night, he'll no know where he is. Tipperary, Dundee or Timbuktu, it'll be immaterial.'

Then at a quarter past twelve, just when I thought I could no longer stay awake, we heard Grandad's step in the lobby. He swept in, gave Mum a peck on the cheek and picked me up. I felt the rough bristles of his moustache against my face and his breath smelled different. It was similar to the smell that wafted out from the various pubs on the Hilltown. He was carrying a small piece of coal and a calendar with a fat, sleek black cat on the front. It had a smug expression on its whiskered face, as much as to say how honoured we were to have its picture on our wall.

'A happy New Year,' said Grandad, 'A happy 1942.'

He took down the old calendar and pinned the new one in its place. 'Now, this black cat will bring us lots of luck and good fortune this year.'

Looking back with hindsight, it is clear that he was one of life's optimists.

Lizzie Callender, our neighbour from the next close, arrived at the door. She also had a small piece of coal in her hand and it was obvious that she had kept a lookout for Grandad, giving him time to be the first one over our well-scrubbed doorstep. Lizzie was older than Mum, a small woman, probably in her late forties. I think she must have been a widow because I can't ever recall a Mr Callender. However, she did have one son, George, who was in the army. She was also dressed up. Her frock was a lovely powder-blue shade with stitched-down pleats from the yoke to the hipline, a style which emphasised her ample figure. I was quite surprised by this well-dressed vision because it was the first time I had seen her wearing anything other than her usual shapeless pinafore and the turban which she tied closely around her short hair. Grandad was lamenting.

'Och, it's no the same atmosphere at the City Square these days. Nor the same crowds,' he grumbled. 'Heavens, Eh can mind when thousands of folk would gather on Auld Year's Night to celebrate. There were dozens and dozens of barrows selling everything from hooters and hats to fancy-dressed herrings. Now, since the start of the war, all the fun has stopped.'

Lizzie was sympathetic.

'Eh ken what you mean, Charlie. This war has put the tin hat on the merriment.'

I was intrigued by all this talk of yesteryear.

'Did you bring back a dressed herring, Grandad?'

Before he could answer, Mum snorted and turned to Lizzie.

'Don't mention the word "herring" to me,' she laughed. 'One Hogmanay before the war, Dad brought back a dressed herring and put it on the mantelpiece. Well, in the middle of January when Eh went to throw it out, it had disappeared. Eh thought Dad had thrown it away and he thought Eh had. Well, this awfy smell appeared that almost made me sick, Eh can tell you. We turned the house upside down until we discovered the herring had slipped down behind the mantelpiece. Believe me, Lizzie, this was one fish that wasn't only dead but damn near cremated!'

I was sitting on Grandad's knee and I could see that he was enjoying all this banter. 'Och, don't listen tae your mother,' he said to me. 'She's just blethering. When you're a bit older and the war's over, Eh'll bring you back a herring all tae yourself. They're dressed up in frilly crêpe-paper skirts and you can get them in lots of colours. Red, green, blue or yellow.'

All this talk of the days before the war had put Mum in a reminiscing mood. 'Do you mind when Charlie, my brother, went to sea with the Merchant Navy? Remember the monkey he brought back?'

She turned to Lizzie. 'He arrived back tae an empty house so he put the monkey in the kitchen and went out to the shops. When we got home the monkey had broken umpteen ornaments and was busy swinging from the curtains.'

Grandad laughed out loud at the memory.

'Och, Eh remember that monkey. Eh think we

had to give it to a pet shop in the end. But to make matters worse, on his next trip back he brought a parrot.'

By now Mum was howling with laughter. 'Don't mention the parrot. It did nothing but screech and squawk and we couldn't get near it. It fair frightened the daylights out of all our neighbours. And us as well.'

To say I was fascinated by all these new revelations would be an understatement. 'Eh wish you still had the monkey and the parrot, Grandad.'

He was still chuckling at all the revived memories. 'Well, the monkey and parrot are long gone but one thing Eh learned to do long ago was knit,' he said proudly.

I knew this was true because Mum owned several garments that had been his handiwork – beautiful, multicoloured, wavy-patterned Shetland jumpers and similar knitted scarves. Lizzie changed the subject to a matter that was obviously rankling with her. 'Eh wonder what the rations will be like this year. Eh hope it's no going to be like last year when the government cut the meat ration to one and tuppence [about 6p] a head.'

Mum agreed. 'Eh don't know how we're supposed to keep a family on that pittance of meat and just one egg each a week. It's getting harder to keep body and soul together.'

Mum sounded bitter. 'It makes me mad when Eh hear that Lord Woolton and his daft advice to eat more vegetables. It's easy seen he's never had to stand two hours in a queue for a single onion.'

'It's enough tae give you the scunners,' said Grandad. 'Eh mean it's all very well this "Dig-

27

ging for Victory" slogan. Eh'm sure it's all right for folk with acres of land but what are we supposed to do – plant turnips and tatties in window boxes?'

On this serious note Lizzie stood up. 'Well, Eh suppose it's time for bed. That's another year brought in and it doesn't look like it'll be any better than last year. It's awfy good to have a real moan, though. It makes you feel a bit cheerier.'

After Lizzie left, we got ready for bed. Outside, the voices of homeward-bound revellers still drifted up from the street. There was also the rasping sound from their cheap and noisy cardboard hooters.

'Still some stragglers on the street Eh see,' said Grandad. 'They would be better off going to their beds instead of catching their death of cold.'

Within minutes of being tucked up in the large squashy bed, I was fast asleep, dreaming, no doubt, about swinging destructive monkeys, colourful squawking parrots, digging for tatties and queuing for that precious commodity, an onion. But it was one Hogmanay I was to remember for many years and look back on as one of the happiest times with Grandad and Mum.

Three days later, with the New Year festivities fast becoming a happy memory, we received a visitor. An official from some department of the wartime hierarchy arrived on the doorstep with a gas mask for George. To be truthful this wasn't so much a mask as a box. An oblong-shaped soft suitcase with a clear panel on the lid would be a better description. The man placed this suitcase lookalike on the table and proceeded to show

Mum how to use it.

'Now this is what you do,' he explained in a slightly superior tone. 'If there's a gas attack, you put the bairn in the respirator and close the lid.'

Then, before Mum could stop him, he went over to the cradle where George was lying contentedly gazing at the blue rattle that dangled from a piece of wool. He lifted him up and carried him over to the container. At this point George gave a piercing wail as would any self-respecting baby who had been unceremoniously lifted from a warm crib and dumped into a cold rubbery-smelling case. The man ignored his distress. 'Never mind about his crying,' he said while closing the lid. 'It's better to have a greetin bairn than a gassed one.'

He laughed loudly, no doubt pleased with his witty way with words. By now the muffled howls had reached din force. Mum stood this for a fraction of a second more before pushing him aside and almost knocking the man over in her anger.

'Right then,' she fumed. 'You can just take this contraption away. The poor wee soul doesn't like it. Shut up like some sardine in a tin.'

She paced back and forth trying to pacify the baby while the man babbled on and on. He insisted that the box had to stay but this official demand fell on deaf ears. Mum wasn't having anyone tell her what to do with her own child. 'You can yap on till you're blue in the face, mister, but Eh'm no putting him in that thing.'

Although she sounded calm, a hint of stubbornness in her voice was unmistakable. By now the poor official was red-faced and very annoyed that his authority was being questioned. 'Eh'm just telling you this for your own sake, missus. You have to keep it. It's the law.'

'All right,' said Mum, conceding ungraciously, 'Eh'll keep it but Eh don't care if Winston Churchill says it himself – Eh'm no putting my bairn in it.'

A look of relief spread over his face when he realised he had won the first round of the battle. He now turned his attention to me. 'Now, the wee lassie here will have her Mickey Mouse gas mask, Eh suppose?'

Mum nodded. 'Aye, she does but she doesn't mind wearing it because she's older.'

Personally, I couldn't understand what age had to do with it. Mum was wrong in her assumption that I didn't mind wearing the ghastly gas mask. In fact I hated it so much that I dreaded the day I would perhaps have to wear it during a real gas attack. It felt like a cold clammy wet hand against my face and the filter cone lay like a heavy and unwieldy lump under my chin. Apart from the claustrophobic feeling I always experienced on wearing it, I found it difficult to breathe when it was on and the glassy goggles always steamed up, even after a few minutes. Then there was another thing: I had seen a picture of the real Mickey Mouse and this gas mask resembled the Disney character like I resembled Shirley Temple.

Now that his task was completed, the official made his getaway, no doubt glad to escape. He was just out through the door when Grandad appeared. Strangely enough, he was unsympathetic to Mum's tale of woe and he took the side of the official.

'Eh think you should persevere with it, Molly. Eh mean, it's for the bairn's safety.'

Because of this attitude, George was lifted up at various intervals during the afternoon and placed in the rubber box. This resulted in furious howls every time and Mum was triumphant.

'See what Eh mean,' she said, pleased that she had been vindicated in her dislike of the contraption. 'You can see for yourself that he's never going to settle down in that, never in a hundred years.'

Grandad had no choice but to admit defeat, but he warned her, 'Well, put it away but remember if there is a genuine gas attack then we'll just have to put up with his howling.'

The object was duly stashed away at the back of the kitchen cupboard and I don't think it ever saw the light of day again. I suppose someone must have collected it after the war's end but I can't recall it. Maybe I was out of the house at the time.

Our second clash with officialdom came a couple of nights later. We were listening to the wireless when an almighty knock clattered against the wooden door. The knock was so loud that the door almost rattled on its hinges and we all jumped up in fright. Standing outside in the dark lobby was an ARP warden who looked really furious and was almost dancing with rage. It was Mum who had opened the door and she was also annoyed by the noise. 'Heavens above! You'll waken the dead with all that clatter. Is it an earthquake or a fire you're announcing?'

The warden was a small man with a sour-looking face and an important manner. 'You're showing a light!' he shouted. 'You must have a hole in your blackout curtain.'

He strode into the room without an invitation and marched over to the window. In the middle of the blind was a tiny half-inch tear. 'There it is! That's the culprit,' said the wee man triumphantly. 'That's the light Eh saw from the street.'

While we all peered at the hole, Grandad tried to humour the man. 'Och, don't be a blether. That wee hole doesn't let out much light,' he said flippantly.

'No much light! No much light!' shouted the warden, repeating himself in his anger. 'There's enough light here for a Jerry plane to beam in on. Do you no ken that Nazi planes have been spotted on the east coast?'

Although this was true he made it sound like our tiny light was sufficient to alert the entire Luftwaffe to descend on Dundee and at this very moment the military might of the German army was now marching up the Hilltown. Grandad disputed this hotly. 'Och, don't be daft man! There's hardly enough light here to attract a moth let alone a Nazi plane that's a mile up in the air.'

The warden, who was still dancing with annoyance, ignored the logic of Grandad's argument. After all, his job was an important part of the war effort and he was one who had to be obeyed. 'That's no the point,' he said. 'What matters is the fact that you're showing a light and if Eh can see it then so can a Nazi plane.'

During all this hassle Mum had quietly taken a needle and thread and quickly stitched the offending hole. 'There now,' she said to the warden, 'that's it stitched up. Does that satisfy you?'

The man studied the repair for a moment then went downstairs and gazed up at the window. We heard his voice calling up the stair. 'That's better. Now make sure you check your blackout blind every night in future.'

'Hmm,' said Mum, as we settled back at the fireside, 'it makes you wonder if there's maybe more than one Hitler in the world.'

Every household had their own way of dealing with the blackout restrictions and Grandad had made our blind from thick black material which he stitched to a home-made wooden roller at the top of the window. The only disadvantage with this was that it had to be rolled up by hand every morning. Whoever had done that chore had caught the fabric on one of the sharp tacks. Mum admitted it was her fault. 'Eh heard it ripping but Eh didn't think it would be seen. Eh might have known the great dictator was on duty.'

Not long after the departure of the warden we had another visitor – Auntie Ina. She wasn't a blood relation but she was one of Mum's best friends. They had known one another for years and had worked together as weavers in the mill. Auntie Ina had married a French naval Petty Officer at the start of the war and she was waiting patiently for the war to end so they could be together again. I was always fascinated by her high platform shoes and her flowery turban – not to mention her delightful tongue-rolling name,

Madame Le Corvec. I thought she was exotic. Ina, however, was on a mission. 'The gaffer in Little Eddy's jute mill is wondering when you'll be back to work, Molly. The mill is needing all the workers it can get.'

'Well, Eh've put George's name down for a place in a nursery but places are very few and far between it seems. And another thing, Ina, Eh'm still no feeling awfy well yet and Eh don't like to ask Dad to look after Maureen.'

Ina nodded sympathetically.

'Maybe when the better weather comes Eh'll be able to get back to the mill,' Mum said doubtingly. 'Maybe Eh'll be feeling much better by then.'

But instead of getting better Mum was to get worse.

CHAPTER 3

It was the last Saturday in January when the spectre of Duncarse Children's Home blew into my life like a cold north wind. As is usual with life, troubles never come singly and so it was on this occasion. Earlier that week Grandad had departed with the Home Guard to some training course. George was seven weeks old but Mum had never really recovered from his birth. On that fateful Saturday she began to haemorrhage and was rushed to the Royal Infirmary as an emergency case. Lizzie had to summon help immediately from Auntie Ina, who had no choice but to make hurried arrangements for our care. As a result, George was put into Armistead Home while she accompanied me to Duncarse.

I remember we took a tramcar then walked along the Perth Road to the large imposing-looking building. At least it looked large to my eyes, this severe house set in its own grounds. I think she did tell me that my stay was merely a stopover until she could contact Grandad, but to be truthful I didn't take much notice at the time, mainly because my mind was on the small dolly she had bought in Woolworths before boarding the tram. Because of this inattention my first clear memory of the home was traumatic. Memory can be selective, and for some reason the first thing I can recall about the place is awaking the following morning in the strange narrow bed that resembled Grandad's bed at home.

I was wearing a long scratchy nightgown and the sheets weren't the cosy flannelette ones we had but stiffly starched linen, white and cold and slippery. The room was quite large, with a window that let in long fingers of watery sunlight which spread like a yellow stain over the dark green linoleum. A row of beds faced me. There was also a strange alien smell of antiseptic everywhere, even on the thin threadbare blankets. Surrounded by all this unknown territory I reacted by bursting into tears. My flood of loud rasping sobs seemed to disgust a small boy in the opposite bed.

He sat up and surveyed my distress with a mixture of annoyance and glee. A young nurse hurried in, no doubt anxious to trace the source of all the howling.

'It's the new lassie, nurse,' said the boy, 'She won't stop greetin'.'

'Eh can hear her, Jimmy, without you giving me a running commentary.'

She stood at the foot of the bed and frowned. She had a round, well-scrubbed face which looked pink and flushed and her hands smelled strongly of carbolic soap. She lifted me from this alien bed and ushered me into an equally alien bathroom. It was a starkly clinical, white-tiled place and the linoleum felt cold under my bare feet. Soon we were joined by a clutch of small children, the residents of the other beds no doubt. They moved dutifully over to the washbasins.

'Get washed – and mind and do behind your ears and your neck,' said the nurse, looking at Jimmy, who grimaced but did as he was told. After she left I burst into another flood of tears.

'What's the matter with you now?' asked Jimmy, in a strange grown-up and cynical voice.

'Eh want my mum and grandad!' I cried. Large wet globules of tears ran down my face and on to the coarse material of the nightgown, leaving large, wet splodgy splashes.

'Well, your mother must be dead or you wouldn't be in here,' he said.

He sounded so matter-of-fact about death and he wasn't much older than myself.

'That's no true! My mum is in the infirmary,' I retorted angrily.

I tried hard to recall what Auntie Ina had said but I couldn't, and the more I tried to remember the conversation on the tramcar the further away and more elusive it became. Jimmy gazed at me thoughtfully for a moment, his thin childish face tinged by a sharp, world-weary expression that for years after I remembered with sadness.

'That's what they tell you,' he said darkly.

On that alarming note the nurse marched briskly back into the bathroom and glared at my fresh bout of tears.

'Eh'll help you get dressed this morning but you have to do it yourself tomorrow.'

As she busied herself with my shoes and socks I could hear the sharp rustling of her starched uniform. Her face looked so stern and I had to choke back fresh sobs when I remembered Grandad's lovely wrinkled face.

We then all trooped down for breakfast. The room was full of long tables and set out with spoons and cups. A bowl of porridge was set down in front of each of us – a thick stodgy mass with the merest trickle of milk smeared over the grey portion. I had never tasted porridge like it in my life. It was full of hard lumps and so unlike the kind that Grandad made every morning. My first mouthful contained such an enormous lump that I knew there was no way I could ever swallow it. This gooey chunk, that felt like a plug of rubber, stuck to the roof of my mouth and there wasn't enough milk to wash it down in one gulp. I was sitting next to young girl called Sheila who I later discovered was Jimmy's sister. She whispered in my ear, 'You better eat it up and don't mind about the lumps, because if you don't eat it now you'll have to eat it cold for your dinner. And if you don't eat for your dinner the Matron will make you eat it for your tea.'

'What? Eat it cold?' I was appalled at the thought.

'Aye, you do.'

With this warning in mind, I tried hard to eat as much of the smooth mixture as I could, quickly skimming around the grey lumps like some obstacle course. Then, when I thought no one was looking, I transferred the five or six hard lumpy balls into my hankie. Later on, when we were out in the garden, it was a simple matter to chuck them on the gravel path.

'What will you do if you have to wipe your nose?' asked Sheila, gazing at my hankie with its traces of cold congealed porridge still clinging to it.

I didn't know the answer to that question but I felt this was the least of my worries. What I did know was that I would sooner wipe my nose on the sleeve of my jumper than eat the revolting porridge.

Later that night the nurse watched over us as we all crawled into bed. But not before we said our prayers. I knelt on the cold floor by the side of the bed, feeling close once more to tears at the thought of being alone and abandoned. I began to recite, 'God bless Mum and Grandad and George, Auntie Ina and Lizzie.' Then I remembered my unknown father and I included him in the list.

'Where is your dad?' asked the nurse. 'Is he a soldier?'

I shook my head and kept my voice at a whisper.

'No, he works in a boatyard.'

I didn't want Jimmy to overhear as he would tell me Dad was dead as well as Mum. Although I didn't entirely believe him, on the other hand I didn't disbelieve him either. The bed was hard and cold, not like our squashy bed at home. I tucked my head under the blanket and prayed hard to Jesus to let Grandad come and rescue me. Then we heard the wailing sound of the air-raid siren.

The nurse rushed in and darted from bed to bed, getting us all on our feet. I suppose Duncarse Home must have been adequately provided with shelters in the grounds but for some reason that night we were all herded into the bathroom. As we crouched under the wash-hand basins I could feel the damp coldness from the tiled wall seep through my nightdress. I had always been frightened by the eerie wail of the siren at other times but on that particular night I could only recall being bored. My grandstand view of the basin's u-bend did nothing to dispel this feeling. Then the nurse began to sing. 'There'll be blue-birds over the white cliffs of Dover.'

Her clear soprano voice was richly resonant in the small confines of the bathroom. Our thin childish voices joined in but I couldn't keep my teeth from chattering. When we reached the line about Jimmy going to sleep in his own little room, I looked at him and he was crying. He quickly dashed the tears away as if realising that boys didn't cry but his eyes remained wet. It was then I wondered if he would ever go home with his sister again. Muffled whispers came from the boys. 'Eh wish Eh could be outside to see the Jerry planes,' said one.

Jimmy made the sound of a Spitfire plane. 'Vroom! Vroom! Vroom! When Eh'm older Eh'm going to be a pilot.'

'So am Eh,' said the first boy eloquently.

As I listened to the dreams and hopes of Jimmy and his pal I wondered if I would ever become resigned to this terrible place and if I had really been abandoned. I doubted it.

After what seemed like hours but was only thirty minutes according to the nurse, the all-clear sounded and we all trooped back to bed. I dreaded the thought of the coming morning and the spectre of the porridge loomed large. Most of all I still couldn't understand why I had been left there. I sobbed quietly, pressing my face into the pillow and soaking it as a result. But I didn't care about the lecture that would follow in the morning. I just didn't care.

I fell into a fitful sleep until the middle of the night when I realised I had to go to the toilet. The routine at home was simple. Either Mum walked with me across the lobby to our toilet or else I used the large potty which was kept in case Mum was fast asleep. But I was now in this strange new environment and although I knew my way to the bathroom I didn't relish the thought of making my way in the dark. Still, I knew I couldn't wet the bed so I had no choice but to slip my feet on to the cold ground. The room was full of dark shadows and strange sounds. I heard a small voice crying for his mother and I stopped, my heart full of dread and sadness at our shared loss of mums and grandads. Then nature urged me towards the door of the bathroom and I quietly tiptoed towards it.

At the window I pulled aside the curtain and saw a moon peeping out behind scurrying clouds. Being well aware not to show a light during the blackout hours I made my way to the toilet with the help of this watery moon, making sure I pulled the curtain tightly closed again. I wondered if I should flush the toilet but decided against it. If one of the nurses heard it then they would come rushing in and I would get another telling-off. I had overheard two of them discussing my never-ending crying and I hadn't liked what they said. 'That bairn will have tae settle down some time. Eh've never met such a crabbit child before.'

At first I didn't realise they were discussing me until I saw them both look over at me. I was miffed. I wasn't crabbit, merely bewildered at my abandonment. Did children ever accept this I wondered. Was I the odd one out?

The next morning brought another ordeal with the porridge. I was in the process of transferring one of the hard lumps to my hankie when one of the assistants noticed. She marched over and stood behind me, her arms crossed over her ample breasts and her face like granite. 'What do you think you're doing?'

Faced by this wrath I had no option but to tell the truth.

She came round to the opposite side of the table and stared at me, her face red with anger. 'Well, now you'll just eat that porridge like the rest of us.'

She stared as I skimmed the smoother parts on

to my spoon, which like the previous day was a big mistake on my part. I was now left with six lumpy balls and hardly any milk. She glared at me and I was forced to put one in my mouth where it stuck firmly to the roof of my mouth. There was no way I could swallow it.

'Eat it up!' she shouted.

I put another two in my mouth and then realised I was choking. The glutinous mass was immovable and I couldn't breathe. My face must have turned blue because she ran for a jug of milk and literally poured it down my throat. Milk dribbled down my chin and spilled on to the front of my frock, but the porridge wouldn't budge even with this waterfall of liquid. I was pulled from my seat and taken to the bathroom where I was sick. The staff all glared at me as if this whole horrible incident was my fault. No one thought of blaming the cook, who obviously couldn't make porridge properly. I was marched back to my seat in disgrace and scores of eyes watched me. Some, no doubt, felt sympathy but the rest looked gleeful.

The assistant who had started it all muttered to her colleague. 'That bairn has been well and truly spoiled. A good skelp on her erse would do her the world of good.'

I didn't think I was spoiled. I knew Grandad doted on me and I felt the same about him but where was he? And Mum and George? Young as I was, I knew I could never settle in there. Never in a million years.

The breakfasts must have improved because I can't recall any more hassle from then on. But still there were tears and unhappiness and I felt I

42

would never see my family ever again. Perhaps Jimmy was right. Maybe Mum had died in the infirmary and Grandad was too busy looking after George. Maybe he didn't have time for me any more.

But time wore on and after what seemed like years Grandad came to take me home. He was the most welcome sight I had seen since I entered this awful place. Seemingly he had come straight from the station when he heard of my plight, not even taking time to stop for a cup of tea. The Matron was telling him about my bad behaviour, how I wouldn't eat and wouldn't stop crying. Grandad was very pleasant with her, nodding his head as if agreeing, but he held my hand tightly as we walked out of the front door towards freedom. The nightmare of the home was now receding with every step I took and I could even survey the lumps of decaying porridge amongst the gravel with a kind of amusement.

'Grandad, why was Eh left in that awfy place for years and years?' He laughed heartily. 'Years and years was it? Don't be daft! You've just been there for a week.'

A week! I couldn't believe it. It had certainly felt like years and years to me.

He was talking about George. 'Eh think we'll leave the bairn where he is in the meantime. He'll no ken where he is but you on the other hand were no behaving, were you?'

I gazed at him with tear-filled eyes, ready to launch into my tales of woe, but he chuckled. 'Och, Eh don't think Eh would like to be in there myself.'

He squeezed my hand and suddenly life was happy again.

We caught a tramcar to the foot of the Hilltown and made our way up the steep slope.

'Eh think we'll have our dinner in Edmond's café,' said Grandad. 'It'll save me cooking.'

Edmond's restaurant at 37 Hilltown was part café, part takeaway, and was extremely popular with the residents of the surrounding tenements. At dinnertime there was always a long queue of women and children clutching large jugs, waiting their turn to have them filled to the brim with the speciality of the shop, a thick hot broth. This ready-made soup was a boon to the workers, especially the millworkers who had little time to make anything as nutritious as Edmond's broth.

But our destination that day was the small seated area of the shop, which meant we had to stand in a queue. This café didn't cater for fancy Cordon Bleu tastes but there was always the most delicious aroma wafting out of the small kitchen. The menu never varied from day to day. There was broth, mashed potatoes with a thick beefy gravy poured over them and semolina served with half a tumbler of milk. By the time we sat down to this ambrosial meal, I had left Duncarse Home far behind me. However, in the evening, I remembered Jimmy and Sheila. I mentioned Jimmy's theory to Grandad.

'Don't be daft,' he said, 'if their parents were dead then surely they would be living in the orphanage. They wouldn't be in Duncarse. No, Eh think their mother is maybe in the hospital. Just like your mum.'

This explanation suited me because I felt guilty leaving them behind in that terrible place. I snuggled down in the feathery depths of our lumpy mattress, watching the firelight cast flickering shadows on the wall and listening to Grandad as he pottered around the kitchen. He had filled the stone puggy hot-water container and it now nestled cosily at my feet. I felt so happy to be home that my emotion threatened to erupt from my body and shower fragmented pieces of happiness into the air like droplets of joy. I believed in Grandad so much that I never doubted his explanation about Sheila and Jimmy and I hoped they would soon be home again, like me.

Lizzie appeared briefly the next morning to give Grandad the latest bulletin on Mum's progress. It was then arranged that the three of us would visit Mum that afternoon as it was a Sunday. It was raining heavily, so I had to put on my wellie boots and a thick smelly raincoat with a matching hat. In its heyday, the outfit had been a fetching yellow but Grandad had bought it from a second-hand shop and it was now well past its best. I detested wearing it. I hated the awful ochre colour and its smell but as Grandad's word was law I had no choice.

When we reached the foot of the steep Infirmary Brae, a deep puddle of slimy water lay in our path. As I waded through it the water swirled around my wellies and it was difficult to keep my feet from slipping. Lizzie was holding my hand. Peching and panting like some clapped-out steam train, she found this added fidgeting annoying. She stopped and issued a warning. 'Will

45

you stop that larking about and walk straight? Or else you'll get a skelp around your lugs.'

Grandad glared at me and I tried hard to behave. When we reached the Infirmary gate a large queue had already formed and it stretched right up the hill. We joined the end of it and moved slowly forwards, a few inches at a time. I had already been warned about my behaviour so I contented myself by gazing intently at the fat legs of the woman in front of us. Each time we shuffled forward her calves shivered like splodgy pink jelly and when we stopped they quivered to a halt. The fascination of this diversion lasted until we reached the door when the plump legs went off in a different direction.

Grandad took the two visiting cards from his pocket. 'Eh'll take the bairn up tae see her mum then Eh'll come back for you, Lizzie. Eh hope they let Maureen in for a few minutes to see her mum.'

The route to the ward took us along endless miles of corridors with dark green and cream painted walls and shiny polished floors. As we hurried along I could hear the squeaky sound my wellies made against this mirror-like floor. A nurse sat at a small table inside the ward, the rows of visiting cards laid out before her like a game of patience. It was clear that the stiffly starched uniformed sentinel with her pale scrubbed face was determined to adhere to the strict rule of two visitors per bed. Grandad handed over the tickets and I caught a whiff of carbolic soap from her hand. For a brief moment the spectre of Duncarse came rushing back. Sensing my tension, Grandad gave my hand a squeeze and I knew I

46

had nothing to worry about. Mum's bed was in the middle of the long ward, directly under one of the large windows. Her white embossed bedcover was perfectly free from even the merest of wrinkles and I noticed all the beds were the same.

Grandad had also noticed this. 'You look like you're tucked up in an envelope, ready to be posted,' he laughed. Mum's face was glum but he continued, 'You're looking much better, Molly. You've got more colour in your cheeks.'

I was held over the bed to give Mum a hug before being told to sit on the sturdy wooden chair. I sat with my legs tucked firmly under the metal-framed bed. It was obvious that Mum was much better because she put on a wry look. 'Eh'm hoping tae be out of here in the next couple of days, and no before time. What a job Eh've got in here tae get a smoke.' If there was one pleasure she had in life it was her cigarettes.

'Eh've left George in Armistead because he's just a baby,' Grandad told her, 'but Eh knew this wee lass here would be unhappy in Duncarse.'

While Grandad chatted with Mum I was busy concentrating on all the bustle in the ward, looking at the other patients and desperate to know what lay behind the pleated fabric-covered screen that was draped around one of the beds. But on hearing the mention of Duncarse my ears pricked up.

'It was an awfy place, Mum. The porridge was full of hard lumps like chuckies,' I said, blurting out my self-pity in an anguished howl.

Mum sounded exasperated. 'Surely it wasn't as bad as that.'

I was about to tell her it was even worse when Grandad stood up. 'Lizzie is waiting tae see you, Molly, so we'll go and let her in.'

When we reached the door of the ward Mum gave us a feeble wave and I wanted to run back but Grandad steered me back through the miles of corridors. Lizzie was waiting impatiently in the crowded waiting room. A constant stream of humanity moved in and out, handing over cards and taking part in dialogues on their loved ones' conditions. The Infirmary allowed such a short period for visiting that should some lucky patient be blessed with a horde of relations and friends it meant a constant bobbing up and down the corridors and stairs.

Lizzie was unhappy. 'Eh'm no sure how to get to the ward. The last time Eh came with Ina and she took me there.'

Grandad decided he would escort her to the ward. Pointing to an empty space on the bench he left me with a dire warning to stay put until he returned.

The benches were crammed with a variety of people, all waiting in different degrees of anxiety. I was crushed between a very fat woman with a tightly buttoned coat and a voluminous message bag which she peered into every few minutes. On the other side was a ruddy-cheeked man who seemed to be dying, judging from the hoarse bronchial cough which racked his body every now and then. In fact, this spasmodic coughing was synchronised with the woman's anxious inspection of her bag and they looked like Laurel and Hardy.

It was the sharp kick in the small of my back

that made me turn round. A small boy, not much older than myself, was lining up his tackety boot for another kick in my direction. His mother was oblivious to him as she gossiped animatedly with her neighbour. Deciding that retreat was better than being thumped a second time, I jumped off the bench a fraction of a second before his boot crashed against the wooden upright support. This shuddering grating noise caught everyone off their guard and almost dislodged the entire bench, not to mention almost giving some of the older occupants the fright of their lives.

His mother paused in mid sentence and yanked him towards her. 'Will you sit still, you wee besom? Or else you'll get a belt around your earhole.'

She then resumed her conversation with her neighbour. 'It was her fault,' said the little horror without a blush on his face, pointing an accusing finger at me, 'she kicked me first.'

Amid his ever-increasing howls the two women became silent and glared at me, no doubt wondering if the tackety-booted terror was telling the truth.

Then Grandad appeared. Later, when Lizzie returned, we had to pass the waiting room. The boy was now sitting hunched up in his seat, a deeply furrowed frown on his pink piggy-like face. Taking my courage in both hands I quickly screwed up my face and stuck out my tongue, rolling my head from side to side as I did so. Thankfully, Grandad didn't see this display of bad manners. Still, even if he had done so, the look of furious astonishment on the boy's face was reward enough for me, even if it had meant a telling-off.

Mum arrived home the following Saturday. She was still not a hundred per cent better but hopefully the coming weeks would help her recover completely. George came back from Armistead and we all settled back in our cosy house. And one bonus of Mum's illness was the fact that Grandad took me out every day to give Mum some time with George. This was to lead to our many trips to the Overgate and our journeys on the tramcar.

CHAPTER 4

Grandad had a large circle of friends but Tam was by far his oldest and most valued one. From their boyhood days in Liff Road, Lochee, to the muddy trenches of the Great War, their friendship had spanned almost half a century. Tam lived in the Overgate, in a dark narrow close that was squashed like some dismal afterthought between two of the busiest businesses in the area, namely the pub and the pawnbroker.

Standing beside Tam's close on a Saturday was like standing at the world's crossroads, such was the colourful human tapestry of life that unfolded before my eyes. On sunny days the public house normally wedged open its inner glass door, a practice that enabled me to catch a glimpse of a forbidden world of sawdust-covered floors, blue spiralling pipe and cigarette smoke and the sharp, hoppy smell of warm, stale beer.

There was always a constant babble of voices from the clientele, mainly elderly men who, even on the warmest of days, would be dressed in their thick, serviceable suits and flat cloth caps. Judging from the conversations that filtered out through the open door it would appear that everything was discussed, from the current price of ten Woodbines to the latest news on the war front.

Meanwhile, the pawnbroker on the other side was normally the domain of women. These women stood in a patient queue, pale-faced and weary-eyed, clutching their threadbare bags close to their sides. In this corner, the topic of conversation revolved around the shortage of everything from money to the humble onion, and the emergence of the wonderful new commodity: dried eggs. One woman was praising them so much that Grandad remarked cynically that tins of dried eggs seemed to be a gift from the gods instead of part of the food plan from the good old USA.

The pawnbroker had two busy days in his week, one being Saturday. At lunchtime the millworkers disembarked from crowded tramcars, their week's wages in their pockets. They would congregate outside the tiny shop, eager and ready to redeem whatever item held some monetary value in their poor financial lives. Then on Monday the same army of women would make the return journey to the friendly neighbourhood 'Uncle' in order to have a few shillings to tide them over to pay day.

Tam lived on the third floor of this narrow close. Its whitewashed staircase spiralled upwards between walls so low and narrow that it was possible to touch both walls and ceiling with outstretched arms. His single-end flat was always neat and tidy, from the highly polished brown waxcloth on the floor to the pair of wally dugs that sat ever so primly, one at each end of the lace-trimmed mantelpiece. There was just the one tiny window and that overlooked a damp and litter-strewn courtyard. Very little natural light filtered through the four small panes of glass in this minuscule window but that light was curtailed even more by the pair of thick brown chenille curtains that hung from a sturdy wooden pole. Seated on a fat cushion at the window was Tam's sole companion, his cat Mouser. This rotund tortoiseshell cat was apparently the scourge of all the vermin in the close, hence the name.

Tam was a small wiry-looking man with a deeply lined face that resembled dried brown leather, caused no doubt by having to live in this dark, smoky room. He looked as if he never saw any daylight. He admitted as much to Grandad. 'Eh don't get out as much as Eh used to. It must be auld age, Eh guess, but Eh still manage to totter down for my messages two or three times a week.'

He certainly looked old, sitting there in his collarless shirt with the sleeves rolled up, showing surprisingly muscular arms. Still, on reflection, if he was a contemporary of Grandad, then he must have been in his early sixties. I never did discover if he was a widower or if he had never married, but spaced out along the length of the old dresser were lots of photographs. Large dark frames encircled the faded sepia-toned images of upright military men in their khaki uniforms and ladies dressed in long skirts and enormous hats.

I would have dearly loved to know the identities of all the photograph people but I was warned not to ask impertinent questions. My curiosity therefore remained unanswered.

Our routine never varied on these visits, beginning with a cup of tea. Our host would gather three enamel mugs from the little cupboard by the window, put the teapot on the ring by the fire and settle back in his high-backed wooden chair with the knitted blanket as sole concession to comfort. He would spoon a dollop of condensed milk into the strong black tea, turning it into a creamy, sweet drink before bringing over the wooden biscuit barrel. Because of the wartime rationing this container never held more than half a dozen Rich Tea biscuits but as I plunged my hands into the dark depths another of Grandad's warnings flashed through my brain: 'You can have one biscuit but no more. It's good manners tae say no to another one, even if Tam asks you to help yourself.'

After the ritual of tea, the real reason for the visit became clear, namely the chat. The two men liked to reminisce about the good, old far-off days of their youth. But before the gossiping began, Tam would rise stiffly to his feet and bring down from the mantelpiece his tobacco pouch and small tin of Pan Drops. Sadly, and to my intense chagrin, because I had eaten a biscuit I had to decline the offer of a Granny Sooker. Grandad was most insistent about this. I would gaze at the tin with my eyes almost popping out of my head. 'No thanks Tam, Eh'm awfy full up.'

Their favourite tobacco was Bogey Roll, a solid

black wedge which was cut and shredded with a sharp pocket knife before being stuffed into their pipes. This produced an evil-smelling blanket of smog that fortunately only seemed to surround the two men. The smoky atmosphere never bothered me because this was the part of the visit I loved. My two favourite spots in the room were the closet bed and the rocking chair.

This bed was tucked away into a small corner recess and had a flowery curtain suspended from a rail. It looked like another window but this was a wonderful and magical secret corner. Above the bed was a long shelf that held all manner of wonderful things, but it was the brightly painted tin which I loved and I was sure it held loads and loads of mysterious items. I was allowed to kneel on the bed but not to touch this array of treasure. Grandad was shocked when I once wished aloud that I could open the tin.

'It's full of Tam's private and treasured belongings and you're no to be sae nosy.'

Of course this remark only fuelled my desire to know more and I would gladly have given my right arm to learn the secret contents of the tin. Instead I had to content myself by looking at the King and Queen's garishly painted heads, commemorating their silver jubilee around 1935.

After a good half an hour contemplating the shelf I would then turn my attention to the rocking chair. It was made of dark wood, no doubt further darkened over the years by pipe smoke. Its once resplendent upholstery, which in its heyday must have been gloriously magnificent, was now thin and faded. Still, even now it was possible to see fragments of its former wine and emerald glory. It was impossible to sit quietly in this chair because the old wood creaked and groaned in an alarming manner. While the two men sat engrossed in their gossiping amid the foul fog, I could rock back and forth and daydream about owning a chair like this one day.

A couple of hours later, after all the topics of the world had been well and truly discussed, it was time to leave. On sunny days, I was always taken by surprise when we stepped out into the yellow brightness which was a huge contrast to Tam's gloomy flat. It was also a relief to be out in the fresh air after all the pipe smoke. Making our way along the narrow pavements, dodging the crowds of pedestrians either out shopping or merely standing around gossiping, we soon reached Greenhill, the chemist, for our weekly dose of sarsaparilla. Grandad swore by this black obnoxious drink and told me it cleaned out your blood, whatever that meant.

Although I wasn't too keen on the drink I loved the shop with its dark interior and long wooden shelves with deeply ridged bottles inscribed with wonderful gold-painted Latin names. Some even had 'Poison' printed on them and my mind boggled with the thoughts of such exotic contents. We made for the back of the shop where there were benches and sat down with scores of fellow Dundonians, all of us eager to clean out our blood.

Every Saturday we would visit the Buster stall in Mid Kirk Wynd, a narrow lane that lay in the shadow of the Old Steeple. This lane also played host to a Saturday market that was always abuzz with people. Rows of barrows and carts lined the lane. They catered for every human need, from rolls of cheap lino to pots and pans. By the time we arrived, there was hardly any room to move and the crush was made worse by small boys on flimsy scooters made from discarded bits of wood and old pram wheels.

Overlooking this lane were the tenements. On sunny days the occupants would lean out of their open windows and chat to their neighbours. Thin flowery curtains would billow out, occasionally wrapping themselves around the owner but she would remain undaunted. Pulling aside this veil she would carry on with the latest titbit, hopefully scandalous.

Because of wartime shortages this market was a mere shadow of its former self according to Grandad, who remembered the halcyon days when it was impossible to walk along the lane because of the amount of carts and traders. 'Aye, this war is fair putting the clappers on everything,' he muttered morosely while gripping my hand tightly lest I disappear among the plethora of barrows.

But our destination was the Buster stall, a tarpaulin enclosure with rough wooden benches around three sides. Presiding at the entrance was an old woman who was always clad in warm clothing, a big apron tied around her middle. A pile of saucers lay beside the steaming pans of peas and chips and we waited patiently while she shovelled out a few spoonfuls of these delicacies before making our way towards the bench with our ambrosial meal.

The canvas cover was loosely tied to the tent poles and on cold blustery days the gusts of wind swirled viciously around your ankles. On days like these, the woman would mutter discontentedly to her customers about the rotten weather, while gathering up spoons and saucers.

Her customers were sympathetic. 'Aye, where are the great summers like we used tae have?' wondered one old man. 'Eh blame them Jerry bombs for mucking up the weather.'

On the other hand, if the weather was sweltering, the owner would be so wrapped up that rivulets of perspiration would form on her wrinkled face. 'What hot weather this is! One day it's freezing and the next it's sweltering. It makes you wonder what those jerries are doing to the weather. One thing's for sure, this war has turned everything topsy-turvy.'

With this profound statement she proceeded to drop the used utensils into a bucket of water that was placed by the side of the door. With hindsight these washing up arrangements were very unhygienic but at the time no one thought anything about it. It certainly never did me any harm.

If Saturday was our Overgate day then Sunday was our tramcar time. Grandad loved the trams and this love affair rubbed off on me. Standing at the top of the Wellgate steps, we watched as the tramcar appeared, weaving deliciously as if inebriated before stopping in front us with a groaning metallic sigh. We always made for the horseshoe-shaped seat at the front of the upper deck but to be quite honest any seat was acceptable. While the tram moved forward in a series of grunts and

57

bumps, we settled back in our seats and looked down with a bird's-eye view on the passing panorama.

One of our favourite routes was the Blackness trip to the Perth Road terminus. Skirting alongside the Blue Mountain area with its multitude of tenements whose small cramped rooms housed hundreds of jute millworkers, the tram gave a sharp mechanical shudder before tackling the steep incline. Moving past dark, bulky shapes of numerous mills that lined this part of the route, we soon reached neat stone buildings with their primly curtained windows. Occasionally, if the light was right, it was possible to catch a glimpse inside some of these homes.

On one trip I remember, the tram stopped and gave me an eye-level view into a window where a tiny woman was balancing on a chair. She held a minute feather duster and she was flicking it over an enormous aspidistra plant. Instead of being angry at this stranger gazing into her parlour, she gave me a cheery wave. Unfortunately, this gesture was spotted by Grandad who duly gave me a telling-off. 'Will you stop peering into folk's houses? It's the height of bad manners.'

When we reached the terminus we stood up while the conductor leapt upstairs and began to slide the backs of the seats to the opposite side so that they faced the right way for the return journey. Sometimes I would be allowed to help with this important job and I moved down the aisle pushing the protesting slats of wood along the metal groove by the side of the seat. This was always a noisy chore and the clanking, grinding noises echoed against the vaulted roof of the tram. Then, after completing his duties, the conductor joined the driver who at this point was lounging against a garden wall enjoying a smoke.

Grandad and I watched them from our high vantage point while they talked quietly to one another and blew white streamers of smoke into the air. After a few moments they dropped the stubs and ground them with the heels of their boots. As they jumped aboard the tram I watched the playful breeze swirl over the pavement and scatter the golden fragments from the men's discarded Capstan cigarettes.

Usually we were the only passengers on this part of the journey and as the tram moved forwards with yelping, spasmodic squeals and a few metallic grunts we were shaken around like pieces of quivering jelly. Grandad held firmly on to the seat in front, trying not to slide along the polished wooden seat. It wasn't easy. 'Eh think these auld trams get more shoogly every day,' he said.

Personally, I loved them and the shooglier the better. I gazed out at people scurrying like ants down the many streets that branched off from the main road. These were dark, depressing streets with a multitude of dark houses and large, imposing jute mills. I also made a mental promise to mind my manners and not gawk at the woman with the feather duster. Should she still be at her window, then I would look away.

At least that was my intention.

CHAPTER 5

My first day at Rosebank Primary School is a vividly etched memory, due mainly to the itchy vest. Grandad was one of the old brigade who positively believed in the 'knitted garment next to the skin' policy. Unfortunately, because of the war, there were shortages of every commodity, wool included.

Women were becoming more depressed by the never-ending struggle and Mum was no exception. 'Honestly, if it's no queuing for this it's queuing for that,' she complained loudly after one particularly frustrating day. 'You get all this advice to mend everything but what if the thing is full of holes or falling to bits? What do you do then? Stitch up all the holes?'

Grandad could see no problem in the wool shortage. 'What about rattling down that pink jumper you've had in the drawer for years? That would give us a big ball of wool that would maybe knit two vests.'

This suggestion was met with stiff opposition from Mum who owned and liked the jumper and could remember with great fondness the far-off days before the war when she had swanned around in it. But as usual Grandad was adamant and he got his own way. Mum was miffed for a few days but the vests were duly knitted, much to my disgust because what they had both overlooked was the sharp metallic thread that was interwoven with the wool. The garments looked lovely, glinting softly in the gaslight when held up for inspection, but wearing one was another matter. I squirmed as he placed the scratchy garment over my head but he had little patience for my gyrations.

'Will you stop jumping about? Folk will think you've got St Vitus's Dance or something.'

To make matters worse, Mum had also knitted a pair of knee-length stockings. Goodness only knows where she found the wool for these. It was one of life's little mysteries but I had my own suspicions. Judging from the texture I was convinced the yarn had originally belonged to a horse.

Then over this delightfully abrasive ensemble was the nap coat that almost reached my ankles. This was the result of Mum's insistence on having a garment with growing room incorporated in the design. In fact, nothing was ever purchased from McGills or the Star Stores unless the assistant assured Mum, 'Oh yes, Madam, this coat has loads of growing room. Just look at the hem. It's at least three inches.'

This flowery phrase guaranteed that the coat would swirl around my ankles for about four years. Then, when it finally fitted perfectly, the only serviceable part was the buttons. In my case, because Mum had insisted on the word 'plenty', I was unlucky enough to get another year's wear.

On the first day of term Grandad inspected the finished result. 'That's grand. You're happed up for the school,' he said, quite chuffed at the horrible apparition in front of him.

I was certainly happed up. In fact I could have gone on an expedition to Everest without so much as another glove but that was neither here nor there as far as Grandad was concerned. Mum came with me on that first day and we met up with a little army of mothers and their off-spring. We all trooped into Miss Drummond's infant classroom.

There was quite a bit of clinging and crying which, strangely enough, came from the boys but the teacher beamed at the worried women, assuring them in her authoritative manner that they had nothing to worry about. She would soon sort us all out. We sat at small desks, looking like a clutch of perky, inquisitive chipmunks, our eyes shining brightly like well-polished boot buttons and filled with an eagerness to ingest our first taste of learning.

At least that was how I should have been. I'm sure I would have enjoyed that first day at school if it hadn't been for the itchy vest. Sitting still at my desk was almost impossible but I tried hard not to fidget too much. After all, I didn't want the class to know about my bright pink – with added glitter – undergarment. At playtime I was glad to escape to the playground shed where I was soon in ecstasy rubbing my back against the rough stone wall. The stockings were equally bad and my legs had thin red weals where my nails had scraped the skin.

I asked Grandad the following morning if I could go to school minus the two offending items. He was shocked. 'What? Go to school without your cosy vest and stockings? Heavens lassie, you'll catch your death of cold!'

Because I knew his decisions were always final I had no option but to put my plan into operation. Before the school bell rang I made my way to the freezing cold outside toilets, nipped into a cubicle and quickly whipped off the vest. I then folded it away in my utility compressed-cardboard schoolbag with the imitation-leather look. I could do nothing about the stockings except roll them down as far as they would go. That way I had only three inches of irritation to cope with.

Going home at dinnertime posed no problems because I left my bag in the classroom. Grandad was a good cook and his home-made kail was so thick it was possible to stand a spoon upright in it. He always made a big potful, enough to last the week.

'Eat it up. It'll put meat on your ribs,' he would say.

The soup was always followed by a milk pudding. George was now old enough to sit at the table even though he needed a couple of cushions on his chair to lift him to the height of the table. He was also learning how to use a spoon instead of being fed by Grandad or Mum. Because of this I always kept a watchful eye on him in case he splashed my gymslip with splodges of Creamola. If that happened, and Grandad insisted on its removal for sponging, then my secret would be out. He would notice the missing vest and I really would be in trouble.

Meanwhile, back at the school the teacher had sorted us out according to our abilities. The two cleverest girls, Ann Roy and Elizabeth Wilson, were at the top of the class while I was further down the row with my friend Janie Gibb.

Rosebank School was a large grey stone building situated at the foot of Tulloch Crescent, a mere stone's throw away from McDonald Street. The janitor's house lay at the foot of the girls' playground but because it faced the grim side wall of the Hillside jute mill it was always cast in a gloomy shadow. If, as the name suggested, it had once been a bank of roses then this rural idyll no longer existed. Any flowery bower had long since vanished under an acre of grey stone.

Our classroom was large and had tall windows that stretched almost to the ceiling. The walls were painted in a depressing sludge colour but were brightened slightly by a colourful alphabet frieze. Printed in yellow splendour on the 'B' section was a beautiful plump and ripe banana. It was indeed fortunate that we had the picture because no one in the class had ever seen a banana, let alone tasted one.

We were all issued with reading books. The storyline consisted of a family appearing to spend their entire day taking cans of tea to their father. Even on schooldays if the children spotted him through the classroom window then their sole aim was to get permission to take him his tea. This was a totally different world from the one familiar to most of us and a thousand light years away from mine. My father was a blurred photographic image and I couldn't ever recall seeing him in the flesh. Still, maybe it was just as well because I couldn't see Miss Drummond letting us all pop in and out like the fictional family.

In any case, I had other things on my mind at that moment, namely Elizabeth Wilson's shiny black patent shoes. Out of the motley bunch of classmates, she was the one I admired and envied the most. She was completely different from the rest of us and especially me, mainly because her school clothes fitted perfectly. There was no growing room attached to her navy nap coat, which had been bought with a total disregard to permanence. She was the fashionable epitome of juvenile elegance.

During that first week I watched her every move so intently that her dainty ways were almost imprinted on my brain. She never got dirty or rumpled. Even at playtime, when the rest of us were running around screeching like banshees, she stood on the sidelines like some fragile porcelain doll. She was a model of perfection from her shoes and snowy white ankle socks to her lovely teddy-bear-shaped hair slides that held her long fair hair away from her forehead. Even something as prosaic as her mitts were beautifully knitted with colourful clowns prancing over the surface.

What was worse was the fact that I just knew instinctively that her vest would be made from the softest white interlock cotton – a complete contrast from my itchy pink monstrosity which I was still pushing daily into my schoolbag. My dark hair was cut in the short Eton crop style and it was sometimes clipped back with a huge ugly kirby grip. Then there were my knees, permanently grubby and sometimes covered with big squares of tatty Elastoplast. I was neither dainty nor elegant and my envy knew no bounds. But it was her patent shoes I envied the most and I began to include a request for a similar pair in my bedtime prayers. I was careful not to let Grandad overhear this plea. He was very strict about asking Jesus for personal pleasures.

'Make sure you pray for the poor folk bombed out of their houses. Some bairns are no so lucky as you,' he would say. 'A lot of bairns are evacuees and away from their mothers and their houses, the poor wee souls.'

In spite of all this sobering knowledge I couldn't stop chattering on and on about the wonderful shoes. In the end, Mum and Grandad were sick of it all, having heard enough on the subject. Grandad was most displeased.

'There is something you've got to realise, young miss. There's more to life than a pair of shiny shoes.'

I stared at him in blank amazement and I couldn't honestly imagine what could be more important in life than pretty shoes. But as usual he was right. As the weeks sped by I soon forgot about Elizabeth and her haute couture. If my knees were forever adorned with grimy plaster then my coat with oodles of growing room and a three-inch hem was long enough to cover them.

At the end of the month it was announced that a medical examination would take place for all new pupils. On the appointed day Mum arrived at the school along with a dozen or so other mothers. They were ushered into a small side room where they sat side by side on narrow chairs, all dressed in their sturdy thick coats and sensible if somewhat shabby shoes.

'Aye, it's a hard job keeping a family dressed these days,' said one woman morosely. 'The coupons don't seem to stretch to everything they need. As for us poor mothers, we have tae take a back seat and resign ourselves to wearing the same old coat day in and day out.'

The group of women were sympathising with this philosophy when Mrs Wilson appeared. Later that night Mum related the incident to Lizzie.

'Speak about being dressed in the height of fashion! Eh wish you had seen the woman's coat, Lizzie. Musquash by the look of it, and she was wearing a wee round pillbox hat with a spotted veil. She also had a pair of real leather gloves. Real leather gloves!' said Mum, emphasising the words in case Lizzie hadn't got the picture. 'And to complete the look and finish off the outfit, she was wearing a pair of suede booties trimmed with astrakhan fur. Compared to her the rest of us looked like we had just fallen off a bus. We were just saying that if her man's a soldier then he's got to be a general or major at least.'

While Lizzie listened open-mouthed to this story, Grandad was trying to read his evening paper. Being totally unimpressed with female fashion and wanting a bit of peace, he said gruffly, 'Heavens, Molly, you're as bad as your daughter! Going on about fur coats and booties when there's more important things going on in the world.'

But Mum wasn't listening. She had a bee in her bonnet about Mrs Wilson's outfit and she wasn't prepared to stop her narrative now she was in full flow. 'Eh'm telling you this, Lizzie. If a braw fur coat like that ever came within my reach Eh would grab it,' she said unrepentantly.

However, as things turned out, I never did discover what Elizabeth's father did for a living as she left school at the end of that term. I mentioned this to Mum.

'Och, maybe she thought her lassie was mixing with tinkies,' she laughed. 'Come to think about it, Eh remember her look when she came tae that medical. Her face changed colour when the doctor mentioned the problem of head lice, saying we had to check every week for nits. Maybe Elizabeth is now a pupil in the high school or somewhere suitable for their social bracket.'

Whether this was the case or not, I don't know. By now most of the class were falling prey to the usual childhood illnesses that beset every infant class when they are all lumped together. It was just my luck that Grandad had a homespun remedy for everything. I was no sooner in the door complaining of a sore throat than he was heating salt in pan, tipping it into one of Mum's discarded lisle stockings and tying it tightly around my neck. Trying to breathe with this contraption under my chin was difficult, not only because of the tingly heat against my skin but also because of the weight of this unwieldy salty lump.

Another homely remedy was the bowl of saps. This gruesome gruel of bread and hot milk was Grandad's staunchest ally in the case of an upset stomach, a bout of sickness or just simply feeling off colour. He would soak a huge slice of bread in the steaming milk then put this obnoxious mixture under my nose. Needless to say I had no option but to eat this pappy delight. His word was law and had to be obeyed.

Sometimes, if I was unlucky enough to suffer from a really sore throat with a high temperature, he would produce, like a rabbit from a hat, another precautionary treatment from his *Dwyer's Homely Cures Almanac*, in this case a lump of margarine rolled in sugar. Seemingly, before the war it had been a lump of butter but the rationing had put a stop to this bit of luxury. This was another cure I detested and I could never understand why his remedies had to taste absolutely revolting. I soon suspected that this was the secret of his medicine. It was a case of the remedy being worse than the pain, and after a while I learned not to mention any feeling of illness. Grandad was also a great believer in 'Friday night is syrup of figs night'. According to him, this gave the medicine the entire weekend to clean out your insides. Another boon was malt extract with cod liver oil, a big spoonful of which had to be taken before facing the hazards of the day.

Sunday night was bath night, with the oval tin bath being brought out of the cupboard with a great deal of clanking and banging before being filled with endless kettles of hot water. Because he was the younger and presumably the cleaner, George was bathed first. The bottle of camphorated oil was placed by the side of the fire to make sure it was warm when Mum spread it liberally over George's chest and back. My treatment after my bath was Vick's ointment. I could feel its warmth penetrate my skin like an internal hot water bottle.

As a finishing touch Grandad would put a thick smear of this balm under my nose. 'To keep the cold snuffles at bay,' he would say but, as I lay in bed, almost passing out from the pungent vapour fumes that assaulted my nasal passages I felt the balm wasn't so much clearing my nose as blasting a huge hole through the top of my head.

It was at times like these, when confined to bed with the salty sock, the awful saps or the margarine and sugar ball, that I used to think darkly about Elizabeth Wilson. In my imagination I could picture her lying ill and pale and ethereal in her elegant bed, eating deliciously cooked morsels especially prepared for her and receiving pleasant tasting medicines from an attentive doctor.

But doctors cost money.

'Where would we get the money for a doctor?' was Grandad's theme tune. 'No, you mark my words, my medicine is better than any doctor's. We'll see what you're like in the morning and if your cold's no any better Eh'll go along to Young's the chemist and get you a bottle of glycerine, lemon and epickeky (ipecacuanha) wine. If that doesn't cure you, nothing will.'

In the classroom one day Miss Innes, the sewing teacher, produced skeins of the same coarse wool as my stockings were made from. She also handed each of us a set of four sharp knitting needles and announced that because of wartime shortages we were to knit a pair of socks for our own use. My heart sank at the thought of a twin for my dreaded stockings and maybe it was this thought that made me hopeless at knitting. No matter how hard I tried I couldn't get the hang of the four

70

needles. It was like playing an imaginary set of bagpipes. As a result of this ineptitude I spent many afternoons rattling down and picking up stitches till at the end of the week my sum specimen was an inch of sludge-grey knitting.

Thankfully, I wasn't the worst knitter in the class because, in her wisdom, the teacher had included the boys in this recreational pursuit and they were marginally worse than me. Still, I struggled on painfully with my tube of puckered-up greyness until it came to turn the heel. In an effort to help the stragglers, namely the boys and me, she drew a diagram on the blackboard, but I couldn't transpose her drawing to the three sets of stitches on my needles. This sorry state of affairs lasted for a couple of weeks, until one wet and miserable afternoon she announced that the socks had to be finished by the following Monday – a mere few days away.

This statement threw me into a situation bordering on panic because I was still on sock number one and what a sorry sight it was. After class I pushed my lap bag in beside my books and rushed home, almost knocking Grandad over with my haste and my tale of woe. 'Grandad, these socks have tae be finished by Monday. Do you think you can turn the heel for me?' I asked, more in desperation than hope.

He surveyed the snarled-up bundle with amazement. 'Heavens! Eh've never seen such a mess before. You're obviously no one of life's natural knitters,' he said in that superior tone often used by people who know they are good at something.

And I knew Grandad had a talent for knitting.

After all, I had the vests to prove it. Mum was also critical when she saw the sorry mess, but in spite of this they each took on the task of a sock apiece. Grandad unpicked my work and started afresh.

The following Monday, the look on Miss Innes' face when I produced the pair of perfect specimens was a joy to behold. Grandad had made me promise to own up to the conspiracy, and although she gave me a long hard look she said nothing and neither did I. I would like to think I tried to own up; I even got as far as opening my mouth, but obviously the socks were now past history because she was placing small squares of material in front of us in order to practise some sewing stitches. So I shut my mouth and said nothing.

Apart from this sewing and knitting, most of our learning was done in a collective and chanting sing-song manner, especially the multiplication tables. In fact, on warm sunny days this synchronised hum was almost hypnotic enough to send you to sleep.

Playtimes were the best part of the day and most of us would run up the steep incline of the playground with our rubber balls. These had all seen better days but they were well guarded by their owners because it was impossible to buy another one. Janie Gibb and I had taken the precaution of gouging our initials into the ball's rubbery surface with a sharp pen nib. My ball was the result of a fortunate find by Grandad just before the war and he had put it in the drawer, where in my usual rummaging manner I had found it. I'm sure it had belonged to a dog in its previous life because it had deep chew marks pitted all over its surface, but it still bounced and that was all that mattered.

We threw it against the wall and chanted with each movement. 'Clap your hands, round your back, over your arm, under your legs,' we sang, making gyrations with each chant. Although I can't now remember all the moves I do know they required a great deal of agile activity.

Another enjoyable pastime in the summer was playing a game of scraps. This needed a book, the thicker the better. In fact, if you were lucky enough to own some long-winded saga you were indeed fortunate. On our weekly visits to the Albert Square library I always tried to get Mum to choose a book like *War and Peace* but she preferred the more sensational Crime Club detective novels. And she warned me in no uncertain manner. 'Don't let me catch you taking my library book to the school for your scraps. Eh'll get a hefty fine if the book gets torn.'

Every morning in the warm sunshine we would all line up against the school side wall with our scrapbooks clutched tightly in our hands, looking like a row of midget financial dealers. 'Show us your scraps!' was the usual opening gambit and, with a quick twist of the wrist, we would flick through the pages to show the three prized scraps hidden amongst the pages. A deal would be made with the purchaser and, depending on the size and quality of her proffered scrap, a set amount of tries were allocated. The tries consisted of opening the book at random and, if the page it was opened at had the scraps, your reward was to take them and put them with your own. As with all games of chance there were days when you could be on a winning streak, while at other times a stroke of bad luck could see you losing everything in ten minutes. One day this calamity happened to wee Rita who ran home that afternoon, seemingly crying bitterly.

The next morning, to our consternation, her mother was at the school gate, standing guard like some avenging angel. 'Right then, you lot! Eh want all the scraps you cheated from Rita yesterday!' she shouted loudly, barring the gate with her plump figure.

I don't think we did anything to cheat Rita but because we weren't allowed to give cheek to our elders there was a great deal of searching and scrambling through various scrapbooks, trying to remember which ones belonged to her. Needless to say, she ended up with more scraps than she lost but she had to pay a high price for this. It was a long time before anyone would play with her again.

Quite a few of the mothers gathered every day at the school gate. It was like a social club as they all stood around on the street, praising their children. 'My Jean is really good at her sums. The teacher was saying she's one of the best counters in her class,' said one proud mum to the group but this remark wasn't going to be taken at face value by the other women.

'It's funny you should say that,' replied one stout woman who appeared every morning in her well-worn baffies, with her dinkie curlers peeping out from her floral turban. 'My Mary is getting ten out of ten for her multiplication tables.'

Because I lived such a short distance from school, Mum and Grandad let me go on my own. Unlike Jean or Mary, whose cleverness was being shouted from the school gate, any talents I may have possessed were not so much hidden under a bushel as buried under an enormous avalanche. Still, this didn't bother me. What did bother Mum and was to become a big worry on the horizon was Grandad's health.

CHAPTER 6

As the warm days of May 1943 drew to a close it was becoming clear to everyone, myself included, that Grandad was very ill. Our trips to the Overgate and the trams had come to an end and I felt very sad inside. As usual Grandad wouldn't admit there was anything wrong with him and was determined to trivialise his deteriorating health as something that would soon pass.

And that wasn't the only problem in the house. There was also the matter of the household budget. For months on end Mum had been struggling to make ends meet but the money shortage was becoming acute. I was vaguely aware that my father sent money home but he was very erratic with it and there were some weeks when it didn't arrive. Although Mum got really mad on these occasions she could still rely on some help from Grandad.

Now, because of the worsening situation at home, she had decided to return to work as a weaver in Little Eddy's jute mill. A few weeks earlier she had put her name down for a nursery place for George in the Dudhope Street nursery but she had been warned at the time that vacancies were very few and far between. Although she knew her return to work depended on this nursery place, one that might not come about for months or even years, she still went ahead with her plans for me. To ease the burden from Grandad it was arranged that I would go to a childminder. This was one of Mum's friends, Cathie Ross.

Cathie lived on the Hawkhill with her two children, David and Sylvia. There had been a third child, a baby called Wilma who had died of meningitis a month or so earlier that year. Because of this personal tragedy Mum had wanted to cancel the plans regarding me but Cathie was firm. It would take her mind away from it, she said.

'Are you sure about taking Maureen?' Mum had asked after the terrible event but, as Cathie said yes, the plan remained firmly in place.

Mum contented herself that her return to work was something to consider for the future as it all depended on the vacancy at the nursery. Then, suddenly, Grandad had to be admitted to Maryfield Hospital. He was diagnosed with pulmonary tuberculosis. Two days after this awful news Cathie arrived back in the house with Mum. They were both agitated. Grandad had stated that he wanted to come home to his own bed and he had discharged himself from the hospital, much to

Mum's dismay. The two women were stripping his bed and Mum was crying. I stood at the foot of the narrow bed as I always did, helping with the chore of tucking the corners of the sheet in place.

Mum's eyes were red and puffy, which alarmed me but, when she dropped her voice to a hoarse whisper, I stopped what I was doing and listened. 'The doctor says Dad's got galloping consumption. He says it's because he was gassed in the trenches during the war.' She wiped her eyes and began to smooth the thin blankets over the bed.

I was devastated by this news. 'Mum, what's galloping over Grandad?' I asked, my words sounding extra loud in the tiny room.

Before Mum could answer, Cathie piped up. She was annoyed by my eavesdropping and she said so. 'Will you stop listening to grown-ups' conversation? You've awfy big ears for such a wee lassie. Now run outside and play and don't bother your mum.'

I would sooner have stayed in the room and heard all about my beloved Grandad but as Mum began to cry again I retreated to the foot of the stairs. I sat there in the sunshine with my book, *The Bobby Bear Album* which had been a present from Santa Claus at Christmas, a time that now seemed so far away that it was almost forgotten. But not quite.

Young enough as I was on that morning I knew something was far wrong with Grandad and I sat in the sun with my thoughts centred on him, not entirely leaving the world of illness to the adults. Later, much to my chagrin, Cathie took me home with her and on my return in the evening

Grandad was asleep and I wasn't allowed to disturb him.

The next morning, before anyone was awake, I crawled silently out of bed and tiptoed to his room. I wanted to see for myself this awful galloping disease that had overtaken him. He lay perfectly still and peaceful. His face had a curious white and waxy look that emphasised his deep wrinkles but, apart from that, he looked just fine.

I stared at him so intensely that he woke up. Giving me a weak smile, he patted my hand. 'Eh'll be as right as rain in a few days, wee lass, and then we'll go and see Tam. Would you like that?' His voice was a whisper.

I nodded happily and went back to bed. The doctor had made a big mistake and whatever had galloped over him was no longer there. I fell asleep thinking about all our trips, past and future. Although I didn't realise it at the time because I was just a child, these were to be his last words to me. Later that day he was readmitted to Maryfield Hospital where he died the next day.

Mum was totally devastated, while I was filled with a feeling, not so much of sadness as of horrible emptiness. There was a dull knot in my stomach. I just knew that this wonderful and vital man had gone out of our lives for ever and things would never be the same again. Grandad had been the pivot of our lives. Our world had depended on his quiet strength for all our needs and he was no longer with us.

It's strange, but I can remember the funeral tea as if it were yesterday. I hadn't been allowed to go to the crematorium and I think I cried because of this but I do recall the atmosphere later in the house. It lay like a thick black fog over everyone. Mum was surrounded by people, all her friends and neighbours. Tam had come back to the house but he seemed ill at ease amongst all the women. He drank his tea quickly, gave his condolences again to Mum and then pulled his coat over a well-worn suit.

I had been sent to a corner of the room with a pile of comics and as he passed me he hesitated. 'Aye, wee lass, you'll certainly miss your old grandad,' he said with a sad shake of his head.

Cathie had overheard this remark. 'Och, she's too young to mind her grandad,' she said, 'never mind miss him.'

This stupid statement shocked Tam and me. He patted my head in passing and he was still shaking his head sadly when he went through the door. It was then, after he had gone, that I suddenly realised how final Grandad's death was. Large hot tears ran down my face where they lingered for a microsecond before landing with a splash on the brightly drawn antics of Korky the Kat. But he was only a comic character and I don't think he minded sharing my grief.

Mum's brother Charlie and his wife and family lived down south and they hadn't managed to see Grandad before he died. This upset Mum a great deal. 'At least we saw your grandad every day,' she told me. 'We've been lucky to have him with us all these years.'

If this was meant as a consolation it was a small one. I would have liked to know him for years and years and years. When everyone went home we sat at the fire and Mum cried for hours and hours.

Later that night as I lay in bed and listened to her muffled sobs I had the strangest feeling that Grandad was in the room. The feeling was so strong that I was convinced I could hear his voice. I knew he had gone away to Heaven but that didn't stop me feeling he was still with us. It was a comforting thought.

The next few weeks passed in a blur of grief. Mum was now alone with two children and she missed the help and strength of Grandad. As for me, I just missed him dreadfully. When a letter arrived from the nursery with news that a vacancy had arisen Mum barely read it. In her grief-stricken mind going back to work was the last thing she was thinking of. She was set on turning it down in spite of our pressing money problems. On hearing this, Cathie said firmly, 'You'll feel better if you get out of the house, Molly. Eh ken how you feel because Eh was the same after Wilma died but you've just got to pick yourself up and get on with life. Especially when you've two bairns to look after.'

Mum was mortified. As she said later, here she was crying every day and Cathie had been through so much more. Grandad had at least had some life while Wilma had had so little. Mum told her this.

'Then you'll take the vacancy at the nursery?'

Mum nodded. 'Aye, maybe Eh should. It might be ages before Eh get another place again.'

Cathie was pleased by her decision. 'Well then, that's settled. Eh'll look after Maureen during the school holidays and she'll be good company for Sylvia.'

The following week Mum returned to her job with the South Anchor jute mill or Little Eddy's as it was commonly called. Every morning during the school's seven-week summer holiday she would strap George in his pushchair and we would set off for the warm and cosy day-nursery before heading for West Henderson's Wynd. We walked briskly along the warren of narrow streets, all lined with tall grimy buildings. The streets that spawned out from Lochee Road and the Scourin-burn all had the same murky, depressing atmosphere. It clung to the many jute mills that lay in this area. It was as if the sun never shone on these streets. If it did it never lingered.

I could never understand why Mum chose to work so far away from the house, especially when the Hillside Works mill was right on our doorstep. It seemed it was all down to loyalty. When she had left school at fourteen she had become a weaver in Little Eddy's.

There was also the fact that wages hardly ever varied from mill to mill. 'It's six of one and half a dozen of the other where you work,' she often said. 'They all pay a pittance.'

During that long summer holiday she would part company with me at the foot of the Hawk-hill. As she hurried towards Brook Street she left me with two warnings. 'Now mind and go straight to Cathie's house and don't get into any scrapes with Sylvia.'

Sylvia was a boisterous girl who, apart from being strong and athletic, was very headstrong. I was hardly the original shrinking violet myself but Sylvia left me far behind. There was nothing she wouldn't tackle and she was forever jumping or climbing over dangerous obstacles. Being no angel myself, I was quite adept at getting into mischievous situations that were always rewarded by a sharp smack on my bottom, but Sylvia left me breathless most times.

The entrance to Cathie's flat lay along a dark and sunless pend and it was four flights up. I was always out of breath when I reached Cathie's door and by that time Mum's warnings had been long forgotten. Cathie's kitchen, because it faced a different direction from the pend, was a delightful place full of sunshine. Her window overlooked an ocean of rooftops that spread out into a landscape of smoking chimneypots. Up until then, I thought chimneypots all looked the same but, when viewed like this in their hundreds, each one had a distinctive and unique character. Sylvia and I would sit on cushions on the coal bunker and gaze at a plethora of tall, yellow-bricked ones and short, stubby specimens. Our particular favourite was one magnificent structure which had smoke pouring out from a multitude of cracks that pockmarked its surface. We nicknamed it 'Puffing Billy'.

Another favourite had a steel hood similar to a bonnet and we christened it 'Grannypot'. 'Grannysooker' was one that let smoke escape briefly before sucking it back again and 'Grannyfatbelly' had a wonderful, obese rotund shape. Then there was 'Grannyhaha'. Every morning we would gaze in awe at this chimney with its tin helmet swinging lazily around. Even in the slightest of breezes it would sing out in a wailing 'hahaha' sound almost as if it were laughing.

Sometimes, if her mum wasn't looking, Sylvia would try to open the window to get a better view but, because we were so high up, this used to throw me into a panic. Fortunately, the wooden frame was so warped with dampness and age that it would have taken an elephant to open it. I would often gaze down at the far-off ground and be grateful for this small fact

As well as the sun-filled kitchen, the flat had another room which, because it faced the high wall of the pend, was dismally dark. For some unknown reason I detested it. Cathie called this room her parlour. It was hardly ever used but it contained the best furniture. Compared to our house this room was pure luxury but I think my dislike stemmed from its cold, unlived-in look. There was a pristine floral carpet square with an edging of well-polished linoleum. The shining grate with its pattern of fancy tiles had the cold, clammy appearance of never harbouring a cosy fire. In an attempt to disguise the unwelcoming hearth, a painted screen with three huge claw-like feet stood like a sentinel guarding the black hole of the grate. I always thought this was a fussy and prissy room with its neatly arranged oak dining-room suite and the strategically placed easy chairs. An overall musty odour was evident in the chill air and a ribbon of mildew clung to the sides of the thick chenille curtains.

There was, however, one thing of exquisite beauty in this ugly room. The most gorgeous doll I had ever set eyes on sat on the mantelpiece. Its creamy porcelain face with the vivid blue eyes and rosebud mouth peeped shyly from under a frilly lace bonnet, while its podgy, flesh-coloured fabric arms stuck out from the puff-sleeved, full-skirted, frothy white dress. I never discovered who actually owned this doll but one thing was always made clear to us: the doll could be looked at but never touched.

Of course Sylvia, being the girl she was, never took a blind bit of notice of any warning and she would drag one of the heavy chairs over and lift the doll from its pedestal. We were then able to hold the doll for a few precious moments before she would clamber back on her perch and place it in its original untouchable position. To be quite honest, I was always on tenterhooks during this ploy in case either of us should drop it. I knew without a shadow of a doubt that I would get the blame, whether I was the culprit or not.

Every morning Cathie would take us out shopping. 'Will you two hurry up?' she would shout from the open door. 'Eh've got to get my messages from the Sosh.'

The 'Sosh' was the nickname for the large Co-operative Wholesale Society shops. Maybe the Dundee tongue couldn't cope with the word 'Society' and had simply shortened it over many decades. At least that was Cathie's explanation. Buying groceries was a ritual in this large shop and so different from our small family-run grocers on the Hilltown where Mum had lodged our ration cards.

To shop at the Sosh, you had to be a member. Members were issued with a membership number and their own members' book. Inside the Sosh with its roomy interior was a long wooden counter with a small box placed in the centre. On entering, the customer placed her 'society book' in this box before retiring to the dubious comfort of a row of ancient-looking kitchen chairs that were set out on the sawdust-covered floor. Here shoppers waited for the assistant to call them to be served once their books reached the bottom of the pile. Every time the door opened a sharp smell of resin wafted up from this floor and sometime a billowing breeze would play havoc with the sawdust, whipping it into a frenzy of minute particles as they were caught up in the draught.

This shop was nearly always busy and six assistants darted to and fro, making up the rations for the waiting women. At the back of the counter and running along its entire length was a marble slab with dark wooden shelves above. According to Cathie, in pre-war days these shelves literally groaned with a magnificent array of food. Huge mounds of butter, fat and cheese had sat in glorious ostentation while whole sides of bacon hung from the steel rail. I tried to visualise this scene but couldn't. It just looked like an empty space to me.

Two young apprentice lads, dressed in long white aprons that almost reached their ankles, watched attentively while one of the trained operatives deftly manoeuvred a lump of yellow butter between two wooden pallets. After a great deal of patting and pummelling, this little mound was placed on a small sheet of greaseproof paper and handed over as the week's ration for one large family. The large, circular bacon slicer seemed to be the domain of another expert who sliced a small side of bacon with his usual practised hand. After a few slithering motions the rashers were slapped on to the weighing scales.

Then there was the biscuit stand. Standing in splendid isolation by the end of the counter it had, in Cathie's words, once boasted a positive cornucopia of chocolate fingers, chocolate creams and other unknown delicacies. Now it was pathetic, holding only a few tins of Rich Tea and Ginger Snap biscuits. It was the same with the brightly coloured enamel tea boxes that had once held aromatic teas from China, Ceylon and India, not to mention other exotic locations.

We waited patiently until one woman left the counter, clutching a tiny bag of groceries. The assistant then meandered slowly over to the box, pulled out a book and hollered, 'Mrs Carmichael! You're next.'

Mrs Carmichael rose stiffly to her feet and hobbled over to the counter while the rest of the women chatted amiably. 'Eh'm telling you, Cathie,' said one woman, 'if these rations get any less than they are now, my family will be starving and Eh'll be bringing in my hankie tae carry them home instead of a message bag.'

Cathie sympathised with her. 'Eh'll be glad tae see an end tae this war. Then maybe we'll see an orange or a banana again.'

'Eh wouldn't mind getting my fists on a couple of onions,' put in a voice from the side.

The women all nodded wearily, glum-faced at

the thought of another imminent mealtime looming and not enough in the larder to feed their families, not even a humble onion.

Most of this wartime talk of rations went over my head. If the shop was exceptionally busy, Sylvia and I would amuse ourselves by drawing patterns in the sawdust with the toes of our shoes. This pastime, however, usually ended up with Sylvia jumping on my drawing and twisting her feet around in an effort to erase it. My retaliation was swift. I would immediately leap on to her masterpiece and scatter particles of sawdust into the faces of the waiting women. This state of affairs was always greeted by a lot of annoyance and muttering from the seated clientele, who reminded us in no uncertain terms how children used to behave in their young day. Not like us, the new generation.

Cathie would stand our nonsense for a few moments before grabbing our collars. 'Right then, you two! Be quiet or you'll both get a belting.'

During term time, Sylvia's brother David would arrive home from school at four o'clock and retire to the kitchen table to do his homework. I don't think I ever met Cathie's husband during my many trips to her house. I had the vague notion he was an insurance man but I'm not certain. Cathie never mentioned him, so he could have been in the army, fighting the Germans, the Italians or even the Japanese. This was something children took for granted, growing up in a strange man-less society. The world seemed to be wholly populated by women, children and old people. I know I never gave much thought to it.

Mum finished her shift at five-thirty and as the time grew near Cathie would bring my coat down from the ornate coat stand and I would rush off down the Hawkhill to meet Mum. I loved this noisy and bustling thoroughfare which, like its counterparts the Overgate, Hilltown and many other communities, absolutely teemed with life. Hundreds of families crammed into grimy and poky tenements and as I passed the 'Blue Mountains' area, I would see lines of washing stretched across windows like the ceremonious bunting in the grand displays put on by the residents of Bernard Street at times of national rejoicing.

When I reached the mill, I waited until the wailing sound of the 'Bummer' died away and I knew she would soon appear amongst the throng of mill workers. She knew the nursery liked to discharge their small residents by six o'clock and it was always a rush to meet this deadline. Still, we always got there in time. This routine lasted until school resumed in August but when Christmas came I was back with Cathie again.

On Christmas Eve we appeared at the nursery as usual, only to discover that the nurses had organised a party for the toddlers. We peered through the window and saw the tiny children with crudely made paper hats on their heads. They were tottering around on small legs, playing a game. Then they scampered towards the table which held a couple of plates of bread and marge. George and another small boy came into view. They were both dressed in the regulation smocks and they were squabbling over something.

It soon became clear that the boy wanted not

only his own sandwich but George's as well. My brother, with a fierce obstinate look on his face, held his bread high over his head and took to his heel with the little bully close by. Suddenly and without warning the boy slipped and landed on his own sandwich. How he managed this acrobatic feat was anyone's guess but as he stood up we could see the doughy white square glued firmly to his bum like a bread poultice. His face crumpled and he threatened to erupt into a flood of tears. His expression was priceless as he searched for the lost sandwich, looking on the ground and under the benches, but in vain.

Meanwhile George rubbed salt into the wound by standing on the sidelines stuffing his bread into his mouth like a stoker shovelling coal into a boiler. By now Mum and I were reduced to fits of laughter at the innocent antics of the two toddlers and for a brief moment we almost forgot that this would be our first Christmas without Grandad.

As Christmas Day was a normal working day at the mill we had the usual routine of getting up early and hitting the road. Still, I was full of anticipation at the thought of a visit from Santa. Jumping out of bed on Christmas morning I found to my delight that he had left me a tiny bag of sweeties, a couple of pennies and a newspaper-wrapped parcel. I opened this parcel with trembling fingers and to my intense delight there was a lovely black doll which, before the word 'racist' entered our vocabulary, was popularly known as a 'darkie doll'. However, this doll was dressed in a tartan outfit – it was a Scottish darkie doll with a kilt and a dashing tammy with a real feather. It was a lovely present and I couldn't believe my good luck that Santa had chosen me for its owner.

George's parcel held a tinplate train set. While Mum hurried around getting ready for work she had just enough time to put the rails in a small circle and wind up the train. George sat in wide-eyed fascination as it clicked its way around the track, disappearing for a brief second under the tiny tin tunnel. Unfortunately, there wasn't time to let him play with it and as we hurried along the cold street with the bitter December wind whipping in our faces, he wouldn't stop crying for his train.

I was lucky because I was allowed to take my doll to Cathie's. I clutched it tightly in my arms, keeping a watchful eye on the feather, which happily was firmly attached to the tammy.

Mum tried to console George. 'You can play all night with your train set, my wee pet. You can't take it to the nursery in case it gets mixed up with the other toys. You might never see it again.'

I was really dubious about letting Sylvia see my doll in case she either broke it or tore its clothes off. But I needn't have worried because Santa had also brought her a doll. Her doll wasn't as pretty as mine but that was just my opinion. Hers was a plain doll with pink cheeks and a floral dress and pants, not so nice as my kiltie. Cathie kept asking me if I liked my present, especially the outfit. 'What do you think about the kiltie outfit? Do you like it? What a braw tammy and a feather! Do you like it?'

Mere words could never describe my liking for

my doll and I simply nodded, my eyes alight with pleasure. I thought nothing about this questioning at the time, and it was only years later that I discovered Dad had sent the two gifts to George and me, but, like all dolls sold then, mine had had no clothes. Cathie had volunteered to make the wonderful outfit from an old tartan scarf. She had even gone to the bother to extract a feather from her pillow with a pair of tweezers. It had taken a few extractions before she had obtained the fat and imposing specimen that had adorned the tammy.

As she had also made the outfit for Sylvia's doll it would appear that our wide-eyed love for the parlour doll hadn't gone unnoticed. Later that night George played endlessly with his train but, although she tried to hide it, Mum cried because she missed Grandad. I missed him as well, in a terrible sad way that even the wonderful doll couldn't quite erase.

That was how our first Christmas without him ended - with laughter turning to tears.

CHAPTER 7

Living in the next close was a family called Doyle. Mr and Mrs Doyle had five daughters, ranging from May and Rose who were ages with George and myself down to a baby a few months old. There wasn't a woman in the street that Mum admired more than Mrs Doyle. She was small and pretty with an industrious nature and she kept both her home and her family in a spotless, bandbox fashion. This cleanliness no doubt would be taken for granted nowadays but back in wartime Dundee it was no mean feat. Although the family had the same accommodation as us, namely a cold-water tap, two small rooms and an outside toilet, the girls were always turned out like new pins.

Also like us, Mrs Doyle had no outside drying facilities and had to hang clothes on a wooden pulley in the kitchen. She extended her drying capabilities by stretching a rope across her window which every night without fail held a row of white ankle socks, vests and pants. Placed along the length of the windowsill were five pairs of white sandshoes which had been whitened with Meltonian chalk paste and left out in the evening sunshine to dry.

May and I were chums but we were as different as chalk and cheese. This difference was evident after such boisterous games as 'tig' or 'kick the can' from which May would emerge as crisp as a mountain daisy while I looked as if I had been down a coal mine. Mum soon noticed this state of affairs.

'Would you look at yourself, coming in here like some mucky toerag! Eh can't understand why you can't keep yourself as clean as May,' she said, throwing a disgusted and baleful look in my direction.

It was the same story when she noticed the family going off to the chapel on Sunday. The girls would be immaculately dressed in cotton frocks and the ever-white socks and shoes while their hair fell in long, rippling ringlets. This soft, spiral hairstyle was achieved by their mum spending an hour or more the previous evening winding long strips of material around thin strands of hair.

'Would you look at the Doyle lassies going away to the chapel? Eh don't know how their mother keeps them so clean. Eh've a hard enough job with just the two of you.' Mum shook her head in wonder.

I had a theory about this and it all boiled down to the sandshoes. I had rotten old black ones while May had the spanking white ones.

'Well, if Eh can maybe get white sandshoes Eh could look like May,' I suggested, quite pleased by my perceptive insight.

Mum treated this statement with the derision it deserved.

'White sandshoes! White sandshoes! Am Eh hearing you right?' She shook her head in amazement, 'If you had white sandshoes, Eh would have to spend half the day whitening them and you would have to sit with your feet hanging out the window for the entire night. And another thing, what has white sandshoes to do with that huge rip in your frock and that tousled hairstyle?'

Actually, I was hoping she hadn't noticed the inch-long tear in my frock, a gash that had been caused by the barely submerged nail in the shed at 108 Hilltown where Jessie Matthews, Amy Ross, Marlene Blacklock and myself had all squeezed during a game of hide-and-seek. Mum was now ranting and she seemed to have a bee in her bonnet about this small rip. 'Eh wouldn't mind so much if Eh had bought it but you got it as a present from Mrs Knight. What do you think she's going to say when she sees how badly you've treated it?'

Mrs Knight also lived at 108 Hilltown and her windows overlooked ours. Every night after school I would pick up her shopping list and collect her messages along with our own. She was an elderly woman who, as far as I know, lived alone. I don't remember ever seeing her dressed in anything other than a black dress over which was tied a tea apron with huge, gaudily printed flowers bursting colourfully over the cotton surface. I think she must have owned an entire wardrobe of these aprons because I can't recall seeing the same one twice. It was rumoured by the neighbours that these aprons were changed hourly but whether that was true or not I didn't know. What I did know was that she was a lovely, kindly woman who really appreciated my help with her shopping.

There was only one thing wrong: I suspected that she thought I suffered from malnutrition. This was the only explanation for her habit of reaching into the bread bin the moment I showed my face in the house. While I watched in fascinated revulsion, she proceeded to spread the bread with a thick layer of margarine and a sprinkling of sugar. 'Now, Maureen, Eh ken you must be hungry so just tuck in,' she said as she handed over the obnoxious sandwich.

I must admit to feeling hungry most of the day but for some unknown reason I couldn't stomach this culinary delight. Perhaps it was memories of

Grandad's sugar-coated balls of marge that he dished out so regularly when I was ill as a small child that damped down any hunger pangs on my part. I often tried to tell her that I didn't like sugar on bread but she never listened.

'No, no, just you eat it up. After all, you run tae the shops for me so it's the least Eh can do.'

As a result of her inability to listen to my protests, I had no qualms about pushing this revolting sandwich through the metal grille of a drain that was conveniently placed at the foot of her close. I watched as the bread dropped to the dark depths and landed with a squelching plop in the pool of stagnant water that lay forever at the foot of this drain. I hated throwing food away but I consoled myself with the thought that it could be worse. She could have insisted that I eat her delicacy in the kitchen, right under her nose.

Our ration books were registered with George Kidd's grocer shop. This shop straddled the corner of the Hilltown and Rosebank Street and was so small that if four customers stood side by side it was like being a sardine in a can. Mum had two pleasures in her life: her cigarettes and her cup of tea. The tea ration of a paltry couple of ounces a week was never enough so Mum had an arrangement with the owner, who allowed her to be a bit ahead with her coupons. If the owner's daughter Rita was behind the counter she would look perplexed at my request.

'A half pound of biscuits, a lippie of tatties, half a pound of marge and our cheese ration,' I said, rattling off the list that Mum had written out before going to work that morning. (A 'lippie'

95

was a Scots measure for dry goods that varied from district to district but was roughly equivalent to one and three-quarter pounds.) 'Mum also says can she have two ounces of tea. We've used up the last four week's rations but she wonders if we can start on next month's coupons.'

Rita held up her hand in despair. 'Wait a minute! Hold your horses till Eh have a wee peek at your ration book.'

She departed into the tiny backshop and I could hear her raking through her file of the government-issued coupons. 'Here we are. Tell your mum that she's now on week two of next month and that makes her five weeks ahead.'

I gathered together my small pile of groceries and placed them in Mrs Knight's voluminous message bag, which had obviously been purchased in the good old days before the war. Now, of course, a whole year's rations could fit comfortably into it with room to spare. Mrs Knight was a customer at Liptons, the shop almost opposite George Kidd's. The founder, Sir Thomas Lipton, would have sympathised with Mum's love of tea and he would have applauded her arrears with her ration because tea was the source of his vast fortune. One of his sayings had been quoted in the newspapers: 'Tea at a rate of 2000 cups apiece per year has turned us into a nation of optimists.'

But that had been long before this wartime shortage of everything. Liptons was a roomy shop with three counters but, like all wartime shops, it had the empty look that echoed the shortages.

'A quarter pound of polony sausage and Mrs

Knight's sugar and cheese ration,' I said, as the assistant hovered into view, '...please.' I remembered to add the last word because Grandad had been most insistent on good manners when he was alive.

I loved watching her cut the muslin-wrapped chunk of cheese. This would be halved and quartered by a thick wire attached to two pieces of wood. A small section would then be placed on the marble slab and she would proceed to cut a thin yellow sliver of cheese that constituted the measly weekly allowance. This sliver was often so thin that it was possible to see the wrapping paper through it.

My next port of call was Harry Dick's butcher shop.

'Half a pound of sausages and a quarter of mince ... please.'

The young butcher, who was Jessie Matthews' older brother, handed over the tiny parcel. 'Tell your mother that she's only got a tanner left on her meat ration,' he said cheerfully.

I promised to pass on this important message. Mum may have been able to wheedle her tea ration but she never tried this ploy with the butcher. By now all my errands were safely tucked up in the roomy bag and I was left with the worst task of all: trying to get Mum's cigarettes.

I made my way to Lottie Henderson's newsagent shop, passing the long, straggling queue at Burnett's bakery as they waited patiently for rolls and bread which were off the ration. Along with potatoes, this bread proved to be a great filler-up for growing families. Yet there were days during these traumatic times when even the bread supplies were scarce. Because of this, Mum would normally nip up to the bakery before going to the mill and buy our supply straight from the bakers. Even at that early time of the morning there would often be a long queue.

But, to get back to the cigarettes... Lottie was another person with a tiny shop. She was partially hidden behind a huge mound of newspapers that threatened to overflow into the backshop. So high was this paper mini-mountain that often the customer would see only her head. She knew what I wanted before I opened my mouth. 'Sorry but Eh've no fags left. Eh sold my last five Woodbines ten minutes ago.'

She sounded apologetic and I knew this was genuine. She wasn't like some retailers who kept all their merchandise, not only tobacco, under the counter for those and such as those.

Mr McConnachie's shop at 93 Hilltown was very different from Lottie's. His counter was not so much bare as spartan. Perhaps in prewar days he had kept a huge stock of goods but now he seemed only to stock a few newspapers. Still, I could nearly always count on getting Mum's cigarettes here. 'Ten Woodbines, please,' I asked hopefully.

He was a small and thin middle-aged man with sandy-coloured hair that had started to recede. He had been great friends with Grandad and because of this he was very good to us. With hindsight this helpful attitude was a pity because if he hadn't been so good in keeping Mum's cigarettes for her she would maybe have had to give up smoking because of the acute shortage of tobacco. 'Eh can let you have Turf or Players Weights but Eh've no Woodbines,' he said sadly.

Sometimes May would accompany me on my shopping trips but merely as a bystander. Her mother did all their shopping while May was at school in St Mary's Primary in Forebank Road, a leisurely state of affairs that made me grumpy sometimes.

Once a week, Mum would unhook the accumulator from the back of the wireless so that I could take it over to be recharged at French and Macdonald's radio shop. I hated this task almost as much as the daily trek for cigarettes. Clutching the accumulator in both hands, I walked slowly down the stairs, carefully watching each step in case I tripped with the heavy, ridged-glass container.

May enlightened me one afternoon regarding this cargo. 'That accumulator is full of acid and if it splashes on your hand the skin comes off.'

I was totally amazed by this statement because I hadn't given it a great deal of thought. I had always imagined the liquid inside to be something as innocuous as water.

'You mean Eh'll lose all the skin on my hand?' I was alarmed and it showed.

She nodded. 'Aye, it's acid and it burns you,' she replied coolly.

Her equanimity was fully justified because she wasn't the one holding the dangerous object. I couldn't tell if this revelation was true or not but I was always more careful afterwards than ever before. Sometimes, when crossing the road I would spot the rag-and-bone man with his tiny cart and pony. On these occasions I would have this terrible vision of the animal rearing up and bringing his hooves down on the accumulator, charging around like the horses we saw every week in cowboy films at the Plaza cinema matinee. Fortunately, and much to my relief, the wee pony plodded along with a hangdog expression. This little horse obviously had all the worries of the equine world on his flanks.

When Mum arrived home from the mill, I passed on the butcher's message.

'Heavens! If it's no one thing, it's the other,' she sighed. 'Down to our last bit of beef and no wireless tae cheer us up.'

From the way she emphasised her words I got the impression she was more depressed about being without her beloved wireless than having only a measly sixpence-worth of beef rations left.

This state of mind was understandable because there was little the housewives could do about the amount of food allocated weekly and they were growing tired of this unending situation. At least with the wireless people could forget their daily worries for a short time and laugh and sing along with programmes such as *ITMA* or *Music While You Work* or listen to the rich, treacly voice of Wilfred Pickles sliding down the airwaves. Wilfred hosted a quiz programme with his wife Mabel. On this show, one correct answer earned the contestant two shillings and sixpence and two correct were rewarded with five shillings. Successful contestants would hear Wilfred advising Mabel to 'give them the money'. As it was, it was only well-heeled people who could afford to own two accumulators and have their entertainment non-stop.

While Mum was grumbling I was busy reading the evening paper. I liked the 'Aunt Joan' children's column and 'Button's Biography'. It was then I spotted 'Mona's Topical Tips' and her recipe for a meatless dish.

'Here you are, Mum. You don't need to worry about beef because Mona says you can make a pie with just two pounds of root vegetables, three bottled tomatoes or tomato sauce plus dried egg, marge and flour for the pastry.'

Mum was amazed. 'Bottled tomatoes or sauce? Where does that woman think we all live – Pasadena, California?'

Now Pasadena was the favourite word for Utopia, made famous no doubt by the popular song 'Home in Pasadena' which everyone whistled. Anything glamorous or unobtainable in wartime Britain was no doubt in plentiful supply in far-off Pasadena. Lucky them! Still, there was no doubt about that wonderful commodity, dried egg. It had arrived on Britain's shores during the early part of the war as part of the American Lease-Lend pact and it proved to be the mainstay of many a diet.

A few days later, May appeared with half an orange while Jessie Matthews had a whole one. Later that evening, Mrs Doyle told Mum a story of outright greed. Apparently, the fruit shop in Ann Street had received a consignment of oranges and word of this had spread, as it always did, at the speed of light. Within a half-hour a large queue had formed, with people arriving from almost a mile away.

'You wouldn't credit it,' said Mrs Doyle, 'everybody was tae get two oranges each, on a first come, first served basis. Well, everything went well to start with until a couple of women got greedy and rejoined the queue. They managed to get six oranges each before they were twigged. So, of course the owner stopped selling them. You aye get some folk spoiling everything for the others.'

Mum was annoyed at this practice. 'You would think it would be a better policy for the shop to sell oranges on a Saturday afternoon when the mill workers are no working, instead of the same greedy folk getting everything. It's just no fair.'

But, fair or not, that was the way it was. Food on the ration was fairly distributed but anything off the ration was a different matter. As Mrs Doyle said, there would always be greedy people. While the unfair method of selling oranges annoyed Mum intensely, the new policy of selling cigarettes left her incensed.

Mr McConnachie broke the bad news. 'You'll find that every packet of fags now has tae include two Pasha cigarettes in it.' He shook his head sadly as if this state of affairs had been dreamed up by him. He pointed out the alien tobacco to me.

'These two oval ones are Turkish. That's why they're called Pasha.'

Lizzie, our neighbour, was in the house when I broke this latest bit of news on the tobacco front. Mum surveyed the cigarettes with suspicion before venturing to light one. A slightly sweet and sickly smoke rose in the air with a strange blue haze. It made us all feel queasy.

'Och, for heaven's sake!' spluttered Mum, 'Eh've never smoked anything as revolting as this. It's like being in a harem in the Casbah.' As Mum rarely visited North Fife, let alone North Africa or Turkey, this was pure supposition. Nevertheless, these oval cigarettes were relegated to the sideboard drawer to be used only in the direst of emergencies.

Lizzie, being a non-smoker, couldn't understand this passion. 'Do you no think this would be a good time to give them up, Molly?' she suggested.

Mum agreed with her but admitted that it wasn't easy to give up. She did say she wasn't as bad as some people she knew who saved all their fag ends in a tin before making a new cigarette out of them.' Mum shuddered. 'They must be smoking pure nicotine.'

Meanwhile May had discovered a shop in Ann Street, that catered for the Catholic community had received a supply of angel scraps. We all loved playing with our scraps but they were nearly as non-existent as everything else. As luck would have it, I almost jeopardised my chances of buying these desirable scraps because of an unfortunate episode in St Mary's chapel in Forebank Road.

Like all calamities it began innocently enough when I went with May one day to the chapel as she said she had to see the priest. She left me outside and warned me to stay there until she returned but I got bored and wandered inside. It was beautiful with its high, vaulted ceiling, its vast, roomy interior lined with cool stone walls and the lovely statuettes of Jesus and the Madonna and Child. The glorious altar was enclosed with a fretted wooden fenced structure and the entire place was filled with the fragrant scent of old wood and a potpourri perfume from thousands of floral displays over the years.

I was waiting in the quiet hush when I saw the elderly woman. Dressed entirely in black, she was standing in front of a wrought-iron, heart-shaped candleholder which was half-full of guttering and smoking candles. As I watched she tugged out a stub and replaced it with a new one from a box that lay under the magnificent display. After she left I decided to get a better look at this blazing wonder. Most of the candles were flickering gently but others were almost burnt out. They lay in their holders, an inch of melted wax encircling a blackened wick. I decided to remove them and replace them with new ones and I had just completed this action when May appeared with the priest. He was a heavily-built man with a fierce red face and when he saw me he hurried over with a furious expression. 'Did you light those candles?' he demanded.

As I nodded wordlessly he pointed to a money-box which I had overlooked in the splendour of the glowing display. 'You're supposed to put a penny into the box every time you light a candle!' he shouted.

As I shook my head to say that no money had been put in the box he almost threw me out of the premises.

'Get out and don't come back!'

When we were outside May explained the ritual. 'Folk light a candle when they want tae pray for someone.'

'Eh didn't know that,' I said, now totally unhappy about the whole sorry affair. 'Eh just thought that if one candle went out you replaced it with another.'

I decided I should go back in and apologise but I was barely inside the door when the red-faced priest saw me and hurried down the aisle towards me. At that moment a gust of wind whistled through the open door and caught the edge of his long black cassock, making it billow up behind him. This turned his advancing figure into the semblance of a demented bat. I took one terrified look and turned on my heels and ran, almost knocking May over on the pavement in my haste. May was really worried that he would report my misbehaviour to her mother. I don't think Mrs Doyle would have been amused.

As it was I was almost afraid to go into the Ann Street shop for scraps in case the priest had issued a description, a sort of juvenile identikit, to the elderly lady who served behind the counter. However, she handed over a sheet of scraps without batting an eyelid.

Then another incident occurred, this time with George and Rose Doyle. One minute they were playing in the street and the next they had vanished, almost right under the noses of the two mothers. Everyone was in an uproar and people were dispatched to search for the two toddlers. It seemed as if they had disappeared completely. A few hours later someone suggested going to the

police station in Bell Street. The two women
headed off and found the refugees sitting quite
happily drinking lemonade and playing with a
train set. They were so engrossed in it that they
screamed and howled when it was time to go
home.

Mum and Mrs Doyle were definitely not amused. After the recalcitrant pair were tucked up in
bed the two women discussed the day's events.
'Eh've never had such a red face in all my life,'
said Mum, 'with all those outraged howls and
antics from the bairns.'

Mrs Doyle, who was equally annoyed, agreed.
'That bobby will think we're bad to them. Maybe
he thinks we give them a good hammering every
night.'

May had her first communion the following
Sunday. She appeared dressed like a miniature
bride in her lovely white frock, with a small veil
on her pristine ringlets. Mrs Doyle was carrying
the baby but also keeping a tight grip on Rose's
hand.

As usual, Mum was peering from the window.
She was full of admiration. 'Eh see Mrs Doyle is
keeping a tight rein on Rose, making sure she
doesn't run away again. She was saying she never
felt so black-affronted as she did at the police
station. She was saying she hopes never to have
such a red face again.'

At that point I had been toying with the idea of
going to the chapel door to witness the spectacle
of all the little girls dressed like brides but in the
light of Mum's words I decided to stay put. What
if the red-faced priest should spot me within a

mile of the chapel? Who knew what he might do! Somehow I didn't think Mrs Doyle would relish the thought of another Macdonald child causing havoc in her well-organised family life.

CHAPTER 8

It was VE day, 8 May 1945, and Dundee, like the rest of the country, exploded into a frenzy of celebrations at the news of Germany's surrender. Mum took us down to the High Street in the early evening and the City Square was packed with people, all singing and dancing. Although we stood on the fringe of all this gaiety, the unrestrained joy of the gathered crowd was highly infectious.

However, there were still parts of the world that were at war. The Allies were still fighting Japan, but according to the local gossip this was a mere formality and that warring nation would soon capitulate just like the mighty Germans. Also, in spite of all this ecstatic display in the city, there were citizens who had nothing to rejoice in. Those families that had lost husbands, sons, mothers, daughters, sisters and brothers in the carnage were thankful it was all over, but nothing could ever bring back their loved ones.

During the war years the local paper had printed stories and photographs of servicemen and women who had been killed in action. These were young people who had grown up and lived their pre-war lives in peace in Dundee and the surrounding districts of Angus, Perthshire and Fife, young people who were now buried in some strange foreign corner. One such picture that made Mum cry told the story of a pretty Dundee girl who had met and married her dashing Canadian pilot. Their wedding picture was shown along with the joyful script of their future plans as a married couple. A short time later the same paper reported the tragic death of the young pilot.

Another tragedy which happened almost on the eve of war ending was the death of Sylvia. Always a headstrong girl, she had been running around the edge of one of the gigantic water containers that were placed strategically around the city. The contents of these man-made ponds were to be used in the event of fire caused by bombing. It seems that she slipped and fell in and, although a young man risked his life to jump in and save her, she had broken her neck in the accident. Shock waves ran round the street and no one could take in this terrible event, especially after Wilma's early death in 1943.

Cathie was inconsolable and I don't think I ever went back to her house. Perhaps I reminded her too much of her daughter who was the same age as me. Who knows? Mum kept in touch with her old friend but I was never asked along, so I never saw again the sunny kitchen or the gloomy parlour or the beautiful doll. I still had my darkie doll with its kiltie outfit as sole reminder of a happier time.

One night I overheard Mum talking to Lizzie.

'Maureen was always with Sylvia and, if it had happened through the week, then Eh'm sure Eh would be without my lassie as well.'

As it was, the accident had happened on a Saturday evening. I think she was wrong with that statement because I don't think I would ever have played so close to water as I was always wary of it. My last clear memory of Sylvia was of her standing on top of a wall like some conquering hero, defiant, bold and totally fearless. Poor Sylvia!

Still, on this festive night, nothing could really restrain the relieved and happy feeling that it was all over at last. The city councillors announced that Dundee would hold a Civic Week in honour of the ending of hostilities. Various events were planned, ranging from the planned release of thousands of homing pigeons to the planting of a white, flowering cherry tree in the City Church's garden.

I don't recall ever seeing any of these events but that may have been because they were held during the day when I was at school and Mum was at the mill. We did manage, however, to visit the Electric Wonder Show which was held in the electricity showrooms in Commercial Street. This exhibition was full of the latest wonders of technology, including a photoelectric cell that opened doors without the aid of the human hand. It was a bit like the story of Ali Baba and his 'Open Sesame'. Although this is commonplace today, in 1945 there was a tinge of magic about this and other wonders on show, especially as the majority of houses in Dundee were still lit by gas-lamps.

Another visit during this special week was a trip

to the museum and art gallery. Along with Lizzie
we joined a motley mass who were intent in putting some culture into their workaday and
mundane lives. We gazed solemnly at the old pictures of florid-cheeked and fierce-looking men
with bushy beards and stern eyes, the tall, statu-
esque women in full-length satin dresses or the
dramatic scenes of the sea, all encased in their
ornate gilt frames.

Without casting doubt on the grandeur of these
old paintings I much preferred the Egyptian
Room. This time capsule set at the back of the
museum contained a wonderful 2,000-year-old
mummy and sarcophagus. There were also
various weird-looking artefacts from the Land of
the Nile as well as a glorious panel inscribed with
indecipherable hieroglyphics. George, on the
other hand, loved the row of microscopes that
showed the greatly enlarged remains of a dead
flea or something equally repulsive.

These events, wonderful as they all were, paled
into insignificance beside the best thing on show,
namely the captured German U-boat which lay
in the calm, oily waters of Victoria Dock. Mum
took us to see it one Sunday evening, a dismally
damp and dreary sort of night that blended well
with the darkly sinister, tube-shaped submarine.
We joined a large crowd that stood haphazardly
along the stone wharf, all gazing in awe at the
boat as it lay in the murky, scummy waters of the
harbour. I think it was open to the public but on
that particular night no one seemed keen to go
and inspect the interior. We all seemed happy to
be standing at a safe distance as mere spectators.

One wee middle-aged woman next to us gave an exaggerated shudder as she turned to speak to her equally small and mild-looking husband. 'Eh don't know how folk can go under the water in a wee poky thing like that! It would make me sick being all cramped up.'

The man pulled himself up to his full five feet four inches and swaggeringly replied, 'Och, it's no as bad as that. Eh wouldn't mind going on one.'

His wife gazed at him in open-mouthed disbelief. 'You?' she emphasised loudly, 'You go in one of these wee things? Don't make me laugh. Heavens! You don't like crossing tae Newport on the "Fifie".' (A 'Fifie' was the flat-bottomed paddle steamer that crossed the Firth of Tay.)

As for me, I was torn between my natural nosiness to see inside this sinister submarine and my fear that the German crew were perhaps still on board.

George had no such qualms. 'Eh want tae see the Jerries!' he cried. 'Will there be any sailors on it?'

Mum, who was unsure if the boat was still manned by the German navy, tried to keep him quiet. 'Will you be quiet? Just mind that we're no at war with the Germany now.'

With that thought in mind we stood in the midst of the spectators, watching the greasy water lap gently against the smooth hull of the boat, spreading watery circles of shimmering iridescence with every wave. These patches of oil were like miniature entrapped rainbows as they swirled around the captured submarine. We all

111

marvelled that this vessel, which, in the not-too-distant past had been one of Hitler's famed fleet, now lay peacefully at anchor in this Dundee backwater.

Soon another treat to celebrate victory was suggested by Mrs Doyle. 'Let's have a big street party! We can have it on a Saturday providing the weather is fine.'

She went round the entire street to drum up support for this great idea and the majority of neighbours promised to help with a contribution towards the party. The children could hardly contain their rising excitement in the days leading up to the great event and when the day finally dawned we were blessed with sunshine. We hung about in tight little groups watching the frenzied activity.

Tables and chairs were negotiated down the steep spiral staircases and laid in a long line on the sun-dappled pavement. The women spread a kaleidoscope of tablecloths that were as diverse as the thirty-year-old damask cloth that had been a wedding gift, the gorgeous multi-coloured embroidered one and the well-used green bordered one that Mum donated.

The plates were stacked with a variety of succulent sandwiches that were filled with scrambled dried egg, fish paste and that other American delicacy, Spam. There were also plates containing a superb selection of fairy cakes, each one topped in coloured water icing that ranged from a vivid shocking pink to a barely discernible and anaemic-looking white.

It was a great adventure and even the tea tasted

different in the open air with the soft breeze wafting over the surface and making delightful wavy patterns in the cup. Mrs Doyle, who had been the galvanising spirit behind this successful venture, then produced her speciality: toffee apples. There was one for each child and everyone marvelled at her expertise in managing to produce these delicious treats. I sat on an ancient and scuffed kitchen chair, feeling the red Rexene seat grow hotter by the minute in the warm sunshine and bit into this completely novel confection which was perched on top of a thin rough stick. The toffee had a slightly burnt taste and the apple was green and sour but it was wonderful. Biting through the brittle carcass into the fleshy pulp of the apple was a taste experience that I had never had before and I thought the gods themselves could ask for nothing better.

Afterwards when the plates were empty and the tables had that forlorn look of having been ravaged by a horde of hungry ants, we decided to play games. A tiring wheelbarrow race soon left us all pink-faced and perspiring. While the children romped around in an orgy of delighted shrieks and howls, the adults sat on their chairs and gossiped about the better times that surely lay ahead.

'What a braw feeling it'll be when we can throw our ration books away,' said Lizzie with a faraway look in her eyes. It was as if she could already visualise the better life. Mrs Doyle had other priorities in mind.

'Well, Eh hope they take the clothes off the ration soon. What a great boon that would be with five lassies to keep clad!'

'Eh'll be glad no to hear that awfy siren going off. What an eerie wail it is and going down to the shelter wasn't much fun,' said Mum, before confessing 'mind you, we haven't been in the shelter for ages.'

Air raid shelters had been provided for the residents of our street in the drying green at 96 Hilltown but because Mum had made up her mind at the start of the war not to use them, George and I had never been inside one.

'If we're going to be bombed Eh want to be in my bed and no in some dark, wet shelter,' Mum had said. Perhaps this philosophy would have been different if we had lived in one of the many towns that had seen the horror of bombing. Clydeside had been razed to the ground and the newspapers had reported with black-and-white clarity the terrible carnage inflicted on the residents during the ghastly blitz of 1941. The papers had also reported the full extent of the twenty-four random raids on Dundee but it would seem that we were lucky to have escaped the same fate as Clydeside, London, Coventry and numerous other cities.

One incident in Dundee which caused a fatality was when a bomb landed on Rosefield Street, sliced through a tenement and killed one woman. Other raids included one which demolished a bungalow in Marchfield Road and a bomb which fell on Taybank Works in Arbroath Road. On that occasion a stone wall deflected the blast away from the workers who were huddled in their shelter.

By now most of the children had grown tired of

running around and we sat and listened to the grown-ups' conversation.

Mum recalled an incident in 1944. 'Do you mind the awfy night when that Nazi plane flew low over the Wellgate?'

The women nodded while I remembered it vividly. That April evening, Mum had taken us to the pictures at the King's Cinema in the Cowgate and we were walking home when we heard the ominous drone of a low-flying plane overhead. For a few heart-stopping minutes the homeward-bound crowd stood in amazement before darting for cover in all directions. Mum was carrying George but she quickly threw the edge of her coat over my head and roughly pushed me into a pend at the foot of the Wellgate. As we ran I lifted the coat and peered upwards. The plane was so low that it was clearly outlined in the sky and the echoing, staccato sound from its machine gun was somehow unreal but still very frightening. After what seemed like hours the plane flew towards the coast and we rejoined the shocked crowds who had moments earlier been pouring out of the cinema.

The rumours were rife the following morning and they ranged from the bizarre to the hilarious. The popular version was that it was shot down in the Stannergate, but one of Mum's workmates, Big Bella, had heard the story that the pilot had parachuted into someone's back garden and had got entangled with a line of washing. Everybody found this very funny but no one believed it. In spite of the rumours that were bandied about, the undisputed fact was that the plane had flown

115

low over the Hilltown and Wellgate area and windows were broken in the Hilltown and also Caldrum Street. A piece of fragmented shell was found in Henderson's Garage in Strathmartine Road.

There was a similar incident twelve days later when another lone plane flew briefly overhead before heading out to sea. Although the first incident lasted only a few moments it did make Mum think twice before she ever maligned another ARP warden.

She confessed as much that day of the party. 'When Eh think how Eh made such a stushie about a blackout curtain one night when my dad was alive! Now Eh can see what an important job they do.'

Lizzie gave a shiver. 'And just be thankful that the awfy buzz bombs didn't reach as far as here.'

She shivered again, but it was hard to tell whether this was because of the thought of the Germans' dreadful invention, the doodlebug, or because the sun had slid silently behind a black cloud. Then someone started to sing 'The White Cliffs of Dover' and we all joined in with the chorus. As the last note died away a heavy feeling of sadness descended on the company. It was as if we all suddenly realised that it was only by the grace of God that we were not among the multitude of war casualties.

The depression was lifted by Mrs Doyle who announced, 'Let's have more games to cheer us up!'

This suggestion was met with a flurry of feet as the children all jumped up, soon throwing themselves into a rumbustious three-legged race. After an hour of this gaiety the moment then arrived when we had to dismantle the tables. When the furniture and tea-cloths had been returned to their respective households and the various tea sets had all been washed and stacked away in kitchen cupboards or the display cabinet, it was time to reflect on the day's glorious happenings.

The street party had been a resounding success. In fact, it was the unanimous decision that it had been one of the happiest days that most of us could recall. The talk turned to the thorny situation of rationing. 'Never mind,' said Lizzie, 'It'll soon be over.'

Mum decided to remove the blackout curtain the day after the party and I was roped in to help. We stood on the wooden coal bunker with a blunt kitchen knife each and tried to prise loose the row of strong tacks that held the fabric firmly to the wooden roller.

Mum looked sad. 'Eh mind when your grandad put this curtain up. We couldn't think how to do it until he had the bright idea of making it into a blind.'

I felt a lump in my throat and tears gathered in my eyes at the mention of Grandad. I wished with all my heart that he could be with us now that the war was over. There was so much we could have done together and never a day went past when I didn't think of him or our wonderful outings. After a great deal of tugging at the deeply embedded tacks and a lot of annoyed mutterings from us both, the black fabric suddenly came free and landed in a sorry-looking and dilapidated heap at our feet.

Mum picked up the curtain, inspected it and gave a deep sigh. 'What a blessing the war ended when it did because this curtain is finished.'

What had been a thick and substantial piece of material at the start of the war was now threadbare and well patched. It was fit only for the dustbin but Mum folded it carefully. 'This is all that remains of your grandad's war,' she said sadly. 'Eh think we'll keep it.'

It was carefully placed in a drawer like some revered tapestry or painting. Grandad's blackout blind ... we both cried.

We weren't the only ones throwing off the shackles of war. Auntie Ina was hoping to join Pierre, her husband, in France soon while her sister Alice was waiting for her husband, Jock, to be demobbed from the Marines. Lizzie's son, George, appeared home from the fighting.

I was in the street one day when she called me in to find a young man was sitting in the armchair. 'This is my laddie back from the war,' she said proudly. 'He's brought you something back.'

George was tall and thin with dark hair. He looked really young and not at all like some of the world-weary ex-servicemen who were appearing daily on the streets. I stood gazing shyly at this newcomer while he brought forward a small suitcase.

'Now shut your eyes for a minute,' Lizzie told me, 'and you'll get a present.'

I hopped about in excitement with my hands over my eyes until Lizzie told me to look. George had opened the suitcase to reveal the top layer covered entirely with chocolate bars. I was mesmerised and speechless.

Lizzie smiled at the wonder on my face. 'You can have one bar for you and one for your brother.'

I hovered over the open case, completely dazzled and unable to make a choice.

'Well, hurry up!' said Lizzie. 'We don't have the entire day tae gawk into a suitcase.'

After a great deal of deliberation I finally chose two Mars Bars. When I took them upstairs, George and I gazed at them for ages, unwilling to eat this wonderful chocolate too quickly in case we had to wait another five years before getting another one. I sniffed it as the wrapper came off and I have to admit that even to this day I smell chocolate before eating it.

Lizzie had accompanied me to the house. She said it was to see the pleasure on our faces but I suspected that she was making sure I handed over one bar to George and didn't scoff the lot.

Later, while we devoured the chocolate, Mum and Lizzie chattered about the demobilisation of the servicemen. 'Och, it's a braw feeling to have my laddie home at last,' sighed Lizzie.

She glanced over at George who was now sitting with a dark-brown ring around his mouth. 'Will you look at the wee soul covered in chocolate! He looks like Al Jolson in one of his "Mammy" pictures.'

She picked him up, took out her handkerchief and proceeded to wipe away the brown ring. While she cleaned his face, she turned to me. 'Well, did you enjoy that?'

To be quite honest, I had enjoyed it so much

that mere words could never convey the intense pleasure I had derived from this unexpected treat. Although we had received some sweeties from our coupons over the last five years, nothing had ever matched the taste I had just experienced.

'Oh, Eh did, Lizzie. Thank you,' was all I could say.

At the end of that week Mum had her usual visit from some of her workmates at the mill. Mum always looked forward to these visits because it gave the women a chance to gossip over a cup of tea. Because of the noisy chatter of the looms in the mill it was impossible to have a normal conversation at work and the weavers, winders and spinners resorted to sign language, a language unfortunately also understood by the gaffer. This group of women comprised Big Bella, Nell and Nan. Big Bella lived in Norrie's Pend with her five grown-up children and a lazy husband who lavished all his care on his two whippets that shared the small, squashed accommodation with the family.

As her nickname implied, Bella was a large woman. Hers was a shape that the wartime shortages had failed to knock a dent into. She had a raucous laugh and a super sense of humour. Her cheerfulness had helped Mum during the grief-stricken months after Grandad's death.

Nell and Nan, on the other hand, were pale-faced and thin-built women with similar droll and laid-back manners. Nan was a single woman but she did have a serious suitor lurking in the background. Nell had been married but that had been in the far distant past and no one ever mentioned her husband. It seemed that he had deserted her after a year or two of marriage and she maintained that any thoughts of him had long since vanished into the mists of time.

On this particular evening Bella was discussing her favourite subject – food. 'Just think,' she said, smacking her lips, 'after five years of rationing Eh'll be able tae have bacon and eggs for my breakfast. No tae mention lashings of butter, jam and marmalade plus spoonfuls and spoonfuls of sugar.'

Nell joined in. 'Don't forget chocolate biscuits, oranges and bananas!' She was almost drooling at the thought.

Nan, who was good at bringing everyone down to earth, protested loudly. 'Och, will you stop speaking about food? You're making me hungry. Anyway,' she said darkly, 'Eh'll believe in the good times when Eh see them.'

The women laughed but Nan had hit the nail on the head with her statement. Instead of life becoming easier now that peace had been declared, there was an unspoken feeling that things would never become plentiful again. In fact, as the weeks went on, the meagre rations were cut even further.

1945 had barely begun when it was announced that coal was in such short supply that customers could not even count on getting the minimum of one bag a week. Then there was a potato shortage. The resourceful Mona, with her meatless, fatless and eggless recipes, would now have to dream up potato-less concoctions.

The mill workers were also disgruntled that

121

their wage claim for an extra fifteen per cent for women and boys and ten per cent for men had been turned down, especially since the announcement that all ex-employees were to register in case they were needed in the now-booming jute industry. One piece of welcome news was the planned introduction of twelve days' holiday with pay, a scheme that would certainly enrich the meagre coffers of the hard-working and low-paid shifters.

As usual it was left to Bella to cheer up the weekly meeting. As the women sat drinking their tea and morosely contemplating their unfortunate lot, she suddenly remembered a titbit of gossip. 'Did you lot know that ice cream is back on sale? The only snag is that a slider that cost a penny before the war will now cost a tanner. Eh just hope that my family don't hear about it because Eh'll have to fork out three-and-a-tanner!'

Although the women didn't know it then, a piece of good news to come was that wages in the jute industry would increase in June 1945 from forty-one shillings and eleven pence to forty-seven and a penny per week. The extra sum would easily have treated Bella and her large family to a slider each.

Then in August of that strange year, Japan surrendered to the Allies. There wasn't as much celebration at this news as there had been on VE day but I think everyone was glad it was all finally over.

And another expression entered our vocabularies – the atom bomb.

CHAPTER 9

I was coming home from school one afternoon in August when I saw a stranger standing at the foot of the close. He was of medium height with fair hair and a moustache and he was dressed in a bright checked sports jacket and flannel trousers. He was very smart. As I approached him, I had the vague notion that he looked familiar but I couldn't think where I had met him or indeed how I could possibly have known him.

'Hello,' he said, looking askance at my puzzled face, 'Eh'm your dad.'

Of course! This was the figure from the blurred photograph, except for one difference – in the photo he was clean-shaven and now he sported a moustache. I glanced warily at this stranger, unsure what to say but he followed me up the stairs.

'Put the kettle on for some tea,' he said, smiling. 'Eh expect your mum is still at the mill?'

I nodded. 'Aye, she is and George is at the nursery.'

As usual Mum had left a list of chores for me to do after school. Today, in contrast to my usual apathy in these tasks, I was glad to be able to hurry round the room with the sweeping brush and duster while Dad sipped his tea.

I gave him a quick glance, this stranger in the house. 'Eh've got to go for the messages now and

123

Eh do Mrs Knight's shopping as well,' I explained in case he wondered where I was going.

He merely nodded and I lifted the pencilled list from the sideboard.

'Just you carry on with your normal routine and don't mind me,' he said. 'After Eh finish this cup of tea, Eh'll head over tae Watery Willie's for a quick pint.'

This was the nickname for Mr Gray's pub that stood on the corner of the street. I don't think this pub sold pints of beer that were any different from other pubs so I've no idea how the publican acquired his nickname. As I ran towards Mrs Knight's house I was ashamed to admit that I was relieved to get out of the house. I didn't know what to say to this stranger who called himself Dad.

Mrs Knight was dressed in her usual tea apron, a hideous creation in purple and green splodges. She was really pleased with my news. 'Och, that's braw that your father is home! Your mum will be pleased.'

When Mum arrived home, however, with George toddling at her heels, she didn't look so much pleased as totally surprised. And a little bit angry.

'Heavens above! Could you no have written a letter to say you were coming home? Eh could have taken the day off work.'

He shrugged. 'The contract is finished so Eh got back a bit earlier than expected. But it does mean that Eh'll have tae look for another job. Eh hear the Caledon shipyard is looking for painters.'

He picked George up and sat him on his knee.

'Would you look at the size of you? You were just a wee baby the last time Eh saw you and as for Maureen here, well, you were just a wee bairn as well.'

I racked my brain in an effort to recall that last meeting but then decided I must have been out with Grandad at the time. As far as I could remember I had never set eyes on Dad before. By now Mum had recovered from the surprise and her mind was on more mundane matters, namely the tea.

'Eh've no got enough in the house for us all so Eh'll send Maureen out for a fish or pudding supper.' She opened her well-worn purse and took out a few coins.

Dad leaned forward and handed over a few ten-bob notes and a piece of white paper that made Mum gasp when she saw it.

'A five-pound note!' she said in wonder. 'Eh've never seen a five-pound note before.'

I ran over to see this wonderful windfall but was quite disappointed with its insipid appearance. As far as I was concerned the ten-bob note was more colourful.

Dad, who was still sitting with George on his knee, looked really pleased by our reactions to his generosity. 'Mind you, Molly, it'll have to last a long time – until Eh get another job.'

While I was dispatched to Dellanzo's chip shop, Mum sat with the five-pound note in her hand. I got the impression she didn't want to hand it back in case she never saw it again. But there again, she knew Dad well whereas he was an unknown man to me and George.

I met Bella waddling down the Hilltown with a huge steaming parcel of hot chips. Like Mrs Knight she was pleased at my news. 'Och, you'll all be pleased at that,' she said as she trundled off homewards, no doubt contemplating another few hours of work before she could put her feet up.

As I stood in the long queue at the chip shop I felt guilty at not being ecstatic at Dad's return. To be truthful, my only feeling was of strangeness.

The next day Dad put his name down at the Caledon yard. Apparently their order books were full and he hoped he would get taken on soon. Until then he managed to get a temporary job as a sign-writer with a painter and decorator's shop in Victoria Road. Over the next few days, I often saw him as I went for the messages.

When he spotted me, he would shout from his high perch on his stepladder, 'Get me ten fags, Maureen. Craven A if possible.'

'Smoke Craven A for your throat's sake' was how this popular cigarette was advertised. This added burden used to depress me because it made life difficult. It was bad enough trying to get Mum's cigarettes without having to scour endless shops for Dad's supply as well. The war may have been well and truly over but supplies of everything were still scanty or even non-existent.

Still, there was one small consolation in the shape of an occasional ice-cream cone. The Italian community owned most of the ice-cream and chip shops in Dundee and were known affectionately as 'Tallies'. I think the older generations of these families were interned during the war but now that it was peacetime these shop owners

126

started to think nostalgic thoughts about their homeland. In the good old days before the war these shops had displayed a surfeit of brightly coloured advertising material in their windows, but now in this sweetie-less and cigarette-less world their windows were bare, bereft of the colourful cardboard pictures. Why advertise the products when they were virtually unobtainable? Which brings me back to my ice cream.

In an effort to brighten these windows a few of the owners had asked Dad, who was a talented painter, to paint a background mural of sun-kissed Naples or some other relevant scene. These backdrops were usually painted in soft misty blues and greys and were probably more romantic than realistic but they did help to attract the attention of passing pedestrians. Whether or not this ploy led to a higher turnover in sales I don't know but if Dad was working on one such scene as I passed, I was rewarded with an ice-cream treat.

By the end of August the weather was still lovely and warm and Dad announced one night that he would take us all to Broughty Ferry beach the following Sunday if the weather stayed nice. I could barely contain my excitement at school the following day and I made the mistake of telling Jessie Matthews all about this wonderful forth-coming trip.

She was quite disdainful about it. 'Och, Broughty Ferry's no that far away. We went to Oban for our holidays in the summer. We took a train and we stayed in a guest house near the sea front.'

I had never heard of Oban before and, much as I hated to show my ignorance, I asked her where it was.

She pretended to look shocked. 'Do you mean to tell me that you've never heard of Oban?' she said in a superior tone that made little impression on me. 'Well, it's on the west coast. Right next to the sea.'

Not to be outdone, I mentioned that we were also planning to go to the beach by rail but Jessie looked scornful. 'Doesn't matter what you go on. We were away for a whole week and you're just going for the day.'

I had no answer to that because it was the truth. Before the school bell rang at four o'clock we managed to get a sneaky look at the classroom atlas and I was dismayed to see that Jessie was right. Oban was much further away than Broughty Ferry but this discovery didn't spoil my anticipation of the trip and the prospect of travelling miles and miles in the train.

Sunday dawned bright and gloriously sunny and we set off for the station in high spirits, George and I clutching our gaudily printed tinplate buckets and spades that Mum had bought from Woolworths the previous day. The East railway station was an arch-shaped building that lay beyond the Customs House on Dock Street and when we reached it that Sunday morning the platform was seething with people. It looked as if the entire population of Dundee was hell-bent on heading to the same destination as us. An air of excitement hung over this mass of humanity jostling amicably for space on the platform.

Mum warned us in no uncertain terms. 'Now, watch you don't stot those buckets against folk's legs!'

Our new buckets had a nasty sharp edge so we held them at waist level, not so much to prevent them injuring folk's legs as to avoid getting them crushed. I loved the railway station with its multitude of unfamiliar noises, like the clanking mechanical sounds and the disembodied voices, not to mention the purposeful bustle. There was a hint of mysterious and exotic destinations in this clamorous cavern with its potent atmosphere of discarded oil cans and smoky smells.

As we watched in silent fascination, a clutch of station porters scurried along the platform. Looking smart and officious in their navy serge uniforms, they weaved in and out through the waiting throng like a swarm of busy bluebottles. Countless conversations hummed over our heads like the dozy, droning buzz from a dozen bee hives. The human clamour rose fractionally louder whenever the rhythmic clattering noise from train wheels passed nearby.

After what seemed hours our train arrived and chugged slowly towards us. It exhaled as it stopped, sending a huge burst of black, sooty steam into the vaulted roof. The sheer power of this delightful whoosh dislodged a flock of pigeons who expressed their displeasure by noisily strutting amongst the feet of the day trippers. We all scrambled on board the train with the charm and decorum of an invading army. The carriages, with their plush upholstered seats, were soon full and George and I had to share a seat. It was by the window, though, and we almost hugged ourselves in anticipation.

On the platform, the imposing and important-looking station master walked down the length of the train, shutting the doors with an echoing thud. The guard then lifted his bright flag and blew hard on his whistle. The train moved slowly forward, just a few feet to begin with as if testing its strength before releasing all its power and energy. It quickly gathered speed and we were soon skimming past the dingy rail yard, the bleak industrial factories and the crumbling tenements of Blackscroft. Meanwhile, no doubt, on the deserted platform the pigeons flew back to their sooty perches amongst the steel girders.

Before long the smoke-hazed skyline of the city disappeared from our view to be replaced with a beautiful, uncluttered landscape of grass and water. I recalled Jessie's scoffing words about the beach being only a few miles from the city but to George and me this beach could have been on the moon, skirting some lunar sea. When we finally reached the little picturesque station at the Ferry, hundreds of passengers leapt from the train and converged on the street that led to the strip of golden sand.

We were a motley mass of crying children, men in their pinstriped and sober demob suits and eager but pale-faced women who, like Mum, were tired after a heavy week in the mills. When we jumped the few feet between the road and the beach I could feel the uncomfortable hot grains of gritty sand squeeze between the leather straps of my sandals. We all trudged forwards slowly to claim a few feet of space. Within a minute or two the once-empty beach filled up with a crowd of people who threw themselves down on to the sand and spread their coats and message bags around them like some vast multicoloured tapestry.

With Mum and Dad now settled on their small square of sand, George and I decided to construct our sandcastle. We began this task with all the fervour of a gang of navvies. Digging so deep that we thought we would see Australia, we dug down into the lower layer of sand which was dark brown and damp, riddled with fragments of royal blue shells that had the sheen of shot silk.

I ran down to the cold waters of the North Sea with my bucket, intent on filling our castle's moat. Sensibly, I had taken the precaution of tucking the hem of my frock in the elastic legs of my knickers. After umpteen trips by the both of us to the sea, our moat was still almost waterless and, being ignorant of the laws regarding seepage, we soon began to squabble. George accused me of pinching his water.

Mum stemmed further trouble by calling us over for our sandwiches and lemonade. Because she had an aversion to people drinking straight from the bottle and leaving small particles of food floating in the liquid she always insisted on using enamel mugs that had once belonged to Grandad. We sat down beside our imposing sand creation and munched our fish-paste sandwiches which were liberally sprinkled with a garnish of sand.

I could feel the sharp grains between my teeth

as could Mum. 'If there's one thing Eh loathe it's sand in your pieces,' she moaned, trying to pick out the particles that clung to the brown fish paste.

Small children with pink chubby legs and moth -eaten woollen bathing costumes ran gleefully to the waves while the majority of men, in deference to the sun's rays, had their shirt buttons undone and their trouser legs rolled up. These men appeared to be immune to all the screeching around them, content to sit in their comical beach wear and read their Sunday papers. The women, tired and depressed by their five years of war and shortages, were happy to lie out on the sand, soaking up the sunshine, thankful that their menfolk were now free from the ravages of conflict.

Nearby, a group of young women seemed eager to impress the clutch of spotty-faced young men who were busy observing them. These girls emerged from the water like blue-toned and wrinkled prunes. Under the appraising eyes of the youths they pranced on the beach until a thick coating of sand clung to their goose-pimpled arms and legs.

'Hey, Marlene! Is the water cold?' shouted one of the boys to the prettiest girl in the group.

Marlene blushed modestly but she was no doubt chuffed at being singled out by this member of the opposite sex. She called out in a casually nonchalant but obviously well-rehearsed manner. 'No! It was braw.'

George and I returned to our castle, working tirelessly until the sun moved westwards and a stiff cold breeze appeared from nowhere. Dad folded his paper and we made our way back to the train station for the return journey. The beach was still full of noise as people stood up to leave, shaking sand from their bodies and their coats. The pristine patch of sand that the beach had been prior to our arrival now looked as if a thousand demented moles had lived and died there. As the train pulled away from the station, I gave a backward glance at the mutilated beach. At that moment I knew this day would remain a happy memory, even in years to come.

It would have been nice to think that our lives could have continued in this same happy vein but it wasn't to be. Although I was too young to know all the ins and outs of my parents' plans, one thing was crystal clear: Dad was restless and eager to try another lifestyle. He had got his job at the Caledon shipyard but he was hankering after the notion of running his own business. He had met another painter during the war years and this man wanted Dad to join him in his shop.

There was just the one big snag as Dad explained. 'It'll mean moving tae Grimsby, Molly. That's where the shop is.'

I was busy with my homework but, as always, having big ears meant that I only ever had half my mind on whatever I was doing.

To say Mum was worried was an understatement. 'But where will we stay down there?'

Dad had the solution. 'Well, if Eh go first, Eh can have a wee scout around for someplace then the three of you can join me later. Still, maybe the deal will fall through.' He sounded quite depressed by this thought.

Grimsby. I let the name roll around in my head.

I'd no idea where it was but it certainly sounded grim. Perhaps it was some seaside bay that was terribly bleak. I made a mental note to look for this place in the school atlas. After this initial conversation the idea seemed to fade away into the realms of wishful thinking. Dad continued with his job at the shipyard and with Mum still employed at the mill everything seemed normal. Some of Mum's workmates told of similar restless longings from their menfolk. It was as if the war had made them discontented with their surroundings. I suppose it was reasonable. I mean, if a man had fought in Monte Cassino or Berlin or the Sahara Desert then a dreary wet day in Dundee wouldn't seem appealing. Yet I was grateful for this calm period.

One Saturday afternoon after Dad had finished work he announced we were all going to the carnival in Gussie Park that evening. It was early December and George's birthday. He was four years old. In high spirits we set off for the wonderful, colourful world of the fair. The place was crowded when we arrived, with people patiently waiting in long queues for vacant seats on most of the rides.

The Hobby Horses ride wasn't too busy and George was soon riding at a gentle pace in a bright red bus with a large silver bell. Dad had tried to put me on this too but I was indignant. I was too old for such childlike things and would have loved a go on the Dodgem cars. The ride was accompanied by a noisy jangling and a very tinny-sounding tune but when it stopped George refused to come off. He wanted to take the bus home with him. Dad paid for another ride for him while I gazed at the speeding Waltzers. By the time we managed to prise my brother loose from the bus, I stated my desire to go on the Waltzers but Mum said no. It wasn't for wee lassies, she told me, much to my disgust.

This made the ride even more desirable in my eyes but by now we had stopped at a sideshow which was presided over by a sinister-looking and very swarthy-complexioned character. 'Three balls for thruppence!' he bawled to anyone within a mile of his stall. 'Score twenty-one and get the star prize!'

Dad bought us three balls each then nudged Mum in the direction of the shooting range. We rolled the balls down a garishly painted board which was numbered at the foot. I counted George's score and was astounded to see he had got a score of twenty-one. I let out a loud whoop and the stallholder came over to see what I was shouting at.

He took one look and tutted. 'Naw, he doesn't have that score. You can't count,' he snarled at me while trying to nudge the balls from their slots.

Fortunately for us, there was a large ferocious woman standing next to me. She leaned over and did a quick count. 'Aye, he does have the right number. The bairn's got an eight, a nine and a four and that makes twenty-one in anybody's book.' She stared the man straight in the eye, daring him to say otherwise.

By now Mum and Dad had appeared in the middle of this commotion, no doubt thinking we were wrecking the stall. They were immediately informed of George's good luck. For a moment it looked as if the man would bilk on his promise of a star prize but by now a large crowd had gathered, eager to see and hear all. He could see his business dropping considerably if he didn't honour his pledge. His face was a picture as he snarled through clenched teeth, 'All right then but Eh still say you were cheating.'

I thought this was the pot calling the kettle black.

'What star prize do you want?' he asked, desperately trying to save face.

The centre of the stall was stuffed full of tatty-looking ornaments and other cheap goods but after a great deal of thought George chose an eighteen-piece tea set. It was made from coarse grey earthenware and was decorated with lavish garlands of puce-coloured flowers but we thought it was as grand as the finest china or porcelain. In fact, Mum thought the same. She said it would be kept for best and it was duly placed in the sideboard.

Dad left for Grimsby the following month, January 1946. He wrote regularly to begin with, enclosing some money or a postal order, saying business was good. Before he left, he had spent Christmas with us. George was delighted to get a big red bus similar to the one at the carnival while I got a tea set. Dad came home periodically during the year, such as when George started school and a couple of other occasions.

As 1946 wore on I overheard Mum confide to Lizzie that this new venture was proving to be dodgy due to the slump in the home decorating business. The majority of people had either got used to doing without or were doing the work themselves.

With the frequency of his letters becoming increasingly erratic, Mum grew annoyed. 'Well, it's like this, Lizzie,' she said to her friend, 'Eh've told him tae come back here and get his job at the shipyard. There's no chance Eh'm taking the bairns tae Grimsby.'

Lizzie nodded in sympathy. She obviously didn't want to give the wrong advice but Mum's mind seemed to be made up. Dad could either return to Dundee or stay in Grimsby, on his own.

Although I missed him terribly to start with, I still felt really ashamed that it wasn't like the all-consuming sadness that had engulfed me after Grandad's death. Over the short time Dad had spent with us I had certainly grown to love and respect this generous, restless and fun-loving father. Like one of his paintings which now hung on our wall, he had filled my life with a bit of colour and pleasure. Perhaps, like the painting which I grew to love over the next few years, my relationship with him would have grown with time. Who knows? The simple fact was he had come into my life too late and he hadn't stayed around long enough to leave any deep and lasting impression, which was truly sad. I didn't realise the finality of this parting at the time. Even if I had, I wouldn't miss Dad in the way that I missed Grandad.

One day at school, a rainy, bleak afternoon when all the tenements had the grey monotone of dreariness and everything was devoid of colour,

Jessie and I sneaked another look at the atlas. If I had thought that Broughty Ferry and Oban were distant places then Grimsby was practically on another planet.

CHAPTER 10

One outing that had become a weekly feature during Dad's short stay was a Sunday visit to his mother, who lived in Isles Lane, a cul-de-sac that branched off the Hawkhill and lay a few yards from Cathie's pend. I couldn't recall ever going to see my paternal grandmother before Dad's sudden reappearance and it all became clear when I realised there had been some family feud between Mum and the Macdonalds.

To give Mum her due, she never said a bad word about them and whatever was the cause of the feud, no one in our house ever knew. In fact, Mum encouraged us to go and visit every Sunday.

'When your Dad comes back again he'll no be chuffed if he finds out you've no been going to see your granny and Auntie Evelyn.'

So it came to pass that every Sunday we were sent off to catch the Blackness tram, our faces scrubbed and our shoes polished. We raced down the Hilltown with our seg-tipped shoes clattering and clacking on the pavement like a pair of demented tap dancers before finally reaching the tram stop by the Wellgate steps. When the tram arrived with its wheezing, shuddering sighs there was always a race to climb the metal spiral stair to the upper deck, a manoeuvre that caused a great deal of shoving and pushing which the conductor wouldn't tolerate.

He approached us as we sat down, his small moustache bristling and his steel-rimmed specs quivering on the edge of his nose. His leather shoulder satchel slapped against his side, making the change jump and jingle inside. 'Right then, you two! If you don't behave yourselves Eh'll put you off and Eh mean it!' he warned.

Duly chastised, we tried to sit quietly as the tram snaked its way through streets lined with stone tenements and grey, bleak jute mills. The mills now lay in silence with blank windows gazing out at the Sabbath landscape.

Although Granny's house was situated a hundred or so yards from the noisy and bustling Hawkhill, the lane had a rural look with a few front gardens and some stunted trees. I loved visiting this house with its inside staircase with a toilet underneath it and lovely poky attic bedrooms with their frilly, floral bed valances and tiny skylight windows. There was a medium-sized living room with an enormous rose-wood sideboard that stretched along one entire wall. In our opinion the crowning glory was the radiogram, an ornate cabinet that not only housed the wireless but also a gramophone. We had never seen anything like it in our lives and I always thought that Granny must be very rich to own something as grand as this. In fact, the whole house looked posh, especially when compared to our tiny two-roomed dwelling.

Granny was crippled with rheumatoid arthritis and she spent a great deal of her life in bed. Her daughter Evelyn looked after her, along with Evelyn's husband Jack, who was a bus driver with Dundee Corporation. Auntie Evelyn had a tough job looking after the house and she seemed to spend most of her time in the tiny scullery that looked as if it had been a cupboard at one time. I'm sure she must have groaned out loud when she saw our silhouettes through the frosted-glass panel in the front door but I don't recall her ever showing any annoyance at our arrival, which always seemed to coincide with the midday meal.

We sat at the table with Uncle Jack and wolfed down a big plate of mince and tatties but always making sure we still had room for pudding. After our meal we were taken through to see Granny who had a bedroom on the ground floor. This tiny room faced the lane and had one of the highest beds I had ever seen. It resembled a built-up dais with its crisply starched white sheets and huge pile of feather pillows. This room always had an antiseptic, hospital-like smell which was in sharp contrast to the rest of the house with its aromatic mixture of old wood and furniture polish.

Then there was Granny. In spite of her being confined to bed, I always thought she looked quite fierce and intimidating with her dark eyes, sharp nose and gruff-sounding voice that fired questions at us.

'Well then, how are you getting on at the school? Are you good at your reading and your sums?' she would bark at me, staring intently in case I was tempted to lie.

I never knew what to say. I was really good with my reading but definitely mediocre with my arithmetic. Still, I soon realised she didn't want to hear about my failures and I simply nodded dumbly while envying George, who wasn't subjected to the same third-degree interrogation.

As well as her keen interest in my school achievements, she was also fond of reminding us about our ancestry which, according to her, could be traced right back to the Macdonalds of Glencoe and the famous massacre.

'In fact, you still have an auntie living in Glencoe,' she would announce, leaning back on her pile of pillows.

George was always more interested in the massacre than the heritage. 'What's a massacre, Granny?'

'That's what happened to the Macdonald clan on the 13th February 1692 when the treacherous Campbells killed them after getting hospitality from them. In fact some Macdonalds still don't have time for the Campbells even to this day.'

There was a niggling doubt in my childish brain. 'Granny, if they all got killed how do we still have an auntie in Glencoe?'

She looked exasperated by this question but maybe she was only tired. 'Only forty or so of the clan were killed and the rest managed to escape but it's the treachery of the Campbells that rankled with everyone.'

Auntie Evelyn noticed she was getting tired so we were ushered out of this cold, clinical room.

To our delight, the table in the living room was set for tea and a delicious aroma wafted out from the scullery. For the second time that day we both cleared our plates before it was time to say goodbye to the paternal side of the family and we set off to catch the homeward-bound tram.

I was barely inside our own door when I pounced on Mum. 'Granny Macdonald was telling us that we come from Glencoe and we still have an auntie staying there. Is that true?'

Mum was usually busy when we arrived, either sewing on buttons or patching our well-worn clothes, and she gave me a look that implied our ancestors were the last thing on her mind. However, she nodded. 'Well, if your granny says it's a fact, then it'll be true.'

Alice Kerr, one of Mum's friends, arrived one evening and the conversation got round to Granny's arthritic affliction. Mum was sympathetic. Granny may have fallen out with her but she didn't like to think of the woman in so much pain. She confided in Alice. 'Eh hear she suffers a lot of pain. She's tried lots of different cures and Eh heard through the grapevine that she's even had a course of bee stings tae help with her painful joints.'

To say I was agog at this news was an understatement. Then, on our next trip to Isles Lane I made the grave mistake of telling George. When we were ushered into the antiseptic-smelling room he couldn't sit still. In fact, he almost fell off his chair in an effort to peer under the bed. Granny noticed this odd behaviour and she smiled warmly. It was obvious she had a soft spot for him.

'What's the matter, George? What are you looking for?'

I knew what was coming but, before I could administer a hard kick to his shins, he asked innocently, 'Eh'm looking for your bees, Granny. Do you keep the hive under the bed?'

She looked in amazement at him for a few moments before deciding he was talking a load of gibberish, no doubt learned from me. 'I'm sorry George, but there's no bees here,' she said, smiling fondly at him.

The look of disappointment on his little face was laughable but when we were on our way home I started on him. 'What did you do that for – asking about the bees? Didn't Eh tell you it was a big secret?'

He was crestfallen but unrepentant. 'Eh only wanted to see them. Eh thought there was a big beehive under her bed.'

'Of course there's no bees under her bed! Don't be stupid,' I said smugly, with all the panache of being three years older.

What I didn't disclose was the fact that I harboured this same notion and thought there must be a beehive in the room with Granny, a huge swarm of buzzing bumblebees under the white valance. I never did discover the truth behind this story of a bizarre treatment. Perhaps I had misunderstood Mum but, of course, I couldn't ask her because she was forever telling me off for listening to the grown-ups' conversation. 'Big Ears' she called me. One thing was clear, however: to our continual and intense disappointment we never ever saw any bees or their hive.

But George and I soon had other things on our mind. One afternoon Auntie Evelyn gave us threepence between us and we made for the nearest shop to buy a bar of Highland toffee. She had also given us the sweetie coupon from her own ration book. On the homeward journey, I tried to break the hard toffee by giving it an almighty thump against the back of the seat. A large, steely-eyed woman was watching this ploy. She was dressed in her Sunday best, a suit of navy-blue serge that was too shiny from so many pressings and a large ugly hat of battleship-grey felt.

She glowered at us. 'If you two don't stop banging on that seat, Eh'll get the conductor to put you off!'

Cowed by her intense glare, I tried to break the bar by bringing my fist down hard on the golden, brittle surface. That didn't work, so we had to suck the toffee, pulling it from our mouths in a long strip. Mrs Blue Serge Suit glared and muttered something about the younger generation while we slunk back in our seats, trying hard not to laugh.

Having money on a Sunday was a novelty as we got our pocket money on a Saturday. Our 'Saturday penny', as Mum called it, was actually a threepenny bit each but she could recall the far-off days when she had received a paltry penny. 'When Eh was your age, Eh was lucky to get a penny and sometimes it was just a maik Eh got, especially when your grandad was out of work. When Eh think though what Eh could buy with it! A lucky bag or two sherbet dips. Maybe six

144

gobstoppers and a visit to the pictures in Tay Street.'

As I listened to this catalogue of goodies I often wished I had been young in those halcyon days instead of these shortage-ridden and expensive times.

George and I usually spent the best part of the week daydreaming and eagerly planning our financial strategy of how best to spend our money. The list of pleasures tended to be a long one. I knew that some of my pals liked to stretch their pocket money over the entire week but we liked one glorious splurge, even when it meant going without for the rest of the week.

Our first port of call was usually Woolworths, where we liked to browse around the high, dark-varnished counters, looking at the prices and trying to get an assistant to climb down from her high, gossiping perch and serve us. I liked to listen to the various conversations under the pretence of looking at the goods.

On one particular day two shop girls were discussing a very important highlight. 'It'll no be long till your wedding, Connie,' said one girl, sounding slightly envious, 'It must be a braw feeling, getting married next Saturday.'

'Oh it is,' gushed the lucky bride-to-be, 'but what a job Eh've had getting my frock, Eh can tell you. The whole family had to put all our clothing coupons together, which means Eh've got this awfy bonny figured taffeta frock. Then, as if Eh didn't have enough on my plate, my fiancé announced he would be wearing his demob suit. Well, Eh soon knocked that out of his head so he's managed to get rigged out at the Fifty Shilling Tailors in the Murraygate.'

She stopped briefly to look disdainfully at us before resuming her tale of impending marital joy. We had been toying with the idea of a purchase but, as Connie was still engrossed in her wedding chit-that, we decided to leave our purchase for another time and treat this visit as an exercise in inside window shopping.

We headed along the High Street and passed The Hub newsagent. It must have ranked as the tiniest shop in Scotland, squashed as it was between H. Samuel's jewellery store and the Maypole grocery shop. Our destination, however, was the City Arcade in Shore Terrace. We both adored this horseshoe-shaped cavern with its small shops that sold everything from hairnets to brightly patterned linoleum and fragrant bunches of flowers. There was always a magical mixture of smells and noises in the arcade and, as we made our way towards the amusements section, I liked to linger for a few moments at one window that to me was like an Aladdin's cave, with its positive plethora of cheap ornaments and shiny trinkets.

The amusements corner was always full of children and their high-pitched voices sounded distorted as they echoed and amplified against the high vaulted ceiling. The owner stood in the middle of the throng, shuffling a pile of pennies in his huge fist and shouting.

'Get yer change here! Does anybody want their money changed?' he called, in an effort to drum up business.

We normally spent one penny each on the

machines and we usually began with 'What the Butler Saw'. Standing close to each other, we placed one eye each against the large viewfinder and watched as a clutch of old-fashioned, faded and sepia-toned postcards flicked quickly over, giving the impression of movement. For half a minute or less the characters moved clumsily in front of our eyes before the light went out. This machine was billed as risqué, but none of the children knew what this meant. We never thought of this entertainment as anything other than a series of postcards.

The 'Gold Digger' machine was next. This contained a huge claw that hovered temptingly over a selection of small toys and chocolate bars. No matter how carefully we worked the wheel, we were always disappointed. We would watch in growing excitement as the claw grabbed a bar of chocolate by the corner but by the time it reached the trapdoor the chocolate would have dropped back on to the bottom of the display and all we got for our penny was a handful of gravel.

Onc Saturday George tried the fruit machine instead and had beginner's luck with a row of shiny cherries. Much to our astonishment three pennies landed with a heavy thud in the tray, and with this windfall we headed straight for another diversion – Ned Smith's Temperance Bar. We hurried past the bus stances at Shore Terrace, pausing to watch with fascination as a double-decker bus skilfully dodged the small pug engine from the docks as it chugged up and down on its own rails. A group of swimmers on their way to the baths strolled through the Royal Arch with their rolled-up towels under their arms. These towels would contain their costumes and 'shivery bites', which were little snacks to be eaten after their swim.

Then it was on to Ned Smith's. Long before the planners had discovered such things as prime sites, Ned's shop was situated on the ideal spot on the steepest part of the Hilltown. It was a mecca for the weary and the thirsty. Many a trauchled housewife with a heavy message bag, a pram and maybe a couple of fractious toddlers found this a quiet haven where she could regain her breath and gather some strength for her final uphill journey. 'Gie me three cream sodies and one sass, Ned! Eh can't go another step with this load,' she might sigh as she deposited her bag and children around her. 'Ye ken something, Ned? Eh swear this hill is getting steeper or else Eh'm getting older.'

Ned, a tall, well-built man, was a bit of a character and always treated his customers with a genial smile and a pleasant manner. His shop was a square and spartan affair with little concession to luxury. Behind the counter were rows of wooden shelves that displayed two sizes of thickly ribbed glasses that were filled with an inch of various coloured liquids. I never discovered how these drinks were made but they tasted like nectar, especially after a hot tiring climb up the brae.

Sitting beside us that day was a small group of men in rolled-up shirtsleeves. They were scanning the newspaper and filling in their horsie lines, as they called their betting slips. There was always a great deal of amicable banter about the form of jockeys, horses and trainers and a lot of deliberation went into picking a possible winner.

'Eh think Katie's Lad has a good chance of winning the two-thirty race,' said one man, confidently.

The choice was not shared by one of his companions. 'Och, away you go! It runs like a cow with three legs.'

Sometimes two large and burly bobbies from the police box at the foot of the Hilltown would appear for some refreshments and on these occasions the betting lines would be made to disappear with the expertise one would expect from a world-class magician. In fact, these scraps of paper vanished so quickly that I often wondered if the men had swallowed them. Also doing a disappearing act on these occasions would be Jeemie, the bookie's runner, who had a thin, pinched-looking face and a furtive manner.

After leaving Ned's shop we usually met up with George's pal, Alex. Because he was normally financially better off than us we would accompany him to the small shop in Ann Street that sold penny Vantas. These were bottles of sugary water that were almost totally tasteless and had to be drunk in the shop.

As we took it in turns to have a swig, the owner kept a beady eye on his precious bottle. 'Will you lot hurry up and finish or are you going tae take the entire day tae drink it?'

As soon as the last dregs were drained, he took the bottle through to the back shop where it would be refilled, no doubt after a cursory wash under a cold tap. No sterilisation in those days.

Our last visit on our spending spree was to the whelk stall. This was merely an old pram or cart with a fish creel perched on top. There were two such stalls near us – one outside the Windmill Bar and the other at the foot of the Hilltown. We always gave our custom to the former.

'Three penny bags of whelks please,' I asked while trying to extricate the pennies from the grubby, bunched-up fists of the two boys.

The fishwife deftly scooped a handful of shells into three small pokes and painstakingly pulled three pins from a long paper strip which she carried in the voluminous pocket of her apron. 'Do you want any dulse?' she asked. Dulse was long strips of khaki-coloured cooked seaweed which hung limply from her creel. They looked awful, like pieces of washed-out rubber, but they were supposed to be very nutritious.

I gazed at the dollops of dulse, as if considering a purchase, then said, 'No thanks. Just the whelks.'

Alex's house was situated up the narrow opening between the Plaza Cinema and Campbell's drapery shop and it was overlooked by the high brick wall of the cinema. We carried our whelks and sat on his doorstep to eat them. On warm days the door of the projection room was kept open and the soundtrack from the latest film drifted down to us. I always thought it a special pleasure to eat my whelks in the prestigious company of Bogart, Bergman and other elite film stars. With the whelks now a happy memory of empty shells we stood up to go. The dramatic strains of Errol Flynn fighting a one-man battle

150

against an army of nasty villains boomed downwards and followed us to the edge of our street as we ran home for our tea.

As Christmas approached, Auntie Evelyn asked us to come to the house straight from school to pick up our presents. Afterwards we ran down to the mill to wait for Mum. Snow began to fall as we waited patiently outside the mill gate, clutching our presents, mysterious wrapped parcels in bright holly-patterned paper with a 'Don't open until 25th December' sticker on the front.

Out of all the depressing streets that surrounded most jute mills, the lane that led to Little Eddy's was by far the most dismally disheartening. The slime-covered road was witness to the fact that this corner was always without the warmth of the sun and on this snowy winter evening it was miserable. Sometimes, if we were lucky, the lodge-keeper would take pity on us and ask us into his tiny office to keep warm. He had the same elderly look as Grandad and he was just as kind. The lodge always had a large fire burning in the grate. Small cinders sometimes spilled on to the tinplate fender where they lay smoking like miniature Vesuviuses. The kettle always seemed to be boiling on the small gas ring and the old man would hobble across with a bashed and ancient teapot to make the tea. This was poured into enamel mugs which were white with a blue rim and, by a small coincidence, looked exactly the same as Grandad's ones.

On this particular night, the mill's siren sounded loudly, casting its eerie wail into the winter air. The large gates opened to disgorge an army

151

of mill workers, most of whom were women. They wore coats over dusty, floral pinnies and the cotton turbans on their heads made a splash of colour under the street lamps. As they all made their way through the narrow street these bobbing heads formed an undulating, techni-coloured sea of humanity.

Because of the snowstorm Mum decided to get the tram home and we walked to the Westport. The tram was already quite full when we scrambled aboard and the conductor had to move niftily in and out to collect his fares. 'Any more fares?' he called, his voice rising over the hum of gossip.

The air was filled with the aroma of wet woollens and damp varnished wood as well as the sweet, sickly smell of jute. We sat with our parcels on our laps while the women complained about the terrible weather. Now and then a voice rose over the general babble.

'Eh just told him if the tatties are no boiling by the time Eh get home then he'll get holy hell.' This came from a small, meek fragile-looking woman.

A ripple of agreement went round the car, and another woman added her lament. 'You can't send our Lizzie out for a simple message. The other night Eh sent her for five pie suppers and a pudding supper for the bairn and what does she bring back? Five pudding suppers and nothing for the bairn! Eh had to share mine with her.'

Of course these were the days when the words diet, calorie or cholesterol were unheard of, and no one gave a thought to the high salt content of the meals. Still, I expect the bairn enjoyed her pudding supper and for all we know might be still hale and hearty. I know I am.

While all this talk of gourmet meals went on I looked out of the window. Big fat wet snowflakes slapped against the glass as the storm gathered strength. Lights from small shops cast golden pools of brightness on to the snow-covered streets while the hissing and guttering street lamps tried vainly to illuminate this increasingly white world. George sat beside me. Chirping with Christmas excitement, we hugged our parcels close to our bodies, dying to know the contents but having to wait till the magic day.

Still, Grandad always said that good things come to people who wait.

CHAPTER 11

The legendary harsh weather of the winter of 1947 began in early February and at first the snow was greeted with loud whoops of joy from the children. Before long an army of imposing-looking snowmen lined the street like some white, snowy guard of honour. Our snowman was a simple affair with pebbles for his eyes and nose but while the snow had still been soft George had drawn a sinister-looking half-circle for its mouth. This grin had an aura of menace which I noticed was missing from all the other snowmen.

If ours had the look of a Chicago gangster then

153

the one at the far end of the street was the ulti-
mate designer model. Made by Nan, a girl who
lived in the second-last close, it was a creation
with a long, flowing scarf and matching hat. It
drew a lot of favourable comment from passers-
by but it cut no ice with the rest of the kids.

'It's just swank, that's what it is,' said Jessie,
who owned a rough-looking model, similar to
ours.

In the late afternoon, after school and well into
the early evening under the pale glow from the
street lamps, the street would erupt into a frenzy
of snowball fights and sledging down a small
slope at Dallfield Walk on tin tea trays. Some
people had the luxury of a proper wooden sledge
but the majority had sneaked the old trays out
from under their mums' noses. All good things
must come to an end, and soon our screams of
delight turned to cries of agony when our gloves
became solidly caked with snow, leaving our
fingers white and painfully tingling.

As we rushed into the house, covered from head
to toe in snow, we complained about the freezing
cold. We peeled off our wet clothes, leaving mini-
mountains of snow on the kitchen floor. Normally
this infuriated Mum, who would tell us off for not
shaking the snow away before coming up the
stairs, but she now seemed to be tired and listless.
She was barely able to drag herself out to the mill
every morning. We had been so pleased by all the
snow that we hadn't realised the enormous
struggle the workers were facing. It was bad
enough having to get to work every morning without the added burden of struggling through a

blizzard. Each day had grown worse with constant snow that left the pavements so deep in slush that even the children became bored with it.

Then one morning, about ten days after the start of this weather, things came to a head in the house. Mum could barely lift her head from the pillow let alone get up for the mill. I was sent to fetch Lizzie and when she saw Mum she was worried. 'You'll have to get the doctor, Molly. Keep Maureen off the school and she can go round to his house to call him out.'

Lizzie sounded quite firm, which wasn't like her. Mum started to protest, her voice a hoarse whisper and her face as white as the pillowslip. 'Eh can't afford the doctor, Lizzie. No, Eh'll just take the day off and Eh'll feel better tomorrow.' This was debatable because she looked and sounded very ill indeed and her words came out in a painful gasp.

Lizzie was adamant. 'Eh'll lend you the five bob for the doctor if you don't have it,' she said hesitantly, as if this offer of charity might offend, but Mum was too weak to argue.

'Right then,' said Lizzie, 'that's settled.'

She gave me my instructions. After taking George to the school I was to go and fetch Doctor Jacob. He lived in Nelson Street and I think he had a small surgery in his large stone-built house. I could understand Mum's hesitation at calling him out because five shillings was a princely sum. It was a recognised fact of life that the poor couldn't afford to be ill and this was probably the reason for all the self-medication they indulged in, like Grandad with all his home-

155

made remedies.

Doctor Jacob was a lovely man. Small-built with a bustling manner, he had a great down-to-earth persona which belied his vast medical expertise and knowledge.

His diagnosis was swift. 'You've got pleurisy,' he told Mum.

I can't recall the exact treatment he prescribed but as he gathered up his well-worn and battered leather bag he gave us his orders.

'Make sure the room is kept warm, day and night. Bank up the fire before going to bed so that the room keeps warm.' Now this was easier said than done. Our coalman, who ran his business from a small shed in Ann Street, could allow his customers only one bag of coal per week.

Things were to get worse. As February dragged its snowy feet across the entire country and held it in a freezing grip, the colliers at the mines couldn't deliver their coal. It had frozen solid, either at the pitheads or in railway sidings. As a result of this national crisis, our coalman's shed, usually filled with black churls (small nuggets of coal), was now completely bare.

With our coal bunker almost empty apart from a thick layer of dross, I simply couldn't light the fire until evening. Every afternoon I would race to the coalman's shed after school, skirting round mountains of piled-up snow, but the story was always the same – no coal. As usual the neighbours were a big help, with Lizzie and Mrs Doyle doing all they could. It was agreed that I would come home every dinnertime and light the gas oven. I would put three pennies in the meter and

156

leave the door ajar, and the room would have warmed up by the time I came home from Edmond's café with a jug of their thick soup. Mum would have her tea and toast in the morning and her soup at dinnertime, then I would just have time to fill the hot water bottle before rushing off to school again.

Lizzie was worried about Mum's thinness. She weighed only six stone and a few pounds and as she lay back on her pillow she looked pale and fragile, not unlike the porcelain doll on Cathie's mantelpiece. Mrs Doyle would pop in during the afternoon to make a pot of tea and have a chat. During that long wintry spell the talk would tend to be about the atrocious weather.

'Folk are saying there's never been a winter like this in living memory,' said Mrs Doyle. 'Eh see from the paper today that a train had to be dug out of a snowdrift at Auchterhouse. It was seemingly stuck for three days. Can you imagine that?'

Mum couldn't. The two women sipped their tea and watched the never-ending stream of snowflakes batter against the window. The cold empty hearth was another reminder of the dreadful conditions.

During the past few weeks when coal was unobtainable, Lizzie had taught me to make briquettes from the coal dross in the bunker. We spent a messy evening shaping the wet dross into bricks and placing them to dry out on newspapers that were spread over the linoleum. Trying to sidestep these black mounds had us moving like an elephant at the circus but they were a blessing during the long cold nights. We also

157

made wet paper twists which when packed around the briquette would keep the fire glowing for a bit longer. But as winter tightened its grip with more ice and snow even these standbys soon ran out.

I was beginning to hate this weather. Everything was being disrupted because of the big freeze. Even our small bottles of school milk would show a frozen inch sprouting from the lid. The teacher placed them by the side of the radiators but that was never truly successful. It resulted in milk that was either half-frozen or full of icy splinters. I also hated the practice of milk-sharing which meant that one person drank half of the bottle and another one finished it. Going second meant a soggy straw or, in the case of some of the sadistic boys who flattened theirs by drawing their teeth down its entire length, no straw at all. The teacher stood no nonsense. Should anyone be daft enough to complain about frozen milk or a flat straw she would point out how lucky we were to get our supplies. She told us that some isolated communities had run out of food for themselves and fodder for their livestock.

I knew other people had problems but I had one of my own. It stemmed from my wet Wellington boots. Jumping through the deep snow would soak the inside of the boots causing them to chafe against my legs. The resulting ring of watery blisters and red raw skin tingled painfully in the warm classroom. While the teacher explained the intricacies of long division, with her chalk squeaking against the blackboard, my attention was solely on my sore legs. I thought longingly of the long scratchy stockings Grandad had knitted for my first term and how I had hated them. I reckoned this pain was my punishment for rejecting them at the time.

Fortunately, Mum noticed this sorry state of my legs and this was just as well because George's legs were also going red. She told me to stuff dry newspaper into our wellies.

'Go into the sideboard drawers,' she went on, 'and get the tin of petroleum jelly. There's nothing better for sore legs.'

As we slapped on a thick layer of this ointment, Mum reached for her purse. 'Now, before you go off to the school in the morning, go over tae the Misses Campbell's drapery and get two pairs of knee-length hose.'

This shop at 99 Hilltown was a long, low-ceil-inged, old-fashioned establishment that seemed to cling to an air of the nineteenth century while somehow having travelled intact into the middle of the twentieth century. It was owned by two sisters who were always helpful and good natured. Nothing was ever too much trouble for them. They would gladly pull open all the wooden drawers from the glass-fronted case and display their merchandise along the length of their counter should a customer be hesitant about a purchase.

I wasn't one such customer. 'Two pairs of woollen knee-length hose, please.'

Behind the counter were tall shelves holding dozens of boxes filled with assorted goods. These boxes jostled haphazardly with cardboard adverts for Vedonis vests and Ballito lisle stockings. One Miss Campbell deftly pulled a box on to the counter and asked for our sizes. Mum had written them down on a note which she had given me along with the clothing coupons needed for any purchase.

In our close-knit community everyone knew their neighbour's business and the sisters had heard about Mum's illness. 'We hope your mum is feeling better now,' they said, not exactly in unison but not far from it.

The stockings were just what we needed and were long enough to pull over the top of our wellies. From now on I was always careful of the snow, making sure I didn't land in a deep patch and soak my boots again. After nearly two months of non-stop snow, I think the entire population was heartily sick of it.

One evening when the stars were glittering like gemstones in a clear black sky and the wind was bitterly cold, Lizzie appeared. She was wringing her hands in an effort to regain the circulation in her fingers. She pulled her chair close to the measly fire although the room was warm due to the fact we had also put the oven on. 'Eh blame the war for this awfy weather we're getting,' she said, 'Eh think it's all the bombs that were dropped during the war that's put everything haywire. First of all we get a braw Indian summer at the end of last year and now it's like the North Pole. It fair makes you wonder.'

Blaming all the bad weather on the war and the emergence of the horrific atom bomb in particular was a common thought. The new word on

160

everyone's lips was radioactivity and the stories that were printed in the papers about the destruction of the Japanese cities of Nagasaki and Hiroshima were horrendous.

Mum cried when she saw them. 'If that's what it takes to end a war, then we live in a sorry world,' she declared sadly

The Japanese army had treated their prisoners of war dreadfully and some folk thought it was only justice to retaliate with the atom bomb. Lots of other people didn't agree. What was clear, however, was that the world now had a weapon capable of destroying entire continents. At least it was in the hands of the Americans and not the Germans, who it seemed had been on the verge of discovering the secret of splitting the atom.

Radioactivity was also being blamed for the saga of the sour milk. For some unknown reason milk wasn't staying as fresh as it should and the papers were full of complaints and accusations that unseen radiation from the atom bomb was the culprit. Denials that anything was amiss came from the poor beleaguered Labour Government Minister of Food, the much-maligned Mr Strachey. On the other hand, a bevy of farming experts had put their oar in, claiming that the milk was as good, if not better, than before the war and the atom bomb. Lizzie spoke the collected thoughts of the entire Hilltown when she said, 'It's this ruddy radiation that's blowing around and the worst thing is you can't see it. No wonder it's turning our milk sour.'

By the beginning of April, Mum was getting better and was able to walk short distances, but she was still far from well. Her pal Nan suggested putting a kaolin poultice on her chest to help with the pain. She duly appeared with this and placed the small can of kaolin in a pan of water, setting it to heat up on the gas stove. When it was hot she spread a thick layer over a square of lint, almost like spreading bread with jam.

When Nan placed this concoction against Mum's skin she let out a yelp of pain as the thick hot clay touched her. 'Heavens, Nan! Are you sure you've made it hot enough?' she said with sarcasm. 'Eh mean, it'll no take my skin off will it?'

Nan was confident in her remedy. 'No, but you have tae leave it on for hours or overnight.'

As it was, it came off within the hour because Mum was convinced her skin would peel away when the poultice was removed. It would appear that I took after Mum with my doubtful opinion of home remedies. Nan did her best to explain that the poultice wouldn't damage anything but Mum wouldn't listen. Nan left feeling slightly miffed.

I knew Mum was worrying about money. With no pay coming in from the mill she was becoming depressed about her illness and the fact that the bills were mounting up. Then she became ill again with pneumonia. On the spur of the moment, and without telling anyone, I wrote to Dad in Grimsby. His letters with a money order enclosed were irregular to say the least and I was convinced he would be overjoyed to hear from me. It was a short letter. I mentioned Mum's illness but, being stumped by the proper spelling

162

of her medical condition, I called it 'numonia'.

Every day after school, I checked for his reply, which I hoped would include a few pounds to help Mum out, but after two weeks I gave up. My disappointment was intense. I was so sure I would receive a letter from him that I even used to lift the small square of lino behind the door in case the letter had somehow slipped under it.

Afterwards I convinced myself that my letter might have been too direct and cheeky. Dad always said I was 'lippy' and I agonised over its contents. Had I asked him how he was keeping? I couldn't remember. Perhaps he had taken umbrage at my impertinence and lack of news about George and our home. Then it dawned on me that his reason for not replying could be something as mundane as having changed his address. To be fair, I still think that was the reason.

Still, life wasn't all doom and gloom. The coalman had received a consignment of coal and he was supplying all his customers with one bag of fuel. Judging by the warm reception he got from everyone he must have felt like King George VI. The greeting he got from one old woman was retold through the street grapevine. 'Och, you've managed to bring me coal at last, son! Eh've been reduced to burning old shoes just to get a glimmer of heat!'

Mum had a good laugh when the coalman told her but she was also amazed. 'Well, all Eh can say is she's damn lucky to have old shoes to put on the fire. Some folk just have what's on their feet. Like me, for instance.'

When the coalman dropped his bag of fuel into

163

the bunker it made a loud clatter because the previous buffer of dross had been used up. 'Eh'm hearing that clatter in everybody's bunkers,' he chuckled, 'but there's tae be no let-up in this weather. Eh just hope the coal doesn't freeze up again.'

'Och, Eh hope no,' agreed Mum, 'otherwise we'll be getting scraped off our beds like frozen mummies.'

Meanwhile the doctor had given Mum some advice which she soon relayed to Lizzie. 'He said that if Eh was a rich woman he would have advised me tae take a sea cruise but, because Eh don't have two brass farthings, the next best thing is a daily walk along the Esplanade.'

Lizzie thought this was an excellent idea. 'Eh hope you take his advice, Molly. As soon as the brighter nights come in you should make a start.'

So it came to pass. By the end of April we had begun to take a daily stroll along the wide, tree-lined Riverside. Sometimes the river would be flatly calm with a brown-tinged, oily, slick look while other days saw the wind whip up the water into a frenzy of salty spume. As the three of us walked along beside the low wall, the sea spray slapped wetly against our faces. It was like walking in a shower of fine drizzle but we stoically braved the elements on our daily march towards the railway bridge.

The sprawling framework of the Tay Bridge marked our boundary and when we reached that point we retraced our steps, hopefully with the wind at our backs. Often to our delight we would see, through the criss-cross tracery of the iron girders, a train puffing majestically across the river from Wormit station with its telltale plume of smoke drawing ever nearer. George and I would make a mad dash to be standing under the bridge when it passed overhead. The rattling, metallic clatter was deafening but this was all part of the pleasure. We jumped up and down and tried to speak but were deafened by the roar of the locomotive as it rumbled towards Tay-bridge station.

Mum could never understand this ploy. 'You wouldn't catch me standing under that bridge for a hundred pounds. No after the last time.'

She shivered slightly and I didn't know whether this was because of her recent illness or the thought of the tragic Tay Bridge disaster of 1879 in which, one stormy December night, a train and all its passengers crashed into the dark depths of the river when the high girders in the middle of the bridge were blown down. As far as she was concerned, the bridge had fallen down once and nothing would convince her that the new structure was safe.

On our return journey Mum liked to sit on one of the benches that were strategically placed along the riverside walk. On these occasions George and I liked to run over to the sea wall and peer at the white-tipped waves as they lapped the stone surface. Clumps of shiny green-brown sea-weed were anchored to this wall, floating on the surface of the river like a mermaid's ribbon. Because of the high tides it was possible to lean over and grab a handful of this and many a happy hour we spent bursting the seaweed's sacs.

Jessie said it was possible to forecast the weather with a small piece of seaweed. 'Just put it on the windowsill. If it's wet then it's going tae rain and if it's dry then it'll be sunny.' This was said with the confident air of one who knows what they're speaking about; an oracle. We tried this bit of amateur weather forecasting but we never knew if her statement was true, mainly because our seaweed specimen had vanished the following morning.

George was disgusted by the lack of foresight on Jessie's part. 'She mentioned the rain and the sun but she didn't say what it meant if it disappeared.'

When tackled about this Jessie had a ready answer. 'Well, it's like this: it's wet if it's rainy, dry when it's sunny and if it's no there in the morning you know it's been windy. Simple.'

CHAPTER 12

One other outing suggested by the doctor at this time was a trip over to Newport-on-Tay. This was one of the great pleasures in the Dundee working-class summer calendar, this crossing of the river on one of the 'Fifies'. They made the journey every half an hour and the two I remember well were the *Abercraig* and the *B.L. Nairn*.

Motorists had to cross the river at this point unless they wanted to make the twenty-mile journey to Perth. This meant that these ferry boats

166

were always full with an assortment of vehicles ranging from the humble motorcycle to cars and lorries. Large queues of people and vehicles gathered outside the Tay Ferries building at Craig Pier. The long line sometimes stretched right up Union Street as scores of families decided to have a day out. The women wore their summer dresses and their husbands were still clad in sober suits.

Our finances wouldn't stretch to weekly trips and we often watched the boats sail out across the water from our vantage point at the Esplanade. George and I would be filled with envy at the carefree passengers who would gaily wave at us. Sometimes Mum managed to save the fares for the three of us and would take us out as a treat. We waited with impatient anticipation and barely disguised excitement on the pier as the ferry approached, to knock gently against the jetty before lowering her large gangplank.

Only then did the stream of passengers disembark, followed by the various vehicles which drove up the slope with such a great deal of petrol fumes and revving of engines that we were left wide-eyed with wonder. I liked to look at the water as it slapped against the side of the boat. These small waves made sucking, gurgling sounds and caused a myriad of rippling patterns that were slicked with patches of oil.

One day, while I was standing too close to the edge, a playful wave slowly curled over my feet. Mum, who was forever warning me about standing too near the water, snapped, 'Have you got your feet wet again?'

'No, Mum,' I lied, 'just a wee bit damp.'

It was one of those typically Scottish summer days – cool, damp and drizzly – and I had to spend my entire afternoon trying to look carefree and nonchalant while my feet got colder and colder. My every move was accompanied by a squelching noise and an eruption of soapy, white bubbles that burst through the black surface of my sandshoes.

Once on board, we gazed over the side of the rails as a throbbing sound from the depths of the boat heralded the cast-off. We watched in fascination as we slipped away from the jetty, the water being turned into a foaming mass by the paddles. The gap between the rails and the jetty widened and we stood in delight as the industrial skyline of the city receded into the distance. Countless chimneys exhaled fluttering ribbons of smoke into the atmosphere, casting a hazy pall over the buildings while ahead the green meadows of Fife beckoned.

The wide upper deck with its glass-panelled salon was our favourite spot. The salon always seemed to be populated by elderly folk, all muffled up against the weather. I could never understand why people wanted to shut themselves away from the exhilarating feeling of standing in the wild blowing wind, the wet sea spray and the tangy smell of the river, not to mention the glorious panoramic view. Mum, however, understood perfectly. Because she couldn't afford the extra penny or so for the privilege of a salon seat, she always made sure she found a sheltered spot, usually near the box that held the lifebelts.

As long as we promised to behave, we were

168

allowed to roam the boat as if we owned it, playing out fantasies like the adventures of Long John Silver and his pirates or Captain Scott voyaging to the South Pole in his ship *Discovery*. On one trip I spotted a pile of debris floating on the murky water, swirling around for a brief instant before being carried out to sea on a wave.

I had seen the Betty Grable film *Song of the Islands* the previous week and it made me wonder. 'Mum, do you think that rubbish will land on a South Sea island beach?'

Mum, who never felt truly happy on the boat because the motion made her feel queasy, replied rather cynically. 'Eh shouldn't think so. It'll be lucky if it reaches Broughty Ferry beach.'

Also on board that day was our pal Alex. Being a fount of knowledge, he remarked to us, 'Do you know something? If you fall over the side and you're drowning, your whole life flashes in front of your eyes.'

George's eyes were like organ stops but I was unconvinced. 'How can a drowning person tell you what they've seen?'

Alex gave this a bit of thought, which meant he frowned deeply and bit his lower lip while making a series of 'tch, tch, tch' sounds. Then his face brightened as he thought of a credible answer – to give Alex his due, he was never stuck long for an explanation of his many theories. 'Well, Eh expect it was somebody who *was* drowning but got rescued at the very last minute. Then maybe they said, "Och, it was awfy. My whole life flashed in front of my eyes."'

We took this explanation with a pinch of salt.

After all, Alex was the one who told us about the 'Dead Man's Handle' on the tramcars. According to him, if the driver felt ill he pulled this handle and the tram came to a stop. We had sat behind the drivers for months after hearing this story, only to find the poor men didn't suffer from as much as a sneeze let alone a tram-stopping illness. Our unflinching gaze at some of the drivers had made them so nervous that they had become quite stroppy.

Still, Alex was forgotten as we neared Newport. The boat docked at another pier similar to Craig Pier and the crowds surged forward in a seething mass into the narrow street that led to the grassy slopes that overlooked the river. This green brae was usually packed with day trippers and it was pleasant to sit there on a sunny day and watch the ferries ply back and forth across the channel, navigating round the exposed sandbanks. From this high vantage point the boats looked tiny as they sat squarely on the water like toys in a bathtub.

After settling us into a comfortable spot, Mum would empty her message bag to reveal the usual fare along with her latest detective novel from the library and our comics. As we sat on the sharp tufts of grass we all agreed that it was lovely eating Spam pieces and reading about the latest exploits of Desperate Dan and Lord Snooty in the company of the river.

The water presented a constantly changing scene as the waves shifted into an endless kaleidoscope of patterns. The waves could change mood from being choppy with white frilled edges to calmly languid and lazy with a mirrored slick finish. Seagulls squawked noisily overhead, diving for almost invisible crumbs which they deftly scooped up in their beaks. It was as if they sensed the food of the picnickers and they massed in furious white clouds above us, filling the air with high-pitched cries. As they fought and jostled for space, their outstretched wings flapped noisily in their desperate bid to grab the tastiest morsels.

We made a few crossings of the river during that summer of 1947. Mum was making a good recovery, which was good news. One return crossing I vividly recall was made on a hot, windless day just as the sun was setting. The sky was marbled with brilliant red and orange streaks that mingled with the ever-darkening azure of the approaching twilight. As we looked backwards, the far-off shores of Newport lay in shadow like an inky and smudgy thumbprint. The fading sun was reflected on the river and turned it into a sea of molten gold.

The normally dismal and smoke-hazed city silhouette of tall chimneys and grey depressing buildings was transformed by a fiery glow that bathed everything in a shimmering opalescent sheen. Long fingers of sunlight probed deeply into the city streets, searching for any west-facing windows to bounce its dazzling, diamond-bright rays against, turning them into gleaming jewels. It was a sight of magical, picture-postcard perfection.

As we walked home, the entrapped heat radiated from the pavements and we felt its warmth through the thin soles of our shoes. The Hilltown was abuzz with people. They sat on their 'pletties' or at the end of their closes. Pletties were concrete platforms that lead off the stairs and they often had front doors opening off them. All doors and windows were opened wide in a determined effort to catch every ray of sunlight. A multitude of chattering voices drifted on to the street along with sounds from scores of wirelesses. There were appetising aromas from a mixture of cuisines as people dined alfresco.

We passed lines of bleak houses that normally glowered like a grey shroud but on this golden evening seemed transformed. Lines of washing hung lethargically from a myriad of criss-crossed ropes that converged towards the communal 'greenie pole', bearing witness to the fact that, although the women were now relaxing, their work had been done first. The greenie pole was a long pole in a back yard that had washing lines attached to it. These lines were connected to windows by means of pulleys and the idea was that, as you pegged the washing on to the line, you fed it out the window.

'What a difference the sun makes!' said Mum as we hurried homewards.

It was certainly a bonus to her as it made her feel a bit better. Regaining good health for Mum was surely just around the corner.

Sometimes on a Sunday, if we didn't want to walk along the Esplanade, we would, like many other city dwellers, take a stroll around the docks. George and I liked to look at the big ships but we were a bit afraid of the exotic-looking

Lascar seamen. These dark-skinned men gabbled away in their own language which we thought was gobbledegook. Then again, they probably thought the same about the Dundee dialect.

On one such stroll we saw an American ship docked nearby. As we passed it, a young fresh-faced sailor came running down the gangplank and rushed past us. In his haste he dropped a big packet of coloured fruit drops. They were encased in a clear cellophane wrapper and we had never seen anything like them before. Our eyes were almost popping out of our heads as George picked them up and handed them to the young man.

The sailor gazed at our faces for a moment before speaking in a super American film-star drawl. 'Gee, sonny, just keep them and share them with the little lady.'

Perplexed, George looked around to see who the little lady was and I hissed at him in a stage whisper. 'That's me, daftie!' I said, sounding more like a furious fishwife than a lady.

Mum was mortified. 'George, hand those sweeties back to the man at once.'

The sailor was nervously consulting his watch.

Mum repeated her command and added, 'Will you two stop gawking at them?'

She turned and addressed the sailor. 'You'll have to excuse them. They look like they've never seen a sweetie before.'

We had never seen sweeties like this before, all wrapped up in clear cellophane and a huge bag-ful at that.

The sailor held up his hand. 'Gee whizz, ma'am!

I sure would like the kids to keep them. I'm sure Mary won't mind and I must rush because I'm late for our date.'

With this he hurried away and Mum looked at us with annoyance. 'Well, Eh hope for his sake that Mary *does* understand about losing her sweeties to two mooching faces like yourselves. Honestly, Eh've never been so black-affronted before. Speak about having your tongues hanging out!'

As we sucked hard on our ill-gotten sweets, Mum was still ranting about being embarrassed. 'What will that young lad think of us? He'll think we're beggars.'

Personally I couldn't see the problem and I didn't think the sailor would be all that bothered. After all, he must have been used to it. Since the war had brought the Yanks over to Britain, if anyone was lucky enough to meet a native of America, that golden land of plenty, the standard phrase was 'Have you got any gum, chum?' or, in the case of the fairer sex at the dancing, 'Have you any nylons, Hank?'

Mum by now was back at work and she always came home tired from the mill. Weary of trying to make ends meet, she expected me to take on extra duties to ease her life a bit. One of these chores was usually on a Tuesday after school when I had to take the weekly washing to the wash-house at the rural-sounding Meadows. Tuesdays were often one of the quieter days at the wash-house.

The preparation for this weekly ritual began on Sunday when the bed was stripped and the sheets and pillowcases were loaded into a battered old tin bath. Then on Monday night our clothes were added to the pile and, as a decoy to any nosy neighbour, a lovely clean cloth was placed over the top. This ploy was used by most women because it didn't do to let your neighbours see your dirty washing. After all, it wasn't the done thing to show people how grubby we really were.

This pretence of taking only clean clothes to be washed was harmless enough unless taken to extremes. One who was guilty of this was a Mrs McDuff who lived at the foot of Tulloch Crescent. She always placed the most lovely embroidered cloth over her washing basket. This delight of linen, lazy daisies and French knots earned her the title of 'Doris the Duchess' or 'that toffee-nosed wee besom'. I thought this most unfair and would have loved to own a similar teacloth myself.

So every Tuesday I would dunt our creaky old pram down the nineteen stairs before loading on the tin bath of washing, the washboard and the Sunlight soap. Our pram had seen better days, but not for many a year. No doubt in its heyday the paintwork had been a work of art and the hood a positive concertina of pleated gaberdine but not now. It also had a wobbly wheel which made pushing it in a straight line very difficult indeed.

I headed for the Hedgie Road, which was very narrow with only a couple of inches clearance at the sides of the pram, then past the Dudhope Nursery before gathering my strength to push my burden up the steep Constitution Brae. The entrance to the wash-house lay directly across from the lovely-sounding Laurelbank, but this name was deceptive. This grim and grey-stoned building looked as if it could be a relic from the Industrial Revolution. It was a ghastly blot, made more unlovely by its contrasting green grassy meadows that swept upwards to the edge of the red-bricked infirmary while a clutch of allotments skirted its lower edge. These were fenced off from trespassers.

On sunny days these grounds were occupied by scores of chattering women sitting outside while their washing flapped in white billows. Squares of white clothes dotted the grass, turning the entire park into a patchwork of green and white. The interior of the wash-house, however, was a stark contrast to the idyllic scene outdoors and entering the building was like entering Dante's Inferno. The steamy heat mingled with the clanking chunter of machinery and disembodied voices. A cacophony of noise echoed from the wet walls while pervading everything was the pungent smell of wet, soapy washing.

A woman sitting in a small cubbyhole collected the admission money and allocated each customer a cubicle. It was then time to start on this long, hot and very tiring job. The cubicles were small but adequate, each containing two sinks, a boiler and a pull-out drying rack. Sometimes this rack would be full of someone's washing which meant we had to wait patiently in the corridor until she pulled armfuls of half-dry clothes from its rails. Pushing the rack back could be hard work and sometimes needed all hands on deck as

176

we pushed the metal contraption back into place, with it protesting and screeching as if it was in mortal agony.

Our routine never varied. Until Mum could join me from the mill it was my job to start the washing. I stood on a small box to reach the sinks but I was never allowed to touch the boiler with its intensely hot water. I hated the washing board and many a skinned knuckle I got from it. Another thing I didn't like was when Mum took the sheets out of the boiler and dumped them into the sink full of cold water. Sometimes they would become inflated with trapped air like giant balloons which, when pushed under the water, would send a cascade all over me and soak me almost to the skin. Some women wore rubber-lined aprons but most made do with strong, serviceable hessian versions which helped to keep them dry. I didn't have that luxury.

One thing I did like, however, were the conversations. In these conditions it was impossible to have a private chat and the voices which floated overhead were anonymous and entertaining.

'Did you see the new picture at the Plaza this week? Eh thought it was braw,' said one.

'Was that Margaret Lockwood in *The Lady Vanishes?*' shouted another voice over the metallic clatter.

Before she could answer, another voice butted in. 'Eh'm really fed up with these coupons. Eh've no sweetie coupons left and no fags.' She sounded down in the dumps.

'And another thing – where's the bananas we're aye hearing about? Eh haven't seen any.'

177

'Och, never mind. We're all in the same boat,' came a sympathetic comment.

Then a modest voice joined in. 'Speaking about *The Lady Vanishes*, some folk say Eh look like Margaret Lockwood.'

There was a moment of stunned silence while we all digested this item of information. Although no one said anything there was an unspoken feeling that we were indeed fortunate to have a glamorous film star lookalike in our midst and we should be thankful she had condescended to use our humble wash-house. As Mum and I made our way to the extractors, which were forerunners of the modern spin dryer, I looked around for this undiscovered beauty. But as in Miss Lockwood's film, the lady had indeed vanished.

I loved the extractors. Sometimes on a quiet afternoon, I would sit on my upturned tin bath and watch the series of wheels and fanbelts that seemed to be the power behind these machines. It was very therapeutic and allowed me to indulge in my favourite pastime, daydreaming. Some women preferred to use the large mangles, which were huge iron contraptions with big creamy-white rollers and a cartwheel for a handle. Sometimes we used one as it cut down on the ironing, but Mum was always careful to make sure that any buttons were well padded in case they shattered.

We often met Nell, Mum's pal from Ann Street, at the wash-house. She was quite a small woman, with black hair and a pale complexion, and the heat, which during the summer months could reach tropical levels, didn't agree with her.

Sometimes she would arrive at our cubicle red-faced and panting as if she was on the verge of a heart attack. On these occasions I would be sent to help her carry her basket to the extractors then help her load the washing on to her pram.

Mum was most insistent about not accepting any reward for any help given. Knowing this, Nell would bring out a 'Chiclet' (a small piece of chewing gum) from a wet pocket and give it to me. 'Now, don't tell your mother Eh gave you this,' she would say with a wink.

I could never eat this piece of chewing gum. It wasn't only soggy but often had thin strands of cigarette tobacco clinging to it. I'm afraid I always used to throw it away, but never in Nell's sight. In any case, I was much too preoccupied admiring the pram belonging to Maggie, another of Mum's pals. It was a Silver Cross high pram and I always thought it looked like Cinderella's coach.

I longed for a chance to push a grand pram as this and I finally got my wish one week when Maggie hurt her back and wasn't able to push it herself. As usual Mum had offered my services and I could barely sleep the night before with my visions of a stately procession to the wash-house. The plan was for me to push it as far as the Meadows, where Maggie would take over. After school I rushed to her door and, sure enough, the grand high pram awaited.

I set off in great style, hoping some of my pals would see me and remark how grand I looked. Sadly, the street was almost deserted that day and my noble progress went unnoticed. It's a true saying that pride goes before a fall, and so it was with me that day. I had barely reached the Hedgie Road when I knew I was having difficulty with the handle. The giant bath of washing perched on top didn't help either as it seemed to have a life of its own as it bounced in disharmony with the pram.

When I reached the steep brae I almost fell flat on my face and had to dig my heels in as the pram ran ahead with me hanging grimly on to the handle. I had this terrible vision of the pram rolling away down the hill and perhaps crashing into the children's nursery. Then there was the added worry that the paintwork could get scratched.

For some unknown reason, George and Alex had decided to come with me and they were trotting along on either side of me like footmen beside a royal coach. I yelled at them like a demented fishwife to help me. With the three of us hanging on grimly, we finally managed to reach the wash-house unscathed. I then had the terrible thought that maybe I would have to push it back home.

Luckily for me, Maggie's husband had been press-ganged into this chore and I could breathe a sigh of relief. There was still the added worry that I might be landed with this job every week and I felt sick at the thought. All the way home I carefully rehearsed my speech about not being able to do it. When I got in, Mum asked, 'Well, how was the braw buggy?'

I burst into tears and a flood of words came spilling out, recounting all the near-disasters I had experienced in the past hour. Mum said not to worry, she would have a word with Maggie. What I didn't know then was that Maggie and her husband were moving to a house in Caldrum Street, a street that had its own wash-house. What a relief! I never complained about our old pram again. Even if I should let go of its handle, the wobbly wheel would soon make sure it stopped against the nearest wall and another scratch on its paintwork would never be noticed amongst the million others.

If Tuesday was washing day, then Friday night was the ironing night. We owned two flat irons and these would be heated on the gas jets of the stove while an old scorched blanket was placed over the table. Mum had the knack of knowing the right temperature of the iron but I was hopeless. That's why I only ironed small items. While we stood sweating over hot irons, George would be sent outside to play.

Often, he wore his Roy Rogers cowboy outfit with its cardboard hat, thin waistcoat and furry-legged trousers. I tended to think a real cowboy wouldn't have been seen dead in this. Then there was the tin gun with caps that didn't explode as advertised. Instead they made a half-hearted crack, nothing like the guns in the cowboy films where Hopalong Cassidy could shoot a sitting target at a thousand paces.

One of the visits to the wash-house that I remember most vividly took place on Hogmanay 1947. The place was solidly packed with women, all hell-bent on getting the washing done before the year's end. I had made my way as usual after school finished at four o'clock but it was six

181

o'clock before I got a cubicle. When Mum arrived she was tired and fed up and her face was a picture of misery when she realised I hadn't even started the washing. We rushed through it but, when we carted the wet washing to the extractors, there was a queue almost a mile long. It was the same story at the three large mangles.

Mum took one look and snapped, 'Right! Put the bath on the pram and let's go home.' As decisions went, it wasn't one of her better ones. We hung the soaking wet washing on the kitchen pulley where it dripped for three days. We placed all our empty containers under these drips and the sound wasn't so much Handel's *Water Music* as a Chinese water torture. The kitchen was turned into a steamy and moist place. Later that night, Lizzie was our first-foot.

'Heavens!' she cried, 'It's like a Turkish bath in here, Molly!'

So we toasted another New Year, without Grandad and without Dad. 'A happy New Year!' we wished one another, to an accompaniment of drips and drops in various naturals, sharps and flats.

CHAPTER 13

Lizzie was excited. Her son George was getting married. Margaret, his fiancée, lived in Lochee but we all knew her well because she was a regular visitor to the street. The wedding was to be held in a church in Lochee with the reception in the Albert Hall at the top of Tullidelph Road.

'You'll be getting an invitation nearer the time,' Lizzie told Mum.

I was more interested in Margaret's new coat when she appeared in the house to show us her engagement ring. It was the most beautiful coat I had ever seen. Pink-coloured, and cut in the New Look fashion, it fell in long swishy panels from her neat waist almost to her ankles. She twirled around in it to show off the amount of material in the skirt. Such a generous amount was almost unheard of in these meagre and still rationed times when all items carried the Utility label. But Christian Dior, the French fashion designer, had stormed the world with his wonderfully opulent garments that were out of many a reach, mine included.

Mum was impressed. 'It's a braw coat right enough, Margaret. And what a length! It fair puts those Utility garments tae shame.'

Mind you, we got a laugh when Margaret left because her lovely new coat trailed along each step as she descended into the street, carrying dust and debris with it.

Although the New Look had arrived with a vengeance, people still needed coupons for everything. The war may have been won but things had become worse instead of better on the home front. People were sick and tired of it. Lizzie told Mum that Margaret's family were having great difficulty in obtaining all the wedding finery.

Mum was undecided about going to the reception, mainly because of the cost. Our faithful old

183

alarm clock had stopped working a few weeks before and Mum had taken out a Provident cheque to buy another one and the 'tickie man' (the man from the Provident who came to collect payments) called every Friday evening. We had tried to do without a clock but Mum was worried about sleeping in for her work. At first she had employed the services of Annie, the 'chapper-up', who, for the sum of a few pennies a week, would stand under the window and either shout, tap the window with a long stick or fling a handful of small stones to rouse people from their beds.

Annie was a true eccentric. Dressed in her own brand of ankle-length coat that had no help from Dior and her shabby boots, she was well known around the Hilltown. She obviously owned a grand alarm clock because she was always on time with her chapping-up. On the Monday morning we were wakened by a loud knock on the window and, completely forgetting our new wake-up call arrangement, thought the house had been hit by an earthquake. Mum leapt out of bed but by this time Annie was already halfway up the Hilltown with her long stick. After a week of this, Mum decided that a shilling a week was a small price to pay for another timepiece.

The alternative was risking being late at the mill and finding the gate shut. This would result in your wages being quartered and if you were regularly late this would make quite a dent in the weekly take home pay.

Mum was telling Nan all our troubles, especially the financial reasons for turning the wedding invitation down. 'It'll mean the three of us getting rigged out,' she complained.

Surprisingly, Nan brushed this enormous barrier aside. 'Just you go, Molly, and enjoy yourself for once. After all it's the summer and the bairns can wear their sandals and something cheap and summery.'

When she viewed it from this angle Mum had to agree that the expense could perhaps be kept to the bare minimum. George had joined the local company of the Boys' Brigade and although Mr Eggo, the leader, had said that any kind of apparel was suitable, Mum had managed to kit him out in a grey flannel suit, complete with short trousers. This meant he had something decent to wear. Mum decided to get her costume from the closet. Although quite a few years old it had hardly been worn, so that was her outfit dealt with. That only left me.

With Nan's words ringing in her ears about putting some enjoyment back into her life, Mum and I set off for the Star Stores. This was a credit shop, with a range limited to whatever stock was available. If they didn't have what you wanted then that was tough luck, as we were about to discover. Some of the older people in the street frowned on any kind of credit, stating quite bluntly that they preferred to pay cash for everything and being extremely proud of this motto. Mum always said that paying a small amount every week was the only way we could afford even the bare essentials.

Top of Mum's list was a wedding present for the young couple and as soon as we entered the shop she spotted a kettle with a copper base. 'Just ideal!' she said and it was quickly wrapped up. A new shirt was quickly chosen to go with George's suit and Mum reckoned a new blouse and perhaps a pair of stockings would be sufficient for her. We were fair rocketing around the store and Mum was smiling at the speed of our purchases.

But then there was me and I was a different story. I must have been in the middle of a growing stage because my meagre wardrobe at home consisted of a few well-worn frocks that were too short. The hems had been let down time and time again until there was no material left. Also, my sandals were old and scruffy with nearly all the original colour scraped away to reveal the scuffed leather backing.

In search of an outfit for me we approached the glass-topped counter and the middle-aged woman who hove into view. 'Can I be of assistance, madam?' she enquired, her head tilted to one side and her hands clasped together as if in prayer. She had a thin colourless face that wasn't enhanced by the severe-looking hairstyle. Her grey hair was pulled back into a giant doughnut of a bun at the nape of her neck.

Mum looked grateful. 'Eh'm looking for a frock and a pair of sandals for my lassie.'

The colourless creature surveyed me with a screwed-up face and pursed mouth, as if I had crawled into her view from under a stone.

'Well, that's difficult, madam,' she observed in her posh voice. 'You see, your little girl is in what we term in the dress trade an in-between size, which means she is too big for the children's sizes

186

and too small for the adults' range.' She gave a little titter as if something had amused her then moved over to a rack at the side of the counter. 'She can try this one on. It should just fit her but there won't be any growing room in it.'

I groaned inwardly when I heard the dreaded words 'growing room' and could visualise myself at Margaret's lovely wedding dressed in something overlong and horribly old-fashioned.

Mum looked dubiously at the proffered blue frock with its smocked bodice. It seemed pretty skimpy. 'There doesn't seem to be much material in it and Eh don't think it'll fit,' said Mum.

The assistant immediately leapt to the defence of the frock, as if Mum had cast a slur on it. 'It's got the Utility label,' she pointed out, turning the garment inside out to show us the black printed mark.

Mum now realised she had upset the woman's feelings by casting doubt on the quality of the frock. To my mind it looked cheap and tatty. 'Och, Eh know it has,' she said, 'but what Eh'm saying is that Eh don't think it'll fit her.'

We had now been in the store for over an hour and Mum was becoming fed up with the lack of stock in the children's department. The assistant, who was now decidedly miffy with us, placed the blue dress back on the rack. 'I'm sorry but I've nothing in stock in a bigger size,' she sniffed 'Try upstairs in the ladies' section.'

Mum decided to buy my sandals first and leave the dress till later. We sat on comfy chairs with my foot on a small foot gauge. A young girl was busy serving two fat women who sat opposite.

She didn't seem to be making much headway because a dozen shoeboxes were strewn around the floor.

'Well, the foot gauge says you're a size six and not a size five, madam,' said the girl, showing the evidence to the clearly unconvinced customer.

'Away you go!' the woman replied. 'Eh've never been a size six in my life. Have Eh, Ina?' she demanded of her companion.

Ina agreed with her. 'No you haven't, Jem, but maybe the war has made your feet bigger. You ken, with all the walking we've had to do?' She seemed completely confident in this unlikely theory and it did the trick with her pal.

'Och, Eh never thought of that. In that case, Eh'll take a size six but Eh don't like any of these shoes. Can you show some more from the back shop?'

The young girl didn't go to the back shop but climbed a ladder to root around on the topmost shelves.

Mum muttered under her breath. 'For heaven's sake! We'll be here all day and we haven't bought everything yet.'

Fortunately for us, the assistant didn't have any more stock and the two women left in a cloud of disgruntled moans. 'Eh'll be glad when these shortages are over. Maybe we'll get a decent pair of shoes then.'

Luckily, the first pair of sandals shown to us fitted and the girl wrapped them up. There was still my frock to find but the selection offered and tried on made me look like a series of thirty-year-old midgets. I was glad when Mum shook her head at each one. 'No, we'll just have tae leave it till another time,' she decided.

I was almost beside myself with misery and Mum didn't help by suggesting that she could maybe sew a band of contrasting rickrack braid around the let-down hem of one of my frocks.

'But Eh'll look awfy at the wedding!' I wailed, feeling quite sorry for myself.

Mainly because of the length of time we had spent in the shop, Mum snapped impatiently. 'Look! It's no you that the folk will be looking at. It's the bride's day – don't forget. It's no Maureen Macdonald's day. Eh'll have to go in my old costume or have you forgotten that?'

On that note, the subject was closed. I seriously considered pretending to be ill on the big day so I wouldn't have to wear the horrible let-down frock.

Then, out of the blue, a wonderful stroke of luck came my way via Mrs Knight. I had received a couple of frocks from her in the past which she was sent by some relative in America. Fortunately, one came a week before the wedding. It was lovely. It had blue ribbons and pink rosebuds printed over the cotton surface and it was edged with deep-blue braid.

To say I was happy was an understatement. 'Imagine Mrs Knight getting a frock from America that just happened tae fit Maureen!' Mum remarked to Lizzie. 'She's got the luck of the devil.'

Lizzie was pleased by my good fortune but, according to her, clothing problems were universal. 'Margaret's mother is in the same boat.

189

She's just about going barmy with all the bother of getting everybody rigged out. Still, Eh've managed tae get a new costume from Style and Mantle at the foot of the Wellgate.'

In spite of my agonies of anticipation, the day of the wedding dawned bright and sunny. For some reason which I can't recall, we didn't go to the church but caught the number 17 bus to the Albert Hall for the reception. A photographer was standing at the door looking flustered and out of breath. He had just arrived from the church where he had taken photos of the bridal party and now he was waiting to take some more. When we arrived he indicated that he would snap us but Mum held up her hand in protest. 'Don't bother about us.'

He wouldn't take no for an answer so we lined up beside the hall railings, looking like three refugees. I was secretly pleased because it meant that my new American frock was now being recorded for posterity.

Then the bride and groom arrived along with their families. The bride looked lovely in her long white satin dress and filmy veil. She carried an enormous bouquet of flowers and long trails of greenery cascaded like a miniature bush in front of her dress, completely concealing the skirt.

We hardly recognised Lizzie. Her floral pinny and cotton turban were replaced by a smart navy-blue costume, sensible-looking navy shoes and a plain felt hat. She was obviously proud of this transformation and as she swept past us she leaned towards Mum and said, 'Eh'm looking right swanky, eh?'

Mum, who looked swanky as well in her plum-coloured suit, agreed. 'You can say that again, Lizzie. You look like a toff and Eh'm no kidding you.'

We all filed into the hall behind the bride and groom. This large room had long trestle tables laid out. A small group of waitresses in their sombre black outfits and tiny white aprons stood against the wall looking like a row of penguins at the zoo. They waited patiently while the bridal party and guests sat down.

A stout man sat down next to Mum and remarked, 'Eh'm starving! Eh could eat a horse.'

He wasn't the only one. We had been looking forward with great anticipation to the wonderful wedding meal and it came as a shock when the plates were placed in front of us.

The children were given half-portions of corned beef, so thinly sliced that it was possible to see the surface of the plate through it, a spoonful of peas and a small mound of mashed potatoes. The adults fared slightly better, being served the gourmet delight of one whole slice of corned beef and a slightly bigger portion of potatoes. This tiny meal was scoffed in moments and a few people, the stout man included, thought that seconds would be forthcoming. Nothing materialised, however.

The pudding was jelly, topped with mock cream and a cup of tea was served to accompany the speeches. Mum gave us a sharp look that warned us not to fidget or complain of feeling hungry in our usual loud whispers. So we sat upright on the hard chairs and let the voices wash over us. There was still the sight of the wonderful three-tiered wedding cake to take my mind off the boring speeches and I longed for the time when it would be cut and we could all have a wedge of it. The bride and groom stood at its side with a sharp knife and I almost drooled in anticipation. Then, to my utter dismay, the three-tiered cake was lifted in the air and placed on a side table, leaving behind, like an orphan in the storm, a tiny iced cake no bigger than a dinner plate. The fancy three-tiered creation was merely a dummy, placed over the small cake for the photographs! I was almost in tears.

At seven o'clock, during a lull in the dancing, Mum went over and wished the happy couple a prosperous life together. She then said her cheerios to Lizzie who was still panting after a dance with the stout man at our table. We then headed for home. I was sent post-haste to Dellanzo's chip shop for three pudding suppers and we sat around the table with mugs of tea and our hot meals.

When Lizzie appeared the next morning Mum told her what a lovely time we had all had. This was true because we had enjoyed the day very much, despite the measly slice of corned beef. Lizzie was annoyed, though. 'Margaret's mother was angry with the caterers. The bairns should have had a whole slice of corned beef instead of a half-slice.'

Mum didn't mention our feast from Dellanzo's because she didn't want to hurt her friend's feelings. Instead she placed the blame for the wedding meal where she thought it belonged, with the government. 'It's these awfy rations, Lizzie.

Grandad Dwyer and Uncle
Charlie, c. 1919

My mother, Molly, with her
brother Charlie, c. 1920

My father (middle row far left), grandfather (middle row far right)
and other members of the Scottish Painters' Society, c. 1938

Grandad Dwyer, c. 1940.
He served in the Black Watch
during World War I and was
medically discharged in 1941

Molly, c. 1930

Auntie Evelyn and Uncle Jack's wedding, 10 September 1942.
My dad, pictured seated, was their best man.

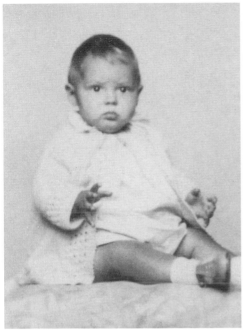

This is me pictured in 1939

And here I am again about a year later

In this one, I'm about three

This is George and me at Rosebank Primary School in 1947

This snap of Mum and me was taken in 1958 at Ashludie Hospital

Here are Mum and George on the day of my cousin Eleanor's wedding in the 1960s

This picture of my parents-in-law, Peggy and Alick Reynolds, with Ally was taken c. 1955

And here are Peggy and Alick again. This time they were snapped at Kinloch Rannoch in the mid sixties

On the left here is my father-in-law in 1922. Before joining the police in Dundee, Alick drove Rolls Royces for the Dunira Estate, Comrie

Mum (second from the right) at work in DPM Dairy. In the middle of the picture is Mum's great friend, Nellie Kilgour

This is Ally in Cyprus, in
1957, during his National
Service days

This is my mum-in-law Peggy
with Ally's sister Ann

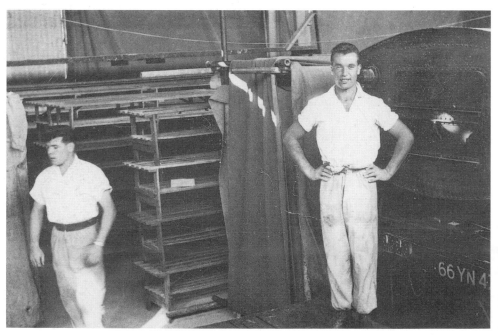

Here is Ally in Cyprus again, this time pictured in the army's
field bakery

Peggy and Alick snapped while out for a drive in the 1970s

Ally and me on our wedding day in 1956. On the left is our bridesmaid, Pat Forrest (now Machir) and on the right is our best man, Dave Gray

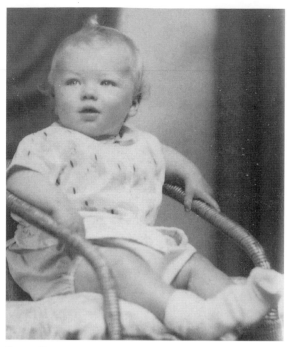

Our first son, Alick, aged nine months

Alick was soon followed by two brothers and a sister. From left to right, they are Steven, Alick, Wendy and George

You would think now the war's over we would be off the ration books. We all thought everything would be plentiful by now but it's still queuing for this and queuing for that. It's a bloody disgrace! It's about time Mr Strachey got himself sorted out in the Ministry of Food and started to get more things in the shops.'

Back in 1945 when John Strachey stood for Dundee in the General Election we had all chanted, 'Vote, vote, vote for Mr Strachey! He's the man to gie you ham and eggs!' This promise was never fulfilled and things were even getting worse instead of better. He tightened the rations even further, going as far as putting bread on the ration in 1946. An item that had escaped rationing during the darkest days of the war was now also in short supply.

The papers had been full of complaints from irate housewives but nothing improved. The war's end seemed ages ago but you wouldn't have thought it in Britain. Apparently it was all down to the American dollar. All foodstuffs were now purchased with the mighty dollar and Britain didn't have the dollars to buy from the world market. Also, the starving masses in Europe that had to be fed put a huge strain on everything. Be patient, the government told us, and good times would soon be back.

'Aye, that's right,' said Mum, 'and Eh'm Betty Grable!'

Lizzie did have a good bit of news. 'George and Margaret have got a key to the empty house below the Doyles and they're moving in right away.'

'That is good news, Lizzie,' said Mum. 'Eh've just been reading about the squatters that are to be evicted. It's a damn shame!'

The papers had reported the plight of homeless families and there was a great deal of bitterness over the planned evictions from all the empty properties. These families had moved to Dundee after the war, perhaps from the bombed cities of Clydebank and Glasgow and other places that had got the worst of the blitz, but there were no spare houses to rent.

'You fight for your country and this is how it treats you!' complained one incensed man when served with his notice to quit his rundown hovel. That was what most of the squatters' dwellings were, old decrepit flats in almost-derelict buildings.

The phrase about fighting for your country echoed the mood of the servicemen after the Great War and it would seem that nothing had changed. Go away into danger and perhaps death for five years but don't bother the Establishment if you survive the fighting, seemed to be the message. This is your eviction notice so out you go.

Plans were afoot to help combat this chronic housing shortage. Dundee Council passed plans for the erection of portable houses, or prefabs as we called them. These were to be built at Blackshade and Glamis Road, and so it was that Mum's brother Charlie, his wife Nora and their two girls were allotted a prefab at 199 Glamis Road.

We went to visit them a week or so after moving in. The houses lay in pristine concrete rows, each with its own front and back garden and tiny

194

garden shed. This new architecture was unlike anything ever seen in the city. Stretching out behind this estate was the lush and leafy green splendour of Balgay Park. Compared to the crowded and cramped conditions of the Hilltown this quiet greenness was like another planet. Before reaching our destination, the number 17 bus had taken us on a scenic tour of the Lochee and Ancrum Road districts. It then deposited us on the pavement right in front of an imposing and grand-looking villa.

George was quite overwhelmed by it all, especially the large house. 'Does Uncle Charlie live in there?'

'Don't be daft!' said Mum. 'He lives across the road in one of those prefabs.'

Once we were inside the house, Uncle Charlie insisted on showing us around their new domain, pointing out the fitted cupboards and the stove fire with its glass doors. He even went as far as opening the cupboards, much to Auntie Nora's embarrassment. 'You're showing up all my clutter,' she said with a laugh.

'Well, how will Molly see what a grand house we've got if Eh don't show it off?' he asked, refusing to be sidetracked.

Although the house was a funny shape from the outside, the interior was well planned with features well ahead of their time. The kitchen had a space-saving drop-down table but as far as Mum was concerned the jewel in the kitchen had to be the fridge. 'Och, it must be braw to keep everything cool, Nora. No more sour milk.' There was a hint of wonder in her voice.

Nora agreed. 'Eh can't think how we managed without it before.'

My cousins Eleanor and Carolyn ran over and yanked the fridge door open. Inside was a container with a row of sticks protruding from the top. 'We've made iced lollies!' they announced. They tugged at one of the sticks until a red oblong appeared.

We didn't say anything but an ice lolly wasn't a novelty to us. After all, we had bought one from Dellanzo's ice-cream shop a few weeks earlier. George and I hadn't been too impressed with it because one long suck removed all the red syrup, leaving behind a white, anaemic-looking carcass of ice. Carolyn soon pulled four ice lollies from the container like a magician pulling rabbits from a hat. As we sucked them outside in the garden my first impression of this new confection was confirmed. Like the ones from Dellanzo's, one suck of these lollies left us with a lump of totally tasteless ice.

We loved visiting this prefab with its homely air and wonderful smell of cooking that always emerged from the kitchen, not to mention the added attractions of the *Girl's Crystal* annuals and the *Film Fun* comics. We never paid a visit to Auntie Nora's house without getting a super meal and although there must have been times when she could have gladly seen the back of us she never showed it. Just like Auntie Evelyn. As we all squeezed round the drop-down table, eating beans and chips, I often thought that paradise must be like this wonderful, funny-shaped house.

Back on the street, the newlyweds moved into

196

their single-roomed flat. The previous tenant had left it clean enough but her tastes had run to dark, sombre paintwork and dismally dingy wallpaper. The young couple were no sooner in residence than they set to work with a tin of cream gloss paint for the woodwork and a sun-shiny yellow distemper for the walls. The small room was instantly transformed into a bright and airy place and once the dining suite and the two Rexene armchairs had been installed from Henderson's furniture store on the Wellgate the effect was stunning and grand.

Mum and Lizzie admired their handiwork while Margaret pointed out the difference a coat of paint could make. 'Do you mind how dark it used to be in here? You wouldn't think it's the same house.' She tried to sound modest but failed.

Mum agreed. 'Eh've just come from my brother's new prefab and everything is brand new and clean looking. It fair makes me fed up with my house.'

Our own flat seemed suddenly dark, with its old-fashioned furniture that had originally bel-onged to Grandad. Very soon after our visit to the new flat, Mum, Lizzie and Mrs Doyle decided to splash out on some home decorating.

'Where did Margaret say she bought the paint?' Mrs Doyle asked Lizzie.

'It was some shop in the Overgate but Eh can't mind its name,' replied Lizzie, trying to remem-ber, 'Eh think it was near Franchi's tearooms.'

At the end of the week, after they got their pay, Mum and Lizzie bought a tin of distemper each and we set to work on the Saturday afternoon.

Mrs Doyle had already finished her kitchen a few days' earlier and it seemed as if the entire street was determined to emulate the newlyweds. Mum rolled up her sleeves with a vengeance before dipping the large unwieldy brush into the cream-coloured distemper and slapping it over the uneven walls of our kitchen.

Mrs Doyle, who was a dab hand at everything, stood in the middle of the floor directing operations. 'You've missed a wee bit in that far corner, Molly,' she pointed out.

Mum was doing a balancing act on a kitchen chair and she reached over and poked the brush viciously into the offending corner. When all the walls were finished we stood in the same vantage point as Mrs Doyle and Mum surveyed her handiwork. It was clear she didn't like it very much.

'Do you no think it looks awfy cold?' she asked doubtfully.

Mrs Doyle shook her head emphatically. 'No, Eh don't. It's just because it's new. Wait till the smoke from the fire makes it brown again.'

However, Mum seemed undecided about the new colour scheme. 'Eh think the walls look awfy bare somehow.'

Mrs Doyle had the answer. 'Eh stippled mine with a wee bit of colour. Eh've got some blue paint left over. Just wait till Eh get it.'

She darted through the door and clattered noisily down the stairs. Within a few minutes she was back, a small tin in one hand and a bunched-up piece of cloth in the other. She began to dab blue patches over the sickly cream expanse.

'Just dab it like this,' she demonstrated, making sure we got the hang of it. 'Eh was really lucky tae get this wee tin of blue paint.'

After she had departed to make the tea for her large family the three of us went wild with our small bits of rag. Soon the walls had the appearance of being splattered by an army of kamikaze pigeons. Mum was still unhappy about this new painted effect but it was now a fait accompli and there was nothing she could do about it. As she prepared to make the tea she shrugged.

'Och well, maybe we'll get used tae it. And as Mrs Doyle says, it'll no stay this clean colour for long. The smoke from the chimney will soon turn it brown.'

She sounded optimistic.

CHAPTER 14

The country was in the throes of change and our street was in a state of excitement. In October 1948, Nye Bevan brought his wonderful National Health Service into all our lives. At a stroke, the worry about the cost of being ill was removed from the working classes and the poor.

The women gathered on the pavement and discussed this latest bit of news. Cissy Murray, who lived in the last close at the far end of the street, was the main spokeswoman on the subject. This was mainly because, although she didn't realise it, her husband Will was the street's hypochondriac as well as being bone lazy. Poor Cissy, with her round dumpling face and thick spectacles which must have been rose-tinted when she married her husband, had but one aim in life – to look after Will. According to her, he had a chest condition and this seemingly made him incapable of switching on the wireless let alone doing a job of work.

Mrs Doyle used to be annoyed by this. 'She runs after him too much,' she claimed. 'She even lights his fags for him! Eh blame it on her no having any bairns. Believe me, if she had a half dozen kids running around her feet she wouldn't have time to buzz around a big healthy man.'

'Aye but that doesn't stop him haring off to Watery Willie's every night for his pint,' said Lizzie, who was also perplexed by Cissy's meek behaviour. 'Eh mean, Eh'm no a nosy person but Eh can't help but see him from my window when Eh'm washing my dishes.'

The clutch of women agreed with her. None of the women in the street had a great or easy life but, compared to Cissy, they were well off. They all felt sorry for this poor, put-upon woman whose face wobbled like a blancmange every time she shook her head. Cissy had a penchant for gingham and most of her wardrobe seemed to consist of garments made in this checked fabric. It also, according to the street grapevine, was very much in evidence in her house.

'She must have bought a whole roll of it before the war. She's got it made up in her blouses and pinnies as well as her bedcover, curtains and tablecloth,' said one sage who seemed to know

200

the house's contents by heart.

Cissy was a woman of many words, never believing in brevity if she could help it. She much preferred a hundred-word statement when half a dozen would have been sufficient. What I liked about her was her wonderful way of mixing up words. I had never heard of Sheridan's work, but I know now that Cissy was a dead ringer for Mrs Malaprop. As she stood in the midst of the women, discussing Nye Bevan and the free health service, she remarked, 'Will has tae watch he doesn't catch bronchitis because his chest gets all congenital. Still, we don't need to worry now. Eh can call the doctor out without having to run down tae Dickson's pawnshop to hock my wedding ring for the five-bob doctor's fee.'

Everyone was of one mind. It was certainly a wonderful scheme. The women's faces were still pale and weary because Mr Strachey had lowered everyone's hopes for an end to rationing. But at least our healthcare was now assured, thanks to the visionary genius of Mr Bevan. After all, didn't we all know about the terrible death toll from tuberculosis, that awful sword of Damocles that hung over entire families in the overcrowded tenements?

Then there was Minnie. She suffered from chronic asthma and was forever being found gasping for breath on the strip of drying green at 108 Hilltown. During a really bad turn she would send for the doctor but her medicine was usually purchased from the chemist under her own diagnostic instructions. I remember how shocked I had been on a rare visit to her damp and dismal single room when I saw her bedside cabinet almost covered by a huge assortment of medicines.

Now the general consensus was that the sun had set on these bad conditions. We were urged to sign on with a doctor of our choice and Mum had no hesitation. After work one evening we were going to sign on with Doctor Jacob's panel. Before the new legislation he had consulted from his home in Nelson Street but in anticipation of an influx of new patients he had opened a surgery in Victoria Road. The premises had been a shop in a previous life but now the big display window was covered with a net curtain to screen his patients from the curious and prying eyes of passing pedestrians.

The medium-sized, square room was spotlessly clean and had rows of pale varnished chairs around the four walls. The floor was covered with the ever-popular and highly polished dark-green linoleum, the same as in the Royal Infirmary and Duncarse Home. When I saw it I wondered if this lino had perhaps been bought, like Cissy's gingham, before the war. Had it been bought in bulk by the Medical Association? There was that antiseptic aroma in the room as well, a mixture of Dettol and carbolic soap, and on this particular night there was also the smell of people.

By the time we arrived the place was already crowded with a good cross-section of Homo sapiens, from the old and infirm to the young couples with a brood of runny-nosed, wet-eyed children. All were eagerly waiting to sign on the panel and receive their free health care. We took our seats between an old man with a deep,

202

hacking cough and a weary-eyed mother with a crying and fractious baby who, judging from his howls, needed either his bottle or his bed. Mum whispered quietly, 'Eh hope we're no going tae be here all night. Eh've never seen such a crowd in one room before.'

George played with his Dinky car, running it up and down his arm and making 'Vroom! Vroom!' noises. I had no Dinky car to play with so I contented myself by studying my fellow patients. It was a strange situation because, although we all faced one another across the small room, no one looked directly at anyone else, preferring to keep their eyes firmly on the floor or on some distant spot above our heads. As I gazed around the room some people shuffled slightly under my intense stare, turning their bodies away with an impatient fidget.

Mum noticed this and gave me a hard dunt with her elbow. 'Will you stop staring at folk? Eh don't know how many times Eh've had to warn you about this. Folk don't like to be stared at.'

Because she sounded cross I decided to transfer my attention to the various posters that decorated the walls. 'Do not tell the doctor his job. He will prescribe what he thinks you should have,' said one epistle, no doubt aimed at the army of well-meaning but tactless people who had been used to years of self-prescribing and considered themselves diagnostic experts. How Grandad would have hated a doctor lecturing him about his weird and wonderful home-made cures.

'Do not ask for aspirins, cotton wool, etc,' stated another poster bluntly. Obviously now that

203

everything was free some greedy people were hoping to stock up their medicine cabinets overnight.

As the minutes ticked by, one of the toddlers began to cry noisily and this high-pitched howl echoed around the room. The harassed mother tried to pacify him by sticking a gigantic dummy in his mouth but this failed to stem his outburst. A couple of hefty-looking workmen, still dressed in checked shirts and cement-grimed dungarees, glanced impatiently towards the surgery door before resuming their scrutiny of the evening papers, turning the pages with rough, callused hands.

Then Big Bella burst in through the door. She stood in amazement. 'Good grief! What a crowd!' she exclaimed as her glance swept around the room.

She spotted us sitting quietly and came over to squeeze into George's seat while he sat on the floor. 'Eh've got this awfy pain in my belly,' she said, holding her hand over her abdomen and indicating the source of pain to all and sundry, 'so Eh just said to myself, "Bella, you have to sign on with the doctor, so go along and do it and, while you're there, let him have a wee keek at your belly".'

She suddenly turned to Mum. 'What are you lot here for?'

Mum, who would sooner have died than let the entire waiting room know of any ailment, whispered her reply. 'We're down to join the panel but, if the queue doesn't move soon, Eh'll come back another night.'

Bella gave a deep sigh and surveyed everyone in the room. For one terrible moment Mum thought she was about to ask them for their symptoms but she merely called out in a loud voice, 'How long have you been waiting?'

'About quarter of an hour but nobody has moved in or out,' said Mum.

Bella looked at her with amazement. 'Are you sure the doctor's in there?' she bellowed.

A suppressed ripple of laughter came from the two workmen.

'Well, all Eh can say is this – whoever is with the doctor must be at death's door.'

This statement brought another wave of laughter and amused looks before the door opened suddenly, almost as if the unfortunate patient had overheard Bella, and the doctor poked his head around the door. 'Next please!' he called out, looking calm and composed in the face of the large crowd.

'Well, now that he's seen this crowd maybe he'll get a move on,' said Bella, with a satisfied smile.

This prediction was true because the room quickly emptied. Soon we found ourselves in the consulting room. This small room looked on to a dingy grey pend which made it dark even with the light on. The dimness wasn't helped by the enormous dark roll-top desk which dominated the space and almost dwarfed the doctor. Undaunted by this desk, the doctor sat and looked at the three of us. Mum explained her reason for the visit and he painstakingly wrote out all our names while still managing to talk in his usual staccato fashion. 'Now, if you are ill, this is my

205

surgery timetable. Every evening from four o'clock till seven o'clock. Except for Sunday.'

When he was satisfied that we had ingested this information he rolled down the top of his glorious desk and saw us to the door. It was almost seven o'clock when we emerged into the dark street and there were still about another six patients to see, including Bella and her sore belly.

'Eh don't know when he'll get home for his tea,' said Mum, who was dreading the climb up the steep hill and the chore of making our own tea.

Later that evening, Lizzie and Margaret were relating their own experiences of joining Doctor Nelson's panel. 'It was bedlam! By the time we arrived, there must have been forty folk waiting,' sighed Lizzie, plunking herself down with a cup of tea from Mum's endless supply.

'It was the same at Doctor Jacob's surgery,' said Mum, 'although Eh don't know how many folk were there.'

'Forty-seven,' I told them proudly, 'Eh counted them.'

Mum gave me a look that said no medals would be forthcoming. 'Aye, you would,' she stated sourly.

As the weeks went by, the health service continued to be the main topic of gossip in the street, especially with Cissy, who folded her ample arms across her gingham-clad bosom and regaled all and sundry with a catalogue of Will's recent trials. 'He took this awfy pain in his chest and the doctor was really worried about him but what a red face Eh got when he gave this loud coarse-sounding burp and it was only indignation he had.'

Poor Cissy seemed peeved by the trivial nature of the illness, more so because of the promising initial symptoms. She was still sounding off. 'Another thing Eh've heard is that there's queues for free teeth and specs so Eh said tae Will maybe he better get seen for his specs and set of falsers.' It would seem that Cissy knew the health service inside out.

The women looked askance at her, no doubt wondering how Cissy could prise Will free from his chair in order to get his teeth out.

Mrs Doyle had heard another piece of disturbing news. 'Eh've heard that folk are coming back on holiday from Canada and Australia just looking for free teeth and specs.'

The women were angry at this news and shook their heads. 'Bloody cheek!' said Mrs Farquhar. 'It's our health service and it's no for the likes of them who scooted away from the poverty gey quick. What Eh say is this, if they've got money to jaunt back here from Canada, then they can pay for their own teeth and specs.'

Cissy, who was becoming slightly miffed now that the subject had moved on to the brass-necked emigrants, butted in, 'Well, that may be the case but, when the doctor came out to see Will, he had this muckle black bag that was full of everything under the sun. What a job he had tae put his hand on what he was looking for! So Eh told him, "You've too many departments in your bag, Doctor. You'll have to get something smaller!".'

As the women laughed at her innocent words, Will's voice bellowed from the open window, 'Ciiisssyyyyy!'

She unfolded her arms and looked flustered. 'Och, for heaven's sake! What does he want now?' she cried, scuttling across the road.

After a few minutes she reappeared. 'Will just wanted me to switch on the wireless. Said he felt a construction in his chest. Eh've told him tae take the two sets of tablets the doctor left that didn't cost us a tosser but does he thump?'

After she left to make Will his afternoon cup of tea, one of the women passed a comment, 'Take his tablets? Eh'd take the toe of my boot and gie him a hard kick up his erse.'

This caused great amusement among the women who all agreed with the idea.

We seemed to be living in exciting times. The street was finally moving into the twentieth century and benefiting from some of its new technology.. Electricity was being introduced to the houses but only if the tenants were willing to pay the connection charge. The street was divided in its opinions. Mum was doubtful but only because of the cost. The papers had reported the story of a prefab tenant who had received a bill for the staggering sum of £19.9s.9d which had sent shock waves through the street. Mrs Farquhar didn't want it and Mum was of the same opinion but Lizzie tried to persuade her. 'Just think how labour-saving it'll be. No more hunting for mantles that only last five minutes. You'll just have tae switch it on and "Hey Presto!" instant light.'

As a result of this logic Mum relented and we were soon connected to the new system, along with three-quarters of the street. To be honest, we didn't like it. The harsh, yellow 150-watt glare probed every corner of the kitchen including ones that the soft light from the gas had skimmed over, making the kitchen a space of semi-darkness. Now this bright light showed up all the scratches on our old furniture. Mum shook her head and hoped we would soon get used to the newfangled light just as we had done with the cream-coloured distemper. And that was another thing – the cream walls and the harsh light were a disaster together.

As usual, Cissy had the last word on the new system: 'What Will and me don't understand is this – where does this power come from? If it's in the wires like everybody says it is, what's to stop us all from getting elocutioned?'

She stopped for a moment to visualise the terrible spectre of electrocution before continuing, 'No, we've made up our minds. We're keeping the gas because it's safer. Mark my words.'

As things turned out, Cissy was lucky in not paying for the power line to be put in because, less than a year after its installation, Mrs Farquhar dropped a bombshell on a shocked street. 'Eh've heard that the houses are to be knocked down,' she announced.

Her window overlooked the drying green of 96 Hilltown and the spare piece of ground that lay beyond this. This tract of land stretched from the Hilltown to Dallfield Walk, the same length as our street, which ran parallel to it. All through our childhood, all the children had played on this site. Foundations had been laid before the start of the war then lain derelict and abandoned for years. This had made it a wonderful place for all our games. Suddenly, this site was now the scene of frenzied activity.

'The workmen are running around all day with their barrows and the rumour is that our street is to be demolished to make way for more houses,' said Mrs Farquhar.

Cissy decided to find out the true situation, using the subtle ploy of giving a cup of tea to two men who appeared in the street outside her door. It turned out that the rumour was true and she relayed the information to the pavement meeting. 'Eh saw these two men looking awfy superstitious like so Eh took them out a pot of tea and asked them what they were wanting.' She had a worried frown on her round, placid face. 'Well, the men were from the town planning department and it's true what Mrs Farquhar says – the street's to be knocked down and we're all being transported to the new housing schemes at the back of beyond.'

Everyone gasped in dismay. Mrs Doyle asked Cissy if she was sure she had got the facts straight. Cissy was annoyed by this slur on her storytelling. 'Of course Eh'm sure!' she said confidently. 'That's what Eh'm telling you. The men were going round eyeing up the street but the plans are going ahead and right facetious they were about the whole thing.'

The ashen-faced women were too worried to laugh at her – all except Lizzie. 'Do you mean they were officious, Cissy?' she prompted.

'That's what Eh said,' retorted Cissy who was becoming increasingly annoyed at this attitude to her fact-finding mission. 'And another thing – Eh don't think we can flit tae another house because of Will. No with the contraption in his chest.'

Mum was really annoyed. 'Imagine moving us just after we've put the electric light in. One thing's for sure, Eh can't afford the big rents that they're charging for the new houses.'

The new housing schemes, such as Kirkton and Fintry, were being built in the distant country-side on the rural edges of the city. It was true that these lovely houses had all the mod cons like hot water, kitchens and bathrooms, but at a greatly enlarged rent, far more than Mum could ever cope with. Most of the women were worried and hoped that Cissy had somehow got the facts wrong.

But she hadn't. Within a few weeks, the tenants received official letters saying that demolition would start in a year and that re-housing would begin as soon as houses were available.

Meanwhile, in the midst of all this upheaval, it was announced that Dundee would host the Royal Highland Show at Riverside Park. The organisers were on the lookout for a permanent home for this show and this meant that the city was eager to highlight its assets and abilities. The site was dubbed 'Canvas City'. We watched all the tents going up as we walked along the Esplanade, marvelling at the progress and purposeful activity. Mum was still worried about the planned moves from the street and she joked about maybe renting a tent at the end of the show.

Unfortunately, a week or so before its opening, disaster struck in the shape of a storm. Gale force winds whipped savagely under the unfinished tents, tearing them to shreds and leaving the site a devastated shambles. Weeks of work had been ruined in a matter of hours but the organisers put on a brave face.

'We'll be OK for the opening day,' they asserted with supreme confidence.

Hordes of Dundonians, including ourselves, converged on the park to view the damage with their own eyes. It was total chaos. The remnants of scattered wooden beams from the collapsed stands lay over the grass while strips of canvas from the ravaged tents hung like cream ribbons on the broken fences. These strips of fabric flapped noisily in the wind like lines of tattered washing.

Yet the newly elected Lord Provost, Mr Richard Fenton, was unbowed when he stated the same as the organisers. Everything would be shipshape and ready for the opening day. And that was how it turned out.

As if to make up for the dreadful wind damage earlier, the weather was glorious. Sun-drenched days brought record crowds and it looked as if the city would succeed in becoming the host of this prestigious show every year. In fact, this wasn't to be and the show finally settled at Ingilston, Edinburgh.

It must be said that none of this glory touched our lives in the street. Although many of us paid a nightly visit to Riverside, we were merely onlookers peeping at the fringes of high society, peering through the wire-mesh fence and imagining all the lovely fashions of the Royal party and the pomp and bustle of the visitors. It was an undisputed fact that the show was way beyond our financial means.

Another of our favourite walks was in Camperdown Park, which was officially opened by Princess Elizabeth after the estate had been gifted to the city. When we made our first visit to it Mum couldn't get over the idea of so much land being owned by one family, that of Admiral Duncan. Still, that didn't stop us enjoying our trips up the long drive towards the white mansion house that wasn't open to the public. I had gazed into all the rooms through the large windows and had been duly impressed, but not as impressed as we were by the monkey puzzle tree. George and I were fascinated by this, never having seen anything like it before. One day we were gazing up at it when an old man appeared. Mum said he might be a gardener in the park as he seemed to know all about the tree.

'Aye, the monkeys can run up it but they can't get back down because of the spikes,' he told us. 'That's why it's called the monkey puzzle tree.' Whether this was true or not is something I have never found out but we loved the story at the time and I still love it now.

The summer was now just a happy memory and autumn was turning all the trees to russet and gold. 'It's really peaceful in this park,' said Mum. 'It makes you forget your worries, even if just for an hour or two.'

Our final walk that year was on one very frosty morning. The trees were sugar coated in white rime and there were hardly any other visitors. As we set off back down the drive on our way home

I remember we left three trails of footprints on the frosty path. In our childlike fashion, both George and I thought they would remain there forever, along with the wonderful monkey puzzle tree.

There was no holding back the tide of change and as the year drew to a close the families from the street were leaving one by one. The Farquhar family moved to Kirkton, the Doyles to Beechwood and Margaret and George to Fintry. Tenants like Mum, who required a cheaper rented house in one of the older housing schemes, had to wait patiently until one became available. The folk from 108 Hilltown watched the mass exodus with peeved faces, gossiping bitterly about it. 'It's all right for some folk to get brand new houses, with hot water and a bath, but what about us? When will our houses get knocked down?'

As far as I was concerned, I wished it was their houses on the demolition list instead of ours because I was missing my pals. At one point, there was a vain hope that the street would get a reprieve but that didn't materialise and Mum soon got a key for a ground-floor flat at Moncur Crescent.

It was the first week of January 1950 – a new decade.

I walked down the Hilltown that evening to look at the beautiful display of glittering Christmas trees in the front windows of the houses at Shepherd's Pend. Each house was trying to outdo their neighbour with the seasonal fairy-light show.

Mum was worried about all the costs of moving but Big Bella, who had a huge circle of relations, came to her rescue. She arranged for a cousin, twice removed, to do our flitting. This cousin owned a battered old van but he was cheap and that was the selling point. Lizzie, who was still in residence in the street, came with us, as did Bella.

We walked through the large and empty rooms of our new abode, hearing our footsteps against the bare floorboards. The big windows overlooked a small garden with a gigantic bushy hedge then onwards to Dens Park football ground where scores of supporters would congregate every second Saturday.

We inspected the kitchen and bathroom with naive eyes, turning on the hot taps which, to our disappointment, gushed forth freezing-cold water. Mum said that the fire had to be lit before the water would heat up. This was news to George and me, who thought it came from some underground hot reservoir.

The kitchen was large, almost double the size of our old one, and it had a bare look. Mum said she would never be able to furnish it so we had to make do with the two large sinks, wooden draining board and cooker. High on a shelf sat the gas meter and underneath was a wooden coal bunker. Grandad's furniture lay in a small and sorry huddle in the middle of the living room, looking forlorn and scratched in the shafts of wintry sunshine that pierced through the smeary windows. Mum looked very unhappy at this new prospect in our lives but Bella, in her usual jovial fashion, made her laugh. 'For heaven's sake, woman! You're no moving to the moon. Eh'll be up to see you every week and so will Lizzie.'

Before moving away, each family had stated the need to keep in touch with one another but, even as the words were being said, they all knew instinctively that this was just a wishful dream. Mum and Lizzie were now saying the same thing.

'Now, Lizzie, no matter where you get your house, we'll keep in touch.'

'Of course we will,' agreed Lizzie.

Then Lizzie departed with Bella – two of Mum's oldest friends. The van drove away and we were left alone in our new domain. Mum looked as if she wanted to cry but instead she began to place the furniture around the room. The only thing was that there was too much of the room and not enough of the furniture so she ended up by putting the kettle on to make some tea.

I think we knew that this mass movement from the street had broken all the old chains of friendship and the camaraderie created by the sharing of hardships through the lean years of the war. This applied even to the communal trip to the tar boiler when any of the children had the whooping cough – according to an old wives' tale, the fumes from tar helped to cure this disease.

From now on we were on our own. No doubt new friends would soon fill the vacuum left behind from the street but one thing was sure. From this new decade on it would be new voices from a different street we would hear.

PART TWO

NEW VOICES FROM A DIFFERENT STREET

CHAPTER 15

Betty had been a blue baby. The daughter of our new neighbours, the Millers, she had been born with a hole in her heart and weighing a mere few pounds. Her first few months had been spent wrapped in cotton wool and it was touch and go whether she would survive the crucial initial weeks after her handicapped start in life. But she did survive and when I first met her she was almost eleven years old, a year younger than mc.

We were now firmly established in our new domain in Moncur Crescent and were slowly becoming acquainted with our new neighbours. Betty resembled a fragile, porcelain doll. Her thin face had, in my first ignorant opinion, a creamy pallor with twin red spots on her cheeks and lips that always had a bluish tinge. The Millers were a lovely couple. Almost equal in height, around five foot two inches, with round, cheery faces, it was difficult to put an age on them. To my young eyes, anyone over twenty was ancient but I guessed they must have been in their fifties.

One day Mrs Miller took Mum aside when they met in the close. 'Will you make sure your lassie doesn't encourage Betty into strenuous games?' she asked. 'Betty isn't allowed to run or jump about.'

Mum made sure I got the message loud and clear. In her opinion, George and I were still noisy, rumbustious individuals with ravenous appetites to match. The fact that we were always growing out of our clothes was another permanent worry.

Betty was a pupil at Fairmuir School, which catered for the physically handicapped, and she attended only the morning session. At the time I envied this arrangement because I was now in the final few months at Rosebank School while George was in Primary Five. The dreaded Qualifying Examination was looming on my horizon. This exam sorted out the clever pupils from the not-so-bright or downright dim and was the yardstick for the entire length of your secondary education. Even then it was regarded as unfair and unequal.

Mr Cuthbert, our teacher, was drumming subjects and facts into our protesting brains like a constant hammer against a brick wall. Whether we retained a fraction of it was another matter. He stood before the class on the day before the exam and told us to have a quiet night at home in order to train our young minds on the task ahead. This would be the most important day in our primary education, he said. This was obviously good advice but it was clear he hadn't reckoned with a gremlin in the works and that the best of plans can go awry. He didn't live at 14 Moncur Crescent.

It all began when we arrived home from school. Betty, who had been standing at the top of the street, saw us and began running in order to catch up with us, because we were racing each other home in order to be the first one with the bread and jam. We didn't see her but by the time she reached the close, she was sucking in great gulps of air and her lips were almost purple.

Mrs Miller almost fainted when we hammered on her door and she immediately rounded on me. 'What did Eh tell you? Betty can't run around like you two. Heavens! You're just like a horse galloping about.'

The woman was beside herself with worry until the doctor arrived and I was dreading Mum's return from the mill. I reckoned I would end up with a smack or a severe telling-off. Neither of these would be conducive to a quiet, contemplative night at home.

When Mum eventually arrived home, I immediately leapt to my own defence, protesting my innocence, with George backing me up. To my amazement, she didn't make a big issue of it but I was told to go and apologise to our neighbour. I thought this a bit unfair, considering I hadn't done anything wrong, but I recalled Grandad often saying, 'You think quickly with your head but you have to make a journey around your heart.' This statement was certainly true at this point because, although my head was full of innocence, my heart was saying something different – that I had had a big fright.

Betty was sleeping peacefully in her room and I was thankful to see her looking pale but normal. Her parents sat hunched up in their large, well-upholstered armchairs, grateful that the doctor had found no lasting damage other than extreme breathlessness.

I began to speak but Betty's mum stopped me.

'Eh ken now it wasn't your fault. It was just that Eh was so worried. Eh'm going to have to warn Betty that she can't run about like you and your brother and she'll just have to accept it.'

I almost burst into tears at this sad statement. I had never given a thought to anyone being different from me or my friends. One of the neighbours in our old street had had a toddler with Down's Syndrome or Mongolism as the women in the street used to refer to it. But I hardly saw him and he died before reaching school age. I was now faced with a different world of permanent disability and I knew that a special eye would have to be kept on any activities that Betty was involved in.

As it turned out, the day's drama was far from over. Later that evening while I was trying some juvenile meditation, our cat decided to surprise us by producing a litter of kittens. This cat had been a thin, waif-like stray who landed on our windowsill a couple of weeks earlier. Mum, being kind-hearted, had taken it in.

There I was, trying to cram as much learning into my head as was humanly possible when Mum rushed into the living room and began to rummage in the corner cupboard. She reappeared with a small cardboard box and an old blanket, calling out to me in the passing to come and help her.

Toots, the cat, had decided that the foot of the bed was the ideal place to give birth and one kitten was already born by the time we lifted her into her new cardboard abode. She gave us a baleful look as if suggesting the cold box was no substitute for the mound of warm blankets but, once she was installed by the side of the fire, she accepted it. With the cat now making strange mewing sounds and Mum fussing around, it was impossible to return to any further study.

Anyway, I was sent to strip the bed. 'Make sure you sponge the blankets even although there's only a wee mark,' said Mum. 'Thankfully, Eh caught her in time.' She cried aloud in dismay as another kitten made its entrance into our already impoverished lives.

The stain was barely noticeable and the blanket was soon hanging over the backs of two chairs, the damp patch slowly steaming in front of the fire. As it was, there were only two kittens and that was a relief to Mum, me and Toots.

Because of all this kerfuffle, George and I slept in the next morning. Mum had wakened me at six-thirty as usual before heading off to work but I had fallen asleep again. As a result, we had to say a quick cheerio to Toots and family before darting down the Hilltown towards the school. We were passing the small sweet factory at the top of Tulloch Crescent when the school bell went. Rosebank School had separate entrances for boys and girls. The boys' gate was in Rose Lane, another 500 yards or so from my gate.

Mum always insisted that I accompany George to the gate and it was a chore I hated. I thought he was old enough to see himself to the playground but it was one of Mum's rules and had to be obeyed. That particular morning, the most important day in my scholastic life, I knew I couldn't be late. Without hesitation I demanded that he should come through the girls' gate.

He was appalled. 'What, go past all the lassies?' he spluttered, his childish face red and obstinate.

With the snake-like queues of children all marching relentlessly towards the open school doors I had no option but to wrap my trench coat around him and pull him across the playground, his little, protesting legs barely touching the ground. Amid sniggering catcalls from some of the boys, he glared indignantly at me before jumping the low wall and running towards his classmates

I had no time to worry about his trivial hurt feelings because I had problems of my own – the exam and my lack of studying. To make matters worse, it was becoming clear from all the lively chatter in the classroom that quite a few of the bright sparks had indeed spent the evening doing nothing but getting into the right frame of mind.

I sat beside Grace and Ruth, who were discussing their chances of passing the exam. 'Did you manage to study last night?' they enquired, gazing at me with button-bright eyes.

I was tempted to tell the truth but I didn't think they would be interested in Betty's drama or the minutiae of our feline population explosion. I just nodded, hoping desperately that all the scholastic facts from the past year had somehow managed to penetrate and cling to the recesses of my brain. At that moment I had to admit it was doubtful.

The exam soon began in earnest as a flurry of bags and books were quietly tucked out of sight. An unnatural quietness descended on the room, only to be broken by the scraping of pens against paper and the occasional, barely audible groan of despair. At dinnertime we all filed into the dining hall, our faces glum and all the bright chatter from the top class absent. We weren't so much shell-shocked as exam-exhausted. Although I didn't know it then, I was about to be faced by another vexing situation.

Ever since Grandad's death, we had been taking school dinners and during that long period, even in times of extreme hunger, I could never stomach sago pudding. Perhaps it was the long-distant memory of the horrible, lumpy porridge at Duncarse Home. The dinner lady knew never to give me any and I was quite content to sit at an empty space while all around me my classmates wolfed down this horrible pudding. At least that was the situation until this stressful day when Miss Edwards overheard the woman saying, 'Oh, Eh just forgot, you never eat sago.'

The teacher's face was puce with fury 'Never eat sago? Am I hearing this correctly, young madam?' At this point, everyone within earshot stopped scooping spoonfuls into their mouths to listen.

'Bring over a plate of sago, please,' Miss Edwards demanded of the open-mouthed server, who protested loudly.

'It doesn't matter if someone dislikes something – there's aye someone who wants a second helping.'

In spite of this backing, the plate was duly placed in front of me. I gazed blankly at it, wishing this awful day was over. It didn't help that my companions, with heads bent low, dutifully scraped their plates clean, as if to emphasise my full plate. By now the mound of sago was growing colder by the minute, taking on a slightly green, bilious appearance. Miss Edwards stood in an uncompromising attitude behind my back while the two dinner ladies muttered under their breaths.

'Blinking shame, making someone eat something they don't like. After all, some things give *me* the boak,' said one, while her pal nodded in agreement.

One thing was clear. I was now beginning to realise that if I couldn't bear to eat sago hot, then it would take a general anaesthetic for me to eat it cold. I considered scooping it into something but, not having had the foresight to arm myself with a hankie or bit of newspaper, I was stymied. It was the afternoon class bell that saved me. Miss Edwards grabbed me by the collar and yelled, 'Get out! And don't ever let me see you refuse food again!'

The dinner ladies gave small, satisfied smiles as I gratefully escaped but I was scared to acknowledge them in case my tormentor was still watching.

George was waiting for me at four o'clock, a furious look on his face, but I was too fed up to argue with him. It had been a day to remember all right. I wasn't sure how well I had done in the exam. Had I passed it?

There was better news about Betty, however. Although the blue tinge was still visible around her lips, she was sitting up in bed with a huge feather eiderdown around her frail shoulders. She was eager to hear about my day and was almost agog when I mentioned the fiasco at dinnertime. She laughed at my exaggerated impression of the teacher, although I didn't add that there had been precious little to laugh about at the time. Distance in this case lent boldness. Then she became wistful. 'Eh wish Eh went tae the same school as you. You're really lucky,' she said, looking like a brittle, fragile doll.

This heartfelt statement suddenly made me feel ashamed of my pathetic moans, especially about something as trivial as a plate of sago, but at that time I really thought Betty would get stronger. It was all a matter of taking life easy, building up her strength and then she would be like George and me.

A few weeks later, Mr Cuthbert stood in front of the class with a list in his hands, reading out the names of pupils who had passed the dreaded 'Quali'. Most of us had passed, thank the Lord. We were now headed for Rockwell Secondary School after the summer holiday. Auntie Nora gave me a new gym tunic that was too big for my cousin Eleanor. One small flaw was the Harris Academy braid sewn around the square neckline. Still, I had seven weeks to unpick it.

CHAPTER 16

Our new house was such a contrast to our old one. The close was situated on a narrow lane that stretched from Canning Street to Moncur Crescent and was always affectionately called 'the cuttie'. This was obviously a shortened version of 'the cutting'. Mum didn't like the large, square kitchen, preferring instead a small, cosy kitchenette, but apart from that it was great to have an inside bathroom and lots of hot water which was provided by the back boiler of the fire.

Each close had six flats and we were on the ground floor. The living room overlooked a tiny, mangy-looking garden with a postage-stamp-sized square of grass enclosed by one of the bushiest hedges we had ever seen. If a square of grass could be described as moth-eaten then that was a good description of our lawn, while the hedge wouldn't have been out of place in the grounds of Camperdown Park. The view then swept down over a triangle of stunted bushes that looked as if they had given up and died, then down to the high wall of Dens Park football ground

We loved to sit at the window on a Saturday afternoon when the local team was playing at home, watching the profusion of tramcars, buses and a small number of cars driving up Canning Street to park. Then there were the thousands of supporters who thronged through the turnstiles, from our vantage point looking like purposeful ants.

Compared to the comfortable, well-furnished domain of the Miller family, our flat was spartan, and in spite of the fire, it had a cold appearance. Mum was a bit worried about the rent, which was in excess of what we paid in McDonald Street. Nevertheless, she had to have it ready every Friday night when the rent man called. Because of this extra demand on our resources we had to make do with Grandad's old furniture, which looked ancient and scratched when viewed in the sunlit room. Because we rarely saw the sun in our old house, the well-worn condition of the furniture had come as a bit of a shock.

Mum had taken out a Provident cheque prior to moving and this had been spent on a colourful square of congoleum, a cheaper form of linoleum. This had been purchased at the City Arcade and three pairs of brightly patterned cretonne curtains bought at Cyril's textile shop in the Westport completed our outlay. This had to be paid back at a few shillings a week, also on a Friday night.

The new lino was bright but, because it was a square, it left an edge of wooden flooring around the edges. Thankfully, the previous tenants had darkened this edge with wood stain, which was more than could be said for the walls. The decor left a lot to be desired, with tatty torn wallpaper on most of the walls and a bilious-looking ochre-coloured paint in the kitchen and bathroom. This colour was so awful that Mum often said it made the food look terrible and the room, during those initial few months, was always freezing. However, because Grandad's table was in the living room, we normally ate our meals in front of the fire and it wasn't a big problem.

Mum had her dreams. 'If Eh ever win the football pools, Eh'll decorate this entire house and get great furniture – just the way Eh want it.'

We realised we couldn't wait for Littlewoods Pools to come to our rescue and, as it turned out, it was Bella who proved to be our benefactor. 'Eh've heard that my next-door neighbour's cousin is selling a three-piece suite – a settee and two chairs. She wanted five pounds for them but she's willing to accept three pounds, ten shillings because Eh told her you were a friend of mine.'

Mum went with Bella to see this suite and was ecstatic when she saw it. The cousin lived in a dark, poky flat in Jamaica Street and the building was more run down than the one we had recently left behind. The suite was brown leather-look, or Rexene as it was called, with large, squashy cushions in brown velvet. Mum snapped it up right away. She had taken her last two pounds with her because Bella had said the cousin would accept payment over two weeks. Mum wasn't sure how she would find the remaining balance of thirty shillings but she said she would worry about that when the time came.

There was, however, the problem of delivery but the indefatigable Bella soon solved this. She persuaded the man of the house to take on the job for an extra half-crown, to be paid with the outstanding balance. It transpired that he knew a delivery man who had access to a small cart and pony, so it was all systems go on the three-piece suite front.

Mum tried to forget about the added half-crown on top of the thirty-shilling burden. All she could think about was how wonderful this new furniture would look in our new house, alongside Grandad's old, scratched but well-looked-after sideboard. She planned to have it delivered the next day after school so that I could be at home to let the man in. Although she didn't say so, I just knew she was glad to be at work. That way, she wouldn't have to worry about what the neighbours might think of a small, tatty cart and pony delivering our suite. 'After all,' she said, 'Eh expect folk around here get their furniture from Henderson's Stores in the Wellgate.'

When the man duly arrived, I was taken aback. He looked like a gypsy, with a deep-brown, tanned face and a red scarf tied around a thin, wrinkled neck like a tortoise's. Seemingly, he was thirty-five years old with a young family of five children. He certainly looked ancient to me but maybe this was the result of his outdoor job, plying his trade in all kinds of sunshine, rain and snow. He had brought another man with him and they both humped our gorgeous new purchase along the path.

Once inside the house, the gypsy-looking man could barely take his eyes away from the large window and the big room. 'Will you show me the rest of the house?' he asked, in a surprisingly soft voice.

I hesitated, taken aback by such a request from a swarthy stranger. George made for the front

231

door but I yanked him back. 'We'll both show you,' I said, alarm obviously showing on my face.

The man held up his hand. 'Eh don't want to frighten you, pet. It's just that Eh have a wee proposition to make tae your mother when she comes to pay the rest of the money next week.'

Mum almost had a fit when I passed on the gist of the conversation. Her poor face was a picture, and the minute our tea was over she set off for Jamaica Street, via Norrie's Pend.

She returned an hour or so later with Bella in tow, both looking crestfallen. The proposition had been a business deal. The couple, along with their large family, were all crammed into two dark and dismal tiny rooms. Because of this desperate situation, they were frantic to get a new house. Although well up on the Corporation housing list, Jamaica Street, unlike our old street, wasn't on the demolition rota.

They offered Mum a sum of twenty pounds plus a complete decoration of their old flat along with all fittings of lino and curtains if Mum would do a swap with them. It wasn't as if we would never get another new house, they said, as it was only a matter of time before all these old and crumbling tenements were demolished. Twenty pounds was an absolute fortune to us, and Mum did admit afterwards that she was tempted but she turned them down.

This decision didn't mean that she was un-sympathetic to their plight, as she explained later to Bella. 'Eh really felt sorry for them, Bella, but Eh've waited years for a house with a bathroom and hot water. Anyway, we've just got the one bedroom here and that wouldn't be enough for their big family.'

Bella, who was still incarcerated in her dark flat at Norrie's Pend, agreed. 'No, just you hang on to your house, Molly. After all, it's just a matter of time before we're all re-housed and we've just tae content ourselves till then.'

Mum was still feeling guilty. 'Eh felt like crying when Eh saw the five bairns all crammed into that wee bed but, after getting a taste of this new house, Eh would hate tae give it up.'

One thing this little episode showed was how desperate the housing shortage was. If it hadn't been for the Corporation wanting the land on which our old houses stood, then we would have all been in the same position. Mum was still upset the following week, so I was sent to pay the balance. She did, however, put in a small note thanking them for a lovely suite and hoping the family would soon be in a new house.

Over the next few weeks, Mum got into the habit of mentioning the lost opportunity, especially when mulling over our money problems. She would sit in the comfort of her easy chair with a piece of paper and jot down all the outgoings, which never seemed to balance with our income.

'Now then, let's see. You'll have your two and six this week from your milk round and the same again next week. That makes five bob. Eh wonder if Eh can maybe miss the rent this week.'

She let this plan mull around in her head for a few moments before deciding the rent should be kept up to date. 'Now, if Eh was out this Friday

233

when the Provident man comes around, then that would save a few shillings.'

She looked at me as if seeking divine inspiration but when it wasn't forthcoming she merely screwed the bit of paper into a ball and lobbed it into the fire. 'Och, something will turn up, Eh suppose.' Like my late Grandad, it would seem she was also an eternal optimist.

The milk round she mentioned was my early-morning job with Sherrit's Dairy on the Hilltown. I had heard through the playground grapevine that a job was going begging, due to the unexpected illness of one of the milk boys. I hurried to the dairy as soon as the school disgorged us, enquiring if the job was still open. It was, and I was told to be at the shop by six-thirty the following morning.

Mr Sherrit was a lovely man. He had the healthy, outdoor appearance of a farmer but his house was actually across the street from the shop. The house lay up a wide pend and there was also a byre with cows, like a miniature farm.

By the time I arrived the following morning, a small group of tired-looking, pale-faced children stood waiting for the heavy metal churns to arrive. Wishing we could all have stayed in our warm beds, we watched as the owner ladled the milk into bottles. To my consternation, I was given a large metal pushcart which held three crates of milk bottles, two firmly encased in the framework and one balanced on top. There was also a metal hand carrier which held six bottles, to be used while climbing the stairs.

The routine never varied. We began with the

234

closes nearest to the shop, returning for a further refill of three crates before toddling off to our outlying customers. And because I was the new girl, my customers were almost on the moon. At six-thirty on a dark morning it felt like that.

My outward journey took in the catchment area from Kinghorne Road in the north then back to the shop through all the small, dark interconnecting streets in between. It was just my bad luck that my time as temporary milk person coincided with the dark mornings. Climbing up three or four flights of stairs with just a solitary, flickering gas-lamp, or worse, no light at all, was very scary.

Sometime my shadow would rise up ahead of me, silhouetted against the narrow walls like the monster from *Phantom of the Rue Morgue*. Another scary time was spent having to circumnavigate the old air-raid shelters in the back lands of the tenements. Being cursed with an overdeveloped imagination made life very difficult as I was convinced that these stark, concrete buildings housed at least one murderous maniac. It was a huge relief when I finished the round unscathed.

There was one strict rule that we had to adhere to because we were still in the land of shortages and rationing. If a customer forgot to put out her empties at the door then that was tough luck, because we couldn't leave a refill. We also had to be careful with all the precious empty bottles. They were like gold dust. I was really proud of the fact that I hadn't broken a single bottle but one thing I've learned in life is never to be smug, because that's when God sends some kind of retribution to wipe the smugness from your soul. Pride goes before a fall, as I was about to discover.

It was a Sunday morning. Lawson's Lane was as quiet as the grave and after heavy overnight rain the road had a shiny wet film over its uneven surface. Suddenly and without warning, the front legs of my cart caught the edge of the pavement and before I could act, the top crate went flying into space, to land with an almighty deafening crash on the stone setts.

I was almost afraid to count the broken bottles but I reckoned there were at least a dozen. Convinced that this ear-shattering noise must have penetrated the walls of the nearby houses, I fully expected to see a crowd of people peeking through their curtains. But the entire street appeared to be firmly entrenched in the Land of Nod.

Lucky devils, I thought bitterly, while trying to hold back tears. Then I realised a sharp shard of glass had cut my hand and bright-red spots of blood were now mingling with the creamy rush of milk as it streamed through a maze of cobbles and into the gutter. No one came to aid me, a positive damsel in distress. I wouldn't have been ignored in one of my storybooks. In this fantasy fictional life there was always a stray passing prince on every page. Alas, he wasn't in Lawson's Lane that morning and I realised delivering milk to the masses was real life. I kicked the remaining fragments of glass into the gutter where they lay amongst the stream of dirty milk.

I considered my plight during the remainder of my round, which was spent delivering milk with one hand and sucking the bloody cut like some modern-day Dracula. Before reaching the shop I decided the best course of action would be to offer payment for the broken bottles. Then I remembered that this week's money had been counted in Mum's calculations. Because of the added outlay on our chairs, she was struggling to keep us afloat in the financial maelstrom of life. I was almost beside myself with anxiety over our predicament at home and what Mr Sherrit would say when faced with a huge pile of shattered bottles.

Then, as if a guardian angel had wafted overhead, my worrying seemed to have been over nothing. He appeared to be more concerned about my cut hand than any breakages. I started to explain about paying for the damage but he waved this suggestion aside and ushered me into the back shop, where a couple of milk boys were sitting. Before my dramatic entrance he had been in the process of baking a large batch of scones which he sold in the shop, along with the milk.

The teapot was sitting steaming on the stove. I was handed an enamel mug of tarry black tea and a hot, thick doughy scone liberally spread with a huge dollop of black treacle. This unexpected snack tasted like nectar and by the time I had wolfed down the scone and licked the sticky treacle from my fingers, my cut hand was almost forgotten until he placed a large chunk of pink Elastoplast over it. 'There now,' he said, with an air of satisfaction almost like some eminent surgeon after a delicate operation, 'that'll keep out the germs. Better tae be safe than sorry eh?'

I was worried about the pile of glass I had

kicked into the gutter, concerned that a small child might fall on it, but it was all gone the following morning. No doubt the scaffie on his early morning round had swept it up. The only remaining trace of my mishap was a thin, white rivulet of dried-up milk now lying like a crazy-paving pattern between the stone cobbles.

Weekday mornings were the best time to catch the customers. Some of them would only just make it to the door with their empties, clattering the bottles together in a glassy din. A lot of the women worked and they were quick to complain about having to wait for delivery. 'Heavens! Eh thought you would never get here. My man and my bairns are shouting for their breakfast,' was a typical moan.

I would have liked to retaliate to these women. I had only two legs and arms and what they were requiring was a human centipede. Strangely enough, it was often the stay-at-home housewives who were the biggest moaners. This thrifty, industrious band of women were mostly nice but now and again one would meet me at her door, one hand outstretched for her milk while the other hand was vigorously shaking a duster, often in my face.

Sometimes, while I recounted these snippets of daily harassment to Mum, she would sigh and say, 'It must be great tae be at home all day instead of going tae the mill!'

This statement was a bit unfair to the stay-at-home housewives who had to cope with young families as well as the daily grind of washing, cooking and housework. All these chores still had to be done by hand and took ages, even in this new decade. There was still some queuing as essentials continued to be in short supply. The war had been won but austerity was still the order of the day. Clothes and sweets were now off the ration but food was often subject to shortages.

There was also the added worry of another conflict, the Korean War. Bella's son, John, had joined up after leaving school and was now a soldier in the 1st Battalion, Argyll and Sutherland Highlanders. An unopposed landing had been made on the coast of Korea and the war went well for the combined UN, British and American forces as they pushed their way almost to the Chinese border. In November, however, China entered the war and they made such an assault on the UN troops that they fell back in disarray.

The Chinese foreign minister, Chou En-Lai, had warned the USA that they would resist if America entered North Korea. He never said a truer word. The newspapers were full of reports of the massive waves of Chinese troops pouring over the Manchurian border. One paper likened it to 'an undulating yellow wave, completely submerging all in its path'. This statement worried Bella and hundreds of mothers and wives all over the country. 'We've just been through one war and here we are fighting another one!' said Mrs Miller. 'We never learn.'

We may have entered a brave new decade but it was still in its infancy. Renewed hope was in the air but the same old restrictions and hostilities were still well and truly with us.

CHAPTER 17

Aggie had been a regular visitor to our old house, mainly because she lived a few hundred yards away, in Arthur Street, but since moving we hadn't seen her for a while. Then, one wet and windy Sunday, she suddenly appeared at the door. The rain was sweeping into the close on the edge of a cutting wind. It was July but we hadn't seen the sun for days. Huge black clouds like funeral pyres hung over the city spoiling the holiday plans of people lucky enough to consider such a thing. Our new door had a bell which worked by twisting it like a clockwork key and the first time we heard it, we thought someone was strangling a hen. The sound hadn't improved with time.

Aggie rushed in, a picture of wetness. 'Oh, for heaven's sake, what a day! Eh thought Eh would be washed away!'

She was wearing her most cherished garment, her musquash fur coat, and she looked like a drowned rat. Inside the living room, she took off the wet fur coat and, holding it by its large tag, she passed it over to me, giving it a few loving strokes and a long caressing glance before placing it in my hands. 'Now, Maureen, mind and hang it up by the tag. Eh don't want the fur to get damaged,' she warned me as I took the object of desire to one of the lobby coat hooks.

I hated this coat. It had a mangy appearance with one or two bald patches, and the smell of mothballs was overpowering. Today, however, there was also the smell of wet fur which was positively nauseating, and the lobby retained this unpleasant smell for ages after her departure. Mum laughed afterwards. 'Aggie's gone but not forgotten!'

Mum, however, was pleased to see her old friend. Their friendship had lasted since the far-off days when, as fourteen-year-olds, they had started at the same jute mill, two youngsters with, hopefully, the world at their feet. In those days, Aggie had been an extremely pretty girl, full of life and fun and forever getting into mischief. At least that was the story according to Aggie, who never grew tired of recalling the happy, halcyon days of yore.

During these long reminiscences, Mum, who was a realist, would nod in agreement at Aggie's tales, later telling me the real truth behind the so-called 'good old days', which were characterised by working long hours in the mill, doing a dirty hard job for little reward.

Still, it had to be said that life had been kinder to Aggie. At sixteen she had met and married a man a few years older and, apart from her housework, she never again had to earn another penny in outside employment. Her husband was a tramcar driver, a job he had held for years. I never knew his first name as he was always referred to as Mr Robb or 'meh man'. Aggie's conversations were peppered with 'Mr Robb did this' or 'Meh man did that'.

On our numerous trips to Isles Lane to see our granny, we often saw him driving our tramcar. Although not a tall man, he was stockily built and had what I thought were enormous feet for a man of his height. 'A man with a good grip of Scotland,' Mum would say.

When we saw him in his tram his feet would be splayed out on the platform, his hand guiding the machine along the tramlines. He sported a bushy moustache and thin, round, steel National Health spectacles that perched neatly on top of his nose.

Apart from Mr Robb, Aggie was blessed with two daughters, Senga and Babs, and it was the former who was the apple of her mother's eye. According to Aggie, Senga was the spitting image of herself. When she was sixteen, Senga met a young American soldier at a dance a few months after the end of the war. Such was the attraction that they wrote regularly to one another after his return to America. On the day of Princess Elizabeth's marriage to Philip, Duke of Edinburgh, Marvin proposed to Senga and flew over with a gorgeous diamond engagement ring.

Aggie and Mr Robb hadn't been keen on the engagement but Marvin soon won them round with his tanned good looks, blond crewcut hair-style, and charming manners. In the beginning he called his future in-laws Ma'am and Sir and Mum always said that did the trick, along with the huge diamond engagement ring.

Aggie had almost swooned with maternal pride. The wedding had been as lavish as restrictions allowed with a ceremony in Wallacetown

Church followed by a grand tea in the Queen's Hotel. Mum had been invited but as we hadn't she didn't go. As Mum said at the time, how could she go to such a grand affair in her old plum-coloured gaberdine costume?

As for Babs, she was hardly ever mentioned in the great scheme of Aggie's life. She had played second fiddle to her glamorous sister at the wedding, dressed in a shiny, satin, powder-blue frock, a colour which did nothing for her very fair hair, pale grey eyes and colourless complexion. She obviously took her looks from the paternal side of the family, big feet excepted, thankfully. Senga and Marvin were now cosily domiciled in California and, from Aggie's never-ending stories, the couple lived a life of luxury.

In spite of Aggie's pomposity, she certainly cheered Mum up. As the first year in our house progressed, it was becoming clear that Mum wasn't well. According to the doctor, there wasn't anything specifically wrong. It was more a progressive combination of hard work, tiredness and lack of money, a condition no doubt shared by the majority of her workmates.

As we sat around the fire that Sunday, I was surprised when Mum announced that she was giving up her job at the mill and taking a new job at the DPM Dairy at the foot of Mains Street, a mere few hundred yards from the house.

Aggie, who of course hadn't worked a day since her marriage, was quite adamant that Mum was making the wrong decision. 'You've been a weaver most of your life, Molly. Do you think it's wise changing jobs now, especially at your age?'

Mum bristled. 'What do you mean, "my age"? Eh'm the same age as you.'

Aggie was taken aback by this information that had somehow become obscured over the years. With a daughter now queening it in California, Aggie obviously reckoned that she was the younger woman instead of being a contemporary. She muttered unhappily, 'Eh suppose you're right.'

It was clear she didn't like this revelation being overheard by me, knowing I was always filled with eagerness to hear everyone's conversation.

'Well, Eh was just thinking of your well-being, Molly, and the different kind of work you'll be doing.'

Mum, who was too tired to argue, said wearily, 'Well, it'll be a damn sight easier than working a pair of looms at Little Eddy's. That's for sure.'

Aggie couldn't argue with that.

With the work subject now dropped, Aggie's good humour was restored and she searched inside her large, squashy handbag, muttering as she rummaged in its interior with the patches of pink face powder clinging to the moiré lining. 'Now where did Eh put the photies of Senga and Marvin? Eh put them in my bag especially to show you, Molly.'

I know Mum groaned silently at another imminent showing of Senga the Magnificent but I was keen to see them. Aggie gave a whoop of delight as her hand closed over the bundle of black-and-white snapshots. For the next hour we looked at Senga with her new house and umpteen poses of one or both of them lying, standing or reclining on bright striped deckchairs which were perched on a tiny lawn with a dried-up, parched look about it. 'Oh aye,' said Aggie, 'the grass is like that because it's always sunny and they hardly ever get rain.'

We turned to watch the rain running down the window while the wind blasted against the wooden frames, shaking the bushy hedge and rattling the metal garden gate. 'Eh wish we could get some Californian weather,' sighed Mum.

Afterwards, with the precious snapshots safely tucked away like the crown jewels and the wet musquash coat closed over her ample bosom, Aggie was ready to go home but not without a last piece of advice. 'Now, mind what Eh said, Molly – sometimes it's better to stick to what you know.'

Mum, who was really fond of her old friend, just nodded. 'Eh'll keep your words in mind, Aggie.'

To be honest Mum's new job was almost forgotten. My mind was filled with the wonders of California as depicted by the small, square photographs. Senga's life seemed so glamorous, just like that of a film star and a thousand light years away from our dismal lives of endless rain and eternal scrimping. I knew all about the love story and I was fascinated by the sheer romance of the whole thing. Marvin sounded and looked like a matinee idol but one thing in his favour was the fact that he never pretended to be rich. This was unlike lots of so-called Wyoming ranchers who spent the war years boasting to their girl-friends about their thousands of acres back home or those who claimed to have glamorous jobs in the movie industry. Many a poor GI bride landed in the USA to find herself the proud owner of some tumble-down shack in the wilderness. Most of the GI brides were happy but some weren't. Some stayed for years while others were back home as soon as they could manage it.

Marvin's honesty had endeared him to Mum and I was totally impressed by this wonderful lifestyle. When Mum arrived back from seeing her friend out, I was still in the land of fantasy and finding it hard to suppress my longing for a similar situation. Perhaps, I thought, if I could conjure up a sliver of glamour then things might be different. I homed in on the word Senga, which seemed an exotic name to me.

'Mum, if Eh called myself Senga, do you think it would make me more pretty?' I asked hopefully, with all the yearning of a thirteen-year-old adolescent.

I was taken aback by Mum's hearty laugh. Tears streamed down her thin cheeks. 'Senga? You daft gowk! Have you no twigged what it means?'

I shook my head, really annoyed by a flippant attitude to my future happiness from my mother who didn't seem to take my aspirations to glamour seriously.

'Well, let me enlighten you. Senga is called after her mother.'

I tried to reconcile Aggie's dull name with that of her chic, sophisticated daughter and failed. Mum explained.

'Aggie is short for Agnes and Senga is just Agnes backwards. Anyway,' Mum went on, 'Eh prefer Babs. She's a much nicer lassie, more like her father.'

With that statement, my little bubble of fantasy was burst and afterwards, any time Aggie prattled on about her daughter, Mum would catch my eye and gave me a huge wink. Thankfully, she always managed to hide this amusement from her friend.

Mum was now on her last week at the mill. I couldn't help feeling a touch of sadness as she prepared for her new job. I went down to meet her at the mill gate at the end of her last shift and I knew I was going to miss this cheery band of women whose resilience never ceased to amaze me. I was also going to miss Tam and the lodge with its cosy interior, the hissing, spitting fire and shrilly boiling kettle, the chipped teapot and enamel mugs. I also hoped his rheumatics would clear up.

Tam always knew when rain was imminent. 'Aye, it'll be raining before night because my rheumatics are real chronic,' he would mutter.

Mum always said the lodge was the quietest spot around. It acted as a buffer between the deafening clatter of the looms and the grey grimness of the surrounding streets outside. On that last evening, I stood at the gate as it disgorged hundreds of women. Mum was with Bella and Nell. Although Bella was still worried about her John fighting the communists on the 38th Parallel, she didn't show it and was as cheery as ever.

Nell, however, was complaining about the forthcoming evening's itinerary. 'It'll be the same old hard grind, Eh suppose, putting the tea on

247

for the family then doing the washing.'

Ahead of us was Mary, fresh-faced and fifteen and in her first job. She turned with a sneer that was aimed at poor Nell. 'Well, it's your own fault for getting married in the first place. Eh'm no going to pander to any man, that's for sure.'

This was said with all the cocky confidence of youth and was actually a sentiment I agreed with. The weavers looked wordlessly at one another until Bella chortled. 'Och, don't fash yourself lass! After all, you've never been asked yet and, who knows, maybe you'll be an auld maid.'

This dire insinuation that she might never see a ring on her finger or have a man in her life greatly annoyed her but she contented herself by glowering darkly at Bella.

'Don't listen to Bella, Mary,' laughed Mum, 'but make sure you marry for money because whoever said love makes the world go round didn't have to live on forty-eight and a tanner a week.'

Bella gave a loud harsh laugh that sounded like a demented crow while her overalls strained at the seams. Trying to keep a straight face, I watched in fascination, wondering if she would burst out from the restraining overalls like some giant quivering jelly. However, to my dismay, the well-stitched seams remained intact.

Nell was still on her high horse. 'Did you see that wee scunner Pete running after me this morning when Eh slipped off for a fly puff of my fag? He had the cheek to tell me he was noting all my comings and goings.'

Bella was also incensed by the gaffer who

obviously thought it was time he put a stop to the workers having a quick smoke. 'Eh just told him to his face that he wasn't going to put a stopwatch on me going to the lavvy.'

Poor Pete, I thought. He would have loved a job in Calcutta as an overseer in charge of a workforce of doe-eyed, docile, dark-skinned and sari-clad girls. Instead all he got was a bunch of smokers, led by big, beefy, belligerent Bella.

As we walked further away from Little Eddy's, I remember thinking that these women deserved a medal, never mind a fly puff of their cigarettes. They were hard working, cheery and got on with whatever the lottery of life threw at them. I had a funny feeling I was seeing the end of an era as far as we were concerned and, as it turned out, I never saw the majority of these wonderful women again.

Prior to starting her new job, Mum contracted a chest infection and she was signed off work for a week. 'Eh only hope this is no a bad omen,' she said, sounding really worried.

In the middle of that week, Aggie burst into the house. Her face red with exertion, she was almost out of breath. For once she didn't insist on the star treatment for the fur coat. 'Oh Molly! Wait till Eh tell you my news. It's good and no so good,' she gasped, trying to regain her breath.

Mum was taken aback by the sudden onslaught and I was positively agog. I prayed that I wouldn't be sent out for some wild-goose message while interesting topics were being discussed but on that particular night I don't think Aggie even noticed me sitting in my comfy chair, my ears twitching and my eyes alight with curiosity.

'Mr Robb and Eh have just got the keys to a new house! A prefab in Blackshade,' said Aggie. Her face was a picture of excitement while I lay back with disappointment. Just a new house, I thought.

'Our house in Arthur Street is to be demolished and meh man was just saying he would love to live in a prefab and here we are, the proud owners of the keys.'

Mum was really pleased for her friend. Although her house in Arthur Street on the corner of Dallfield Walk was vastly superior to our old house it still wasn't in the same class as a prefab. 'That's good news, Aggie,' said Mum. 'You and your man deserve it. What does Babs say about it?'

Aggie's face crumpled slightly and she looked to be on the verge of tears. I perked up immediately. 'Well, Senga and Marvin will just love it when she comes back for a visit.'

She stopped when Mum gave her an enquiring look. 'Och, Eh don't mean they're coming back right now,' she went on, 'but Eh just know they'll be over the moon with it.'

I waited with bated breath for the follow-up. It was clear from Aggie's disapproving tone that Babs wasn't the flavour of the month. With her plain, colourless face, thin, angular body and serious personality, Babs had clearly upset her mother. She had a good job as a clerkess with a potato merchant and the thought flitted through my mind that she had maybe absconded with the entire week's wages.

But no, according to Aggie it was much worse.

250

Seemingly, love had entered her life in the shape of a travelling salesman called Ron. He had a sharp taste in suits, favouring dark grey gaberdine with a cream pinstripe, purchased from the Fifty Shilling Tailor in the Murraygate, and hair well slicked down with Brylcreem. In Aggie's eyes he resembled a spiv.

'Eh don't know what she sees in him,' she confided, 'He's right oily-looking, like one of them dancehall dagos.'

By this time, *my* imagination was doing spirals and little war dances in my brain.

Mum was amused at Aggie's description. 'When was the last time you saw a dancehall dago, Aggie? Heavens, woman! You wouldn't recognise a dago if he jumped out and did a tango with you.'

However, Aggie with her musquash fur coat, her Californian connections and now a brand new prefab, was not going to be easily mollified. 'Well, you know what Eh mean. Maybe he's...' She looked in my direction before cupping a hand over her mouth and whispering, in a stage whisper as it fortunately turned out, 'What if he's already married?'

Mum didn't have the answer to that perennial problem and Aggie's step wasn't as jaunty as usual when she left. It was as if one daughter's foolhardiness was blunting the pleasure gained from the other sibling, and the prefab.

However, as Christmas 1951 approached, Mum was in her new job, while over at Chez Robb in the new abode, Aggie and her man entertained Ron the spiv to Christmas dinner – with most of the ingredients still on the ration.

CHAPTER 18

We were in Miss Calvert's English class, working out the intricacies of verbs, pronouns and adjectives when the news of King George VI's death was broken to us. A pale-faced, sad-looking young teacher was the bearer of this bad news.

Miss Calvert then addressed her motley lot with the dramatic announcement, a grave expression on her face. 'King George VI, after a long illness, has died. Long live the Queen.'

A sea of faces solemnly gazed back at her and I remember glancing around the group of girls who sat beside me in class 2AMC, wondering what this momentous news meant to them. No doubt they were thinking the same. To be honest, it meant little to me. My life was spent in getting through each day and I had no thought for people who had immense wealth. While it was a sad day for the country no matter how hard I tried I couldn't identify with the remote and now deceased royal figurehead.

It was a well-known fact that the late King had undergone a major lung operation and that he had looked increasingly frail. On our last visit to the Odeon Cinema, Mum and I had watched the Pathé News and there had been an item with the King saying goodbye to his daughter and son-in-law as they left London Airport for Kenya on a visit to the Commonwealth. The King stood with uncovered head in the cold drizzle of a February day, and Mum had remarked, quite prophetically as it turned out, 'Eh don't think the King looks awfy well. In fact he's a poor soul.'

Miss Calvert's voice brought me back from my reminiscences. She was informing us that we were now in a new Elizabethan Age and she voiced her hope that this second golden age would be as illustrious as the first, which had been a truly historic age producing such notable figures as Shakespeare, Francis Drake and Walter Raleigh. We were now two years into a so-called 'brave new world' and now that the country had a new young Queen then surely things had to get better.

I was now into my second year at Rockwell Secondary School, a large, attractive, red stone building in Lawton Road. It was so unlike the homely atmosphere of Rosebank Primary. It housed hundreds of pupils in its airy classrooms with their large windows that let in lots of sunlight. The curriculum was also very different from the primary school, the day being divided up into a series of periods, each one teaching a different subject. It was a constant round of shifting rooms as the corridors echoed to the sounds of clattering feet and ringing bells.

It was strange at first but as time wore on I got used to the routine and often longed for the bell to ring, to sound the end of a particularly hard or boring subject. This would include arithmetic or shorthand, a form of writing to my mind that smacked of hieroglyphics. The variety of subjects was quite overpowering at times, ranging from science and the mysteries of the Bunsen burner to typing blindfold to the accompaniment of a Victor Sylvester record. Or we could listen to garbled chattering of a French family on the radio or sing camp songs in the music room. Oh yes, it was all go.

One subject I really loathed with intensity was physical education, especially if it took place out in the playground with us running around in our navy-blue knickers playing netball in full view of leering, grinning pubescent boys. They must have sharpened their pencils down to the bare lead, judging by the time they spent hanging around the sharpener that always seemed to be on the windowsill.

Perhaps if I had owned a pair of chic, designer knickers then I might have felt differently but during the entire three years I spent at the school, half my time was spent making up a whole host of notes with a multitude of excuses. Some worked and others didn't. I had no qualms about this ploy because, in my opinion, whoever devised such a costume for an outdoor activity for adolescent girls was either a fool or a sadist.

In spite of this one bête noire, I enjoyed most of the classes, as did my friend Sheila. We had hit it off right from day one, perhaps because we were alike, not in looks but in circumstances. Sheila lived with her granny and auntie and although she was slightly better off than me, it wasn't to the same degree as the rest of our classmates. Affluence was beginning to creep around the edges of some people's lives and this was evident with a lot of my contemporaries who would appear at the school with crisp, new clothes, nice shoes and smart leather school-bags.

Sheila played the violin and if physical education was my pet hate then playing her violin at Friday assembly was hers. The headmaster had decreed that anyone with a modicum of musical talent was to be encouraged and sent to stand on the stage in a mini-orchestra before the morning prayers and hymn. In spite of all the intervening years, I can still see Sheila standing almost on the edge of the stage, dressed in her jumper and skirt and white ankle socks, looking awkward and ill at ease as if she hated every minute of these recitals. She freely admitted the truth of this at the end of most performances.

If she is still playing her violin, I hope she enjoys it better now.

One thrilling bit of news was the forthcoming coronation of the new queen. The newspapers were full of the coming plans but some Scottish insurgents were targeting pillar boxes with the new E II R logo on them. These purists were at loggerheads with the authorities, claiming that the Scottish postboxes should be emblazoned with E I R because, as they pointed out, the first Elizabeth had been Queen of England and not Scotland.

As it was, in my small corner, most of the historic events went almost unnoticed due to an accident Mum had at work. She was enjoying her job at the dairy and had made new friends with some of the women. It was very different from the mill. Instead of a dry, dusty atmosphere filled with a million particles of jute dust, the bottle-washing department was warm and steamy with an ever-present moist air. Instead of the chattering clatter of hundreds of looms, the dairy echoed to the constant racket of thousands of milk bottles as they marched relentlessly down the conveyor belt towards the huge milk machines.

It was a rogue milk bottle, jammed in the belt, that caused the accident. When Mum tried to remove it, the top shattered and the jagged edges sliced deeply into the palm of her hand, making a large gash at the base of her thumb. The first we heard about it was when she arrived back from the casualty department of the Royal Infirmary, accompanied by Nellie, who was to prove herself a very good friend to us over the following years. Mum's hand was swathed in a mound of white bandages and supported by a stockingette sling. The wound had needed a few stitches and Mum, who hated the sight of blood, looked pale and ill.

Although we didn't know it then, this unfortunate accident was to have effects lasting far longer than any of us could imagine. She was signed off work and we were now back to keeping the house on the paltry sickness benefit. Initially, the wound healed up quickly although the scar had a deep red, puckered appearance. It wasn't until a trip to the hospital clinic as a routine check-up that the doctor confirmed what Mum had known right from the start. Her thumb was now totally useless and she was incapable of grasping anything in that hand.

She was to be admitted to hospital while the surgeon tried to repair the damaged tendons and nerves. Auntie Nora would have looked after us but Mum thought, because I was almost fourteen, I was capable of looking after George and myself with some help from Mrs Miller. It would only be a few days. At least, that was the plan but it turned out to be a nightmare. The few days in hospital stretched out to a fortnight and then another two weeks as the surgeon tried to repair the damaged hand. He probed several times for the tendon but the jagged glass had severed it completely and, being like a strong elastic band, it had retracted, never to be found again.

Mum was in a dilemma. Firstly there were her two children, gamely trying to keep going, and secondly there were her cigarettes. She was almost on the point of despair over the never-ending financial situation at home and the non-existent chance of having a fly puff. The Sister on the ward was very strict, not only to the nurses but also to the patients. She was also dead against the horrible habit of smoking and would regularly inspect the toilets. Heaven help the culprit if she detected even the slightest whiff of tobacco.

On visiting days, George and I would trudge up endless stairs and along the antiseptic passages to the crisply starched ward where Mum lay under the unwrinkled bedcover, smokeless and totally fed up. Once a week I took the green sickness cheque for her to sign and received a list of chores and bills to be paid. At the start of every visit I would silently pray that she would be discharged but it didn't materialise.

Then, a week or so later, she got the bombshell. I could see from her face when I entered the ward that something was amiss. I thought it was something medical and was almost afraid to approach the bed but it turned out to be another financial headache, that old bugbear. Before I had time to sit down on the hard, uncomfortable chair, she said, 'Because Eh've been in hospital all this time, the hospital wants to deduct some money from the insurance to pay for my stay here.'

I was appalled at this statement because the sickness benefit money wasn't covering everything and some bills were being left unpaid.

Her face was red and she looked distressed. A young nurse arrived and pushed a thermometer under Mum's tongue. 'Now, you'll have to stop worrying as your temperature is high and Sister doesn't want you to get an infection,' she said, while looking at the slim glass tube in her hand.

Mum was still vexed. 'Eh can't help worrying, nurse. It's this awfy letter Eh got from the insurance folk,' she said. Then she explained all the sorry state of our finances. 'And the worst thing is there's Mrs What's-her-name in the next ward. Her man is well off but, because she doesn't work, the hospital is no taking a penny off her. It's no fair.' Mum, who was rarely a complaining kind of person, was now in full flow over the financial injustices of the insurance world and the National Health Board in particular.

The young nurse was very sympathetic. 'I would see the almoner about this, if I were you, especially as it's causing hardship.'

I almost told her this was the understatement of the year. It was bad enough living on the breadline but if this sum was deducted every week then we would be in dire poverty. After the nurse left, Mum decided to bypass the almoner, making up her mind to go straight to the horse's mouth, so to speak, namely the National Insurance Office on the junction of Tay Street and the Overgate.

To be more precise, I was to go, post-haste after school the following day. My heart sank at this request. I hated visiting this building which had been erected at the conception of the NHS in 1948-49. This single-storey brick-built building was always overflowing with people, no matter what time of day you went there.

The waiting room chairs lay in pristine rows and faced the various desks of the clerks. Sometimes, if you were lucky, all the desks would be manned and the waiting motley band of sick, newly well, infirm or just downright work-shy would be dealt with quickly. A multitude of human problems and frailties would all be neatly documented on duplicate or triplicate forms to be later filed away in the far blue yonder of a back room, probably in some pigeon-holed cabinet. We were now truly a form-filling nation.

The following day I trudged up the street to the building and was dismayed to see most of the desks unmanned. I settled down for a prolonged stay. Sitting beside me was a family with a husband who clearly suffered from a debilitating illness. He weighed about seven stone and had a thin, drawn, yellow-tinged face with a slender wrinkled neck. His wife, on the other hand, looked a picture of health with red glowing cheeks and contrasted sharply with the emaciated, shrivelled-up man at her side. Two small children sat quietly beside them and they looked like miniature versions of the woman, which must have been a blessing.

The weary-eyed woman at the desk called out sharply, 'Next please!' and I went forward, prepared to do battle over the letter in my hand. Mum had said I was to be adamant that we couldn't possibly live on a reduced amount. But the clerk was merely there to take down all the details and it wasn't her job to reach any decision on anyone's benefit. At least that was what I was told.

I wasn't looking forward to relaying this news to Mum on the next visiting day but she accepted it better than I anticipated. This was because she had been told she could go home in a couple of days. As it was, she got home the following afternoon, down in the dumps because her hand was virtually useless and there was nothing that could be done surgically for it. But she was glad to be home where she could sit with her favourite detective novels and a cigarette.

Fortunately, we never heard another word about hospital charges. Maybe the form disappeared between pigeon-holes or whatever receptacle it had been destined for, preferably the waste-paper bin. Nellie came round with some good news. The foreman at the dairy had been pushing for Mum to get her wages every week. As he said, the accident had happened at work so now she would be paid until able to return to work.

Nellie also brought two tickets for the first

house at the Palace Theatre for the following Saturday. 'Eh thought we could have a night out but just if you feel up to it,' she said.

Mum, who loved the variety theatre and the pictures, was thrilled. Sometimes both of us would go to the Palace Theatre for a treat but the last time had been years ago.

The theatre was at the end of a lane that ran down beside the imposing facade of the Queen's Hotel. How well I remember the dancing chorus girls all dressed in skimpy costumes and black fishnet tights that sometimes had little holes in them, with small pimples of pink flesh poking through. Sometimes, if the theatre was a bit cold, the girls' arms had a goose-pimpled effect that even the orange stage make-up couldn't conceal. Oh yes, I loved the dancing act, as well as the singers and comedians.

Nellie was still explaining. 'Eh'm no sure who's on the bill, Molly. Eh've heard Jack Milroy and his *Braw, Braw Heilan Laddie* is coming but that's at the start of the New Year.'

'It doesn't matter who's on, Nellie,' said Mum. 'You've made my day with your kindness and we'll enjoy whatever is on the programme.'

Meanwhile, back at school, the tattie holidays were looming and I was looking forward to getting out of the classroom and also earning a bit of money. The children had two choices, or three if you counted the fact that you could remain at your lessons. You could go privately and make your own arrangements with a farmer or do what the majority of children plumped for, which was to go under the school's own scheme. Rockwell

School laid on a fleet of buses and we were all allocated a certain farm for the day or, occasionally, for the week. A hot midday meal was supplied in a nearby school or village hall and the pay was eleven shillings and threepence per day. This sum filled Mum with rapture because we could now catch up with our bills after our poverty-stricken times a month or so ago.

I was full of excitement on that first day as I stood beside Sheila in the school hall at an unearthly hour, six-thirty if I remember right. We then filed on to an old-looking bus that slowly drove out of the school playground and on to the far horizons, which was Meigle or Muirhead, but could have been on the moon as far as I was concerned. The morning was crisp with a hint of autumn sunshine peeping through the early mist.

We all tumbled out on to the tattie field and watched as a weatherbeaten grieve with strips of sacking tied around his trouser legs marched briskly up the rows of withered, brown shaws, measuring and marking out each person's bit. The tattie digger churned up the thick brown earth to reveal what looked like hundreds of white-skinned potatoes. It was certainly back-breaking work but not really any harder than Mr Sherrit's milk round which I had had to give up when the regular boy appeared back at his job.

I enjoyed being out in this different world of fields, trees and quietness. It was such a change from the city. Because we were given our dinner at midday, all we had to carry was a bottle of lemonade and two rolls and butter for the morning and afternoon piece-break. This break was always greeted with relief as it allowed you to straighten up for a quarter of an hour. It was a glorious autumn that year and at the end of the three weeks I was almost as weather-beaten as the grieve on that very first day.

Mum commented on my newly rosy cheeks. 'Maybe Eh should go out to the tatties as well and get braw red cheeks.'

We did get some rain but it always appeared at the end of the day or at the weekend. There was an unfortunate accident on one of the farms one day. A boy from another school was determined to get conkers and, unlike his pals who were content to throw sticks at the giant horse-chestnut trees that lined the edge of the field, he decided to climb on to the branches. The result of this foolhardy exploit was that the master daredevil fell and broke his arm.

This threw the farmer into a fury. 'What have Eh told you wee beggars? Never climb the trees!'

I didn't recall him saying that but, apart from this one mishap, it was a very enjoyable experience. Not everyone lasted the course and by the time we returned to school, quite a few stragglers had given up and had returned to their studies.

As usual, Betty enjoyed hearing all the stories about the various farms and farm workers, but most of all she enjoyed listening to the slightly bawdy songs some of the boys used to bellow out on the homecoming bus. Unfortunately, Mum overheard me one evening and she was really annoyed by the words. They were quite innocent but I was warned not to sing such shocking songs again. That just made Betty and me laugh all the more.

A couple of days before Hogmanay, Betty announced that her mum said she could visit a couple of aunts who lived on the Hilltown. At first I didn't believe that Mrs Miller would allow Betty out late at night, even to visit the two elderly women who lived next to Martin's fishmonger shop, but it was true. She could go provided I went with her. Betty started to make secret plans to visit the City Square to see in the New Year and enjoy the celebrations and festivities. I was really worried about this plan because of the cold and the mass of people who regularly crowded into the square at midnight. But Betty was adamant.

I was torn between the desire to be in the throng of things and the worry about keeping Betty away from the place. Many years before, Grandad had always promised me he would take me to see the old year out but his death had put paid to these plans.

By ten-thirty we were ready to leave. Betty was always well wrapped up every time she went outside and she always wore a woollen balaclava with a scarf attached. On this particular night, we wore our best clothes. Mine weren't that new but because Betty was dressed in a slightly more old-fashioned way than me, I reckoned we were equal. We were wearing black net gloves that would have been more suited to a French café than a murky Scottish Hogmanay but Mrs Miller had unearthed them during a spring clean and we had pounced on them like some long-lost treasure.

Perhaps it was our whispering manner but Mrs Miller was suspicious. 'Now, Betty, you've just to go to your aunties' and no further. Now remember.'

Betty nodded. We set off in high spirits, past all the brightly lit tenement windows towards the City Square. By the time we reached the Hilltown clock it was clear that she should slow down her walking pace, and we did. I was getting more worried by the minute. Her breathing was coming in gasps but still she was adamant about getting to her destination. We were at the edge of Ann Street when we heard the bells and within a few minutes we were caught up in a throng of good-natured revellers who were streaming up the Hilltown. To my immense relief we had no option but to turn around and head uphill with this happy, singing band.

Betty's aunties greeted us with undisguised relief. 'We thought the pair of you had got lost!' they cried.

We were handed a large glass of ginger wine which I didn't really like but I had to sip it to be sociable, trying hard not to screw my face up. The parlour of their small flat was furnished in an opulent if somewhat prim manner that matched the two owners. The antimacassars on the three-piece suite were smooth against the uncut moquette fabric and it was easy to believe that a wrinkle never lingered on the crisp linen. Holding them in place were small safety pins discreetly fastened at the back of the chairs.

The aunties raised their glasses of ginger wine. 'A happy New Year to everyone and let's hope we all have health, wealth and prosperity,' was the toast, then, looking at me they observed. 'And we've got a dark-headed first-foot, which will be lucky for us.'

I was surprised. I had never been a first-foot before and I wouldn't have bet half a crown on being a lucky one. Ironically, as it turned out, I wasn't.

During the first few weeks of January, the elderly ladies' wireless set blew two of its valves and I was told in no uncertain terms not to be a first-foot ever again. And, apart from one other time when I was another unlucky first-foot, I make sure I keep well away from doorsteps at midnight on New Year's Eve.

Meanwhile, Betty gave me a big wink. 'We'll make the City Square next year!'

CHAPTER 19

The school was abuzz with plans for the forth-coming coronation. There was to be a school holiday in June to commemorate the glorious occasion. Most of the girls looked on the crown-ing of a new, young Queen as the beginning of new horizons and their feeling was that the world was their oyster.

On the other hand, most of the boys seemed only interested in the gift each child was to receive as a memento. A list was passed around each class and we had to choose between a propelling pencil and a souvenir mug. A bar of chocolate would be given to each child as well.

The Labour government had been defeated in the last election and Clement Attlee, Nye Bevan and company, who had done so much to alleviate the poverty, hardship and ill health that existed in the country, were now out of power. Winston Churchill was back at 10 Downing Street. He announced that a special allowance of an extra pound of sugar and a quarter-pound of margarine was to be allocated to enable people to put on a street party. I could well imagine Mrs Doyle organising such an event in her new street at Dronley Avenue in Beechwood and I quietly wished that George and I could maybe be invited, because it didn't look as if any events were being planned in Moncur Crescent.

According to Churchill, the world now had enough food to end all the rationing but Britain didn't have enough dollars to purchase the necessities. Aggie wasn't impressed by this statement. 'Well, Eh've heard some excuses in my life but that one takes the biscuit. Heavens! You would think we lost the war instead of winning it.'

Nevertheless, everything in the Robb household seemed to be rosy, as she was about to inform us. As always, her musquash fur coat was duly and carefully taken care of. (Mum always said after one of her visits, 'Eh don't think Aggie trusts you with her coat.') Then she sat down, a smug smile on her face. 'What do you think we're getting?' she enquired, waiting with a pregnant pause while Mum and I looked dumb. 'Well,' she said, 'meh man has gone out and bought a television set. For the coronation in June, you ken.'

Her superior tone suggested that we didn't know the date of the forthcoming Royal attraction and Mum said afterwards that she had to bite her tongue. After all, we would have had to be living on the moon to escape all the hype of pomp and pageantry. Still, Aggie was determined to tell the world about her new acquisition and she didn't notice the curtness of Mum's manner.

'We got it out of Watts in the Wellgate. It's just a table-top model with a fifteen-inch screen and it cost meh man sixty-six pounds, five shillings. We've put down a deposit and we'll pay the rest back over the next few months. It's the only way you can get anything for your house, to pay it on the never-never.'

Mum was trying hard not to be envious because she too would have loved a television. She cheerfully agreed. 'Aye, it's well named the never-never. Eh feel like it's never-ending when Eh'm paying the tickie man every week.'

'That's what Eh feel as well, Molly, but meh man says that we would never have furnished our new prefab if we had to pay the money all at once. We wanted everything new so we got a dining-room suite out of Hendersons in the Wellgate.' She stopped as if struck by a thought. 'Eh've just noticed that we seem to spend all our money in the Wellgate. But never mind, where was Eh? Oh aye, my new suite. Well, it cost us twenty-eight guineas but you put down two bob in the pound deposit and pay the rest over easy weekly terms. When Eh finish paying the television set, Eh'm getting a new bedroom suite and a carpet square.'

268

She gave a loud sigh, as if exhausted by all this mathematical and financial talk. She finished off the dregs of tea from her cup, swallowing in the process all the residual tea leaves. This habit of hers always made me shudder.

Mum, who was also totally drained by Aggie's calculations, decided to change the subject. 'How is Babs' romance going then?'

Aggie smacked her lips and ran her tongue over the surface of her teeth, obviously thinking hard before answering this loaded question. It was clear that she didn't approve of Ron the spiv but, to be truthful, following in Marvin's footsteps would have been hard for anyone. 'Well Babs seems happy enough but then her lad's away a lot, him being a commercial traveller.'

Obviously Mum wasn't going to get any more information from her and as Aggie had run out of new possessions or the benefits of various easy terms it was time for her make her way home on the 1A bus back to Blackshade. Before departing, however, she did invite us up to view the coronation on the television and, although I would have loved to have seen it, Mum was working that day.

She was back in the dairy now on the inspection side of the milk-bottling plant. It was a task that didn't require her to use her 'gammy hand' as she now referred to it. Because the dairy opened every day including weekends, the workers were on a three-week rota with a different day off through the week and Mum loved this variety. Still, as she confessed after Aggie's departure, even had she been off on 2 June, she would never have made the bus trip to the prefab, for the simple reason that by the time she made the conducted tour round the house and Hendersons furniture, the coronation could be over and the Queen tucked up in bed.

Meanwhile, back on the school front, the arguments over the commemorative souvenirs was still raging. I was now in the final few weeks of school and as we were studying for our leaving certificates, our noses were to the proverbial grindstone. Should we be lucky enough to win this prized certificate, we could then burst forth on a surprised world as accomplished French-speaking shorthand typists/book-keepers. Or maybe emerge as scientists destined to find an epoch-making cure for humanity's ills. That was the teachers' hope and it was what they had striven for over three long, gruelling years.

As for the souvenirs, the headteachers had ordered these gifts according to the lists from each classroom but there was going to be a spanner in the works. Suddenly and prior to the distribution of the mementoes, a wild rumour swept the school that those who had ordered a propelling pencil did not qualify for a free bar of chocolate. This turned out to be totally unfounded but that didn't stop the majority of the boys suddenly shifting their allegiance to a coronation mug. All previous thoughts of this being a cissy gift were now forgotten in the anticipation of chocolate.

This anarchy threw all the careful calculations out of the window and would even have taxed the dexterous mind of Aggie. In a state of extreme annoyance, the headmaster ordered the return of all gifts. The next morning, at assembly, he appeared almost foaming at the mouth. While trying to keep his temper in check, he announced through clenched teeth, 'Last month I sent the monitors round with a list. At that time we had 500 pencils and 200 mugs. It now seems as if we have 100 pencils and 600 mugs in the school.'

He was obviously so incensed by the entire farce of the situation that he hadn't realised how funny he sounded. Meanwhile, the whole school, standing in dutiful silence, were trying desperately to suppress the laughter which threatened to erupt at any moment.

He resumed his speech. 'Right then, I want all the original names for pencils to come forward today and claim them and we will deal with the mugs tomorrow.'

As we trooped out of the hall, Sheila and I overheard one wag exclaiming, 'Only 600 mugs in the school, did he say? Here's me thinking we're all mugs!'

Thankfully, by coronation day, the situation was sorted out. As soon as the pupils realised that a bar of chocolate went with each gift, calm reigned once more. This may have seemed a big deal about the chocolate, especially in today's world where shops like Woolworths have confectionery stacked up to the roof, but back in 1953 sweets hadn't been off the ration for very long.

Dundee, like many other cities, had a full programme for the big day and the city planners were hoping for good weather. Unfortunately, although the rain stayed off, it was cold and blustery with the temperature well below the seasonal average. In fact, the previous week had seen one of the worst thunderstorms for thirty years. This caused widespread havoc over the Scottish Highlands while the gate at the Western Cemetery was hit by lightning and lots of low-lying streets in the Dock area suffered from flooding.

Betty and I went down the town to see some of the jollities. The town centre had a festive air and there was a feeling of renewed optimism on the faces of the waiting crowds. A thirty-foot-high red, white and blue floral display in the shape of a coronation arch dominated the City Square while another eye-catching sign was mounted above the frontage of Phins' ironmonger shop in the Nethergate.

Although we didn't go there, Riverside Drive was the main showcase for a massed bands display, a twenty-one-gun salute and bonfire, with fireworks planned for later. As we stood on the edge of the crowds in the High Street to see the parade of the Black Watch, Territorial Army cadets and military vehicles, the news reached us that the mighty peak of Mount Everest had finally been conquered by Edmund Hillary and Sherpa Tenzing. While the flags waved in the stiff breeze, I could well imagine Miss Calvert likening these two modern-day heroes to the likes of Drake and Raleigh and it did seem as if we were entering a true golden Elizabethan age. On a more mundane level, G.B. Forbes, who owned the pram arcade in King Street, was donating a free pram for every baby born on coronation day.

Later in the week, Mum and I saw an hour-long

film at the Odeon, entitled *Elizabeth is Queen*. Out of the entire footage of this historic film, the one person Mum loved was Queen Salote of Tonga who braved the wet and windy London weather with a smile that had all the warmth of a South Sea island.

Some housing schemes had organised bonfires and outside dancing but if Moncur Crescent had any jollities then I must have missed them. However, the main topic was the televising of the coronation. Aggie would have been miffed to know that the Caird Hall had installed twenty sets to let an invited populace watch the whole pomp and pageant. It was reckoned that thousands of people saw the crowning of the Queen at first hand, but not us.

Grand as all this pageantry was, it was the following Saturday that produced the biggest and best surprise. Many years before in McDonald Street, we had, for a very short time, a neighbour in the empty flat across the lobby. Her name was Katie and she was engaged to be married. She was young, pretty and had a bubbling vivacity. I thought she was wonderful. Every weekend the flat was full to overflowing with a multitude of her friends, all laughing, singing and dancing. Mum said she made the close cheery and I would lie awake in bed and listen to all the latest tunes on her wireless.

To start with, she always invited Mum into the party but Mum, being the way she was, much preferred to curl up in bed with her latest detective novel from the library. 'Eh'm no unsociable, Katie, but Eh just like lying here listening to your young voices and you've fair cheered up the place.'

Meanwhile, Katie, happy in the knowledge that the noise wasn't causing a nuisance, sailed off in full flow to join her guests while I lay in bed wishing she had asked me to the party. This lasted for two months or so before Katie disappeared. One day another couple turned up and moved in. They were Irish and the husband worked on the Tummel-Garry hydroelectric scheme. He was away from home all week and Vi, his wife, told Mum that they had bought the key to the flat along with all the lovely furniture.

They had met Katie at a party and during the conversation had mentioned how desperate they were for a house. Katie had wanted to move away to another town and a new job and Vi was overjoyed when offered this golden opportunity. Mum, however, was worried about Katie. For weeks after she confided her worries to Lizzie. 'It's no like her to go and no say cheerio to us. Eh mean, we got on so well and Eh just hope nothing's happened to her.'

Lizzie was reassuring. 'Och, Eh expect she's moved away to be nearer her boyfriend. He's in the army, isn't he?'

Mum was still worried. 'There was always so many people in that house and it makes me wonder. Eh mind one day there was this huge white chalk cross on her door and I gave Maureen a right telling-off, thinking she had done it. Well, Eh had just sent her to wash the door with a bucket and cloth when Katie came up the stairs. She nearly had a fit. "Oh no, don't wash off any crosses on the door, Molly," she said. "Eh put them there to warn my friends no to come partying when my lad's on leave!".'

I remembered that incident and how strongly I had protested my innocence, not that I got an apology from Mum. The weeks and months went on and we became friendly with our new neighbours and we never set eyes on Katie again. That is until the Saturday after the coronation. We saw this couple arrive at the close entrance and we were struck by their hesitation. The bell sounded, that unlovely, twisty bell with the sound of a chicken being garrotted. And there stood Katie, looking just as I remembered her.

She was wearing a lovely yellow suit with an elaborate orchid buttonhole and a tiny yellow straw hat with a creamy, spotted veil. Standing beside her was the best-looking man I had ever seen, tall and deeply tanned with bright blue eyes and gorgeous white teeth which flashed every time he smiled. He was also wearing a button-hole, a carnation, on the lapel of a very expensive-looking suit. Mum was completely astonished. She invited them in but not before shoving me ahead of her to hide all the clutter under the velvet seat cushions.

'Eh've been looking all over for you, Molly,' said Katie, as if she had seen us ten minutes before instead of almost five or six years. 'Ricky and me are getting married this morning and Eh wondered if you'd be my witness at the registry office.'

While speaking, she swept a hand in the direction of the Gary Cooper lookalike at her side. Mum was so surprised she had to sit down. And for once she didn't tell me off for staring with my mouth open at this gorgeous guy.

'Oh, Eh can't do that Katie. What would Eh wear for starters?'

'Well it's like this,' explained the radiant bride-to-be, 'Ricky is on leave from Burma and he's got a special licence for the registry office. The wedding is...' she looked at a lovely gold watch on her slim wrist, 'in an hour.'

While all this chatter was going on, Ricky sat gazing at his beloved while I sat gazing at him.

'You were my first choice, Molly, when we made our plans but Eh thought you were still living in the same street. What a shock Eh got when Eh saw it was knocked down but lucky for me Eh met that pal of yours from Norrie's Pend – the big woman – and she gave me this address. Now hurry and put something on because the taxi's waiting.'

Mum almost choked. 'What do you mean, the taxi's waiting? Where is it?'

'Never mind about that. Just get ready. Ricky's got oodles of money, haven't you darling?'

Mum hurried to put on her old plum-coloured costume and a bashed-looking hat that resided at the back of the wardrobe and was the mainstay of my playing at dressing up – when I was younger of course. I was certainly not owning up to any childish pastimes with a film star in our living room. I took my eyes off Ricky for a moment to look at Katie and she caught my eye.

'Maybe you would like to come as well, Maureen.'

Wouldn't I just, I thought, leaping out of my chair to get my coat from the pegs in the lobby.

'You'll have to wait outside because we've got our two witnesses, your mum and Sam. He's Ricky's friend.'

Although I didn't say it, I would gladly have parked myself on Mars in order to go to this grand romantic affair. Mum arrived from the bedroom, looking quite nice I thought. She had put on her pretty blouse and some lipstick.

'This is the best Eh can do for you, Katie,' she said apologetically.

'You look smashing,' said Katie, ushering us out into the close, towards the waiting taxi. We passed Betty who stopped in amazement, her eyebrows nearly disappearing into her hairline. She opened her mouth but I just said a quick hello before whispering that I would tell her everything later that night.

The taxi was lovely. I sat on a small fold-down seat with my back to the driver and we made a speedy progress down the Hilltown towards the City Square. I felt like a queen. At the registry office we were joined by another well-tanned man who looked as if he could have come from Burma as well. After the ceremony, Ricky and Katie took us to the Café Val D'Or for our dinner, or lunch as Ricky called it. It was a really swanky-looking place and I wished I was as well dressed as the bride, but at least I wasn't looking like a tink for once in my life.

'When are you going back to Burma?' Mum asked, between spoonfuls of lovely hot, green pea soup.

It was Ricky who answered. 'We're going away tonight to London then we fly out on Sunday night. I'm on leave from my rubber plantation and the plan was to stay in London until after the coronation.' He stopped and smiled at the man who was the other witness. 'But Sam persuaded me to come to Dundee to see his parents and while I was here I met Katie.' He looked tenderly into her eyes while I almost swooned with the sheer romance of it all.

Sam nodded cheerfully. 'That'll be a couple of hundred pounds for the marriage introduction, Katie,' he said and we all laughed.

Later, when the two men went to the toilet, Katie explained her sudden departure. 'Eh tried to make a go of my engagement but we were two different kinds of people and it didn't work out. Eh've been working in a hotel so Eh didn't need the house, but Eh was really sorry no to say cheerio to you all. It all happened so sudden. Vi and her man would have been good neighbours.'

'Well, Katie, Eh was really worried about you. After all, you could have been murdered or something equally gruesome,' said Mum, with a shudder.

'Och, away you go, Molly!' said Katie, laughing. 'You read too many murder stories for your own good.'

The two men returned. Ricky settled the bill and this wonderful, unexpected day was over. Mum declined the offer of a taxi home, much to my dismay, saying the tramcar was handy. We said goodbye to the newly-weds and Sam, and watched them go off in a cloud of bliss. When we

278

arrived home, Mum still wasn't over the shock and all she could say was, 'What if it hadn't been my day off? Katie would have had to get someone else.'

I almost passed out at the horrible thought of this. That would have been terrible, I thought, until the idea crossed my mind that perhaps I could have been Katie's bridesmaid.

Later, Betty listened to all the glorious happenings with a wide-eyed look and open mouth.

'This has been one of the best days of my life, Betty.'

While Betty agreed with me, she quickly poured cold water over my dream of maybe having been a bridesmaid.

'You wouldn't have been allowed,' she said. 'Eh think you have to be sixteen so you are too young.'

I almost said that if the occasion had arisen I would have cheerfully admitted to being a hundred and six.

CHAPTER 20

Starting work in Keillor's factory was like stepping into paradise, especially to anyone who was raised during the sweetie desert of wartime rationing.

It was July 1953 and this was my first job since throwing off the shackles of school two weeks earlier. The last few days at Rockwell School had been slightly bitter-sweet because I knew I was finally leaving childhood behind. On the other hand, I was gaining freedom.

On that last afternoon, we all trod the hallowed stage in the assembly hall to receive our Leaving Certificate, the piece of paper we had all worked so hard to get. However, before that final moment, I had to face a career interview with Miss Kemp, the headmistress. These personal meetings to discuss our future plans and employment were held in her sanctum. She beamed at me over the top of her highly polished desk. Her homely pink face was topped with a crown of snowy white hair, a colouring which I thought at the time resembled pink and white marshmallows. But there was nothing soft and squashy in her expression when I mentioned my forthcoming job at Keillor's sweet factory.

'What about the vacancy I mentioned to you for an office junior? Or the pre-nursing course at Seymour Lodge?' she enquired, quite annoyed that, in her opinion, the three years' intensive schooling had been a complete waste of time.

I could hardly confess to this pillar of the education system that pre-nursing courses cost money, that the initial expense of books and other miscellaneous items were far out of reach of Mum's pocket. As for the other job, I didn't fancy being cooped up in some little office with just one other person, which would have been my lot in that vacancy.

No, I had weighed up the options and, even if it meant taking on a dead-end job which was obviously being frowned upon in this quiet school office, I knew I wanted to meet people and also earn a decent wage. I wanted to burst forth into this new age and be part of the exhilarating atmosphere of a brave new world. In Mum's eyes, the idea of another wage coming into the house was a happy financial prospect. Regardless of who was right, it was a decision I was never to regret.

Still, as I approached the factory gate on my first morning, I was apprehensive and my stomach was churning. In fact I thought I was going to be sick. The building had the look of being squashed in between two walls, like a stone sandwich. But the narrowness of its entrance deceptively concealed its length, stretching as it did almost to the edge of the High Street.

I passed along a narrow corridor and landed in the women's cloakroom. It was packed with chattering women, all standing or sitting in their own tight, intimate circles. They had a closeness obviously born out of long friendships formed over a period of time. For me, a nervous newcomer, it was like standing on the fringe of some new civilisation, wondering if the aliens were friendly. On that particular day they were not. They were too busy pulling white caps over curled hair to notice a stranger in their midst.

There was one girl whose face looked familiar. Even before she spoke to the people in her group, I just knew what her voice sounded like. It was such a strange feeling of déjà vu but the more I tried to pin down where I had met her before, the more elusive the memory became. She caught me staring at her and gave a friendly smile before I was whisked off to the Personnel Office for a form-filling episode prior to my entrance into the wide spectrum of the workaday world, or 'making a bob or twa', as Grandad often said.

My eventual destination was the Enrobing Department, a room where sweets were made in their entirety. Their origins were in one of the vast vats of bubbling hot chocolate and they ended up on a conveyer belt which terminated in the cold room. As the soft cream fillings trundled under the chocolate tanks, a group of six women waited to stamp each sweet with its distinctive mark using little hand-held metal stampers. Or the women would dip their fingers in tiny pots of chocolate and deftly draw swirls or circles or lines. Then like a battalion of soldiers, the sweets would march under the cool air until reaching the cold room where another group of women waited with fat spatulas in their hands and swiftly slotted the sweets into wooden trays.

My first day was spent in the cold room and I was almost speechless by the sight of so many goodies. I wasn't sure if we were allowed to eat any of these finished products but one of the older workers, a tall, thin woman with a highly strung temperament and protruding eyes that suggested she suffered with goitre, waved this misconception away with a flapping hand.

'You can eat as much as you like but you can't take anything out of the building,' she said, her voice sounding like machine-gun bullets hitting a brick wall.

I was aghast at this remark, especially the suggestion that I would pinch anything. The factory dealt with this problem in its own way, namely a spot search every night as the work force streamed out through the narrow doors. No one knew when they would be picked and I only had one search made during my short time with the factory. I was overjoyed that I could eat as much as I wanted. It was a bit like the later *Charlie and the Chocolate Factory*. At the time, I was puzzled by this lax attitude, thinking that the firm could hardly make a profit because of all the heavy overhead munching costs, but after a few weeks I soon found out that most of the sweeties lost their appeal due to that initial daily intake.

Still, during that first week or two, I hadn't reached the sugar saturation point and I sampled everything that arrived before my fat spatula. Mum would laugh when I got home at night. 'What would you like for your tea?'

Looking quite green and sick, I was unable to face any food. 'Eh'll just have tea and toast, Mum,' I said, not even needing the toast.

The firm allowed the workers to buy a sweet parcel once a month. George liked everything but Mum was partial to chocolate gingers. By now I could barely look a sweetie in the eye and the parcel was divided up between Mum, George, Betty and Mrs Miller. Mrs Miller always ate her sweets with a cup of tea in the afternoon and Keillor's fame was spreading because she started to buy her own from the confectionery shop beside the Odeon.

'What's the name of yon chocolates with the purply centres?' she asked me. 'Eh'm going to buy two ounces tomorrow.' Obviously blackcurrant creams were her favourite.

The factory had a lovely large and airy canteen which served subsidised meals to the workers. It was quite a few weeks before I discovered it. Mainly because of my chocolate-stuffed days, I spent the dinner hour either sitting beside the conveyer belt or on a bench beside the museum gardens. When I decided to pay a visit to it, I immediately ran into the girl who had smiled at me on my first day.

'Hello!' she said. 'Eh saw you on your first day here. Do you no remember me?'

I tried hard to think but the fragment of memory was still proving elusive.

She noticed my frown. 'Eh used to deliver papers in Ann Street and you had a milk round with Sherrit's Dairy.'

Suddenly it all fell into place, like the missing piece of a jigsaw, and I felt stupid for not remembering. We had passed one another every morning for months until the milk boy, whose ailment I never did discover, returned to reclaim his milk round.

'That's right! Eh remember you now. It's Violet, isn't it?' I was relieved to put a name to the face. 'How long have you worked here?' I was curious because she seemed to know lots of the women.

'About a year. Eh'm in the Wrapping Department. You put tinfoil on the sweeties and they get sent to the packing room to be put into fancy boxes. What a pity you hadn't been sent there to work beside us,' she said, pointing out three young girls who were at the table.

As I sat down beside this quartet with my threepenny bowl of soup and slice of bread which cost one penny, Violet informed the three girls which part of this huge complex I belonged to. 'Maureen's in the Enrobing Room,' she told them. Then she turned towards me, 'Do you like it there?'

Alas, that was the crunch! She had hit the nail on the head with her question. As the weeks had progressed, I was certain that the gaffer didn't like me. The reason for this dislike was obscure, at least to me, because I had hardly spoken more than a dozen words to the man since day one. And I was becoming increasingly disenchanted with my brand new first job.

The majority of the women in this department were older than me and they all had their allocated jobs which they went to every morning. Being a newcomer, and a disliked one at that, I was put in the pool which was a small band of workers who were slotted into whatever job was vacant. There were about five of us and I often wondered if the gaffer disliked us all but no, he always kept his special glare for me.

Either because of absenteeism or perhaps just because an extra pair of hands was needed, we were sent all over the place. The gaffer always left me to the last, which meant I got all the grotty jobs. One day I would be sent to the room where the workers sorted through huge mounds of brazil nuts or hazelnuts into trays prior to them being coated in chocolate. I always referred to this room as the Nuthoose, which didn't endear me to Mr Gaffer.

Then the next day I would find myself in the ginger boiling room, a place I hated. I could never understand how anyone could work here for long but I suppose the women needed their jobs. The ginger roots were boiled in vats similar to the chocolate vats which, like the latter, were always the domain of men. When cooked, these roots would be howked out with large slotted ladles and left to cool.

We all sat around a big table, a sharp knife in hand, ready to chop these strange shapes into bite-sized pieces. I thought most of these shapes resembled tiny boiled babies, complete with heads and stumpy arms and legs, and I always dreaded handling these ginger root embryos. Of course, this was all in my imagination because no one else seemed to mind this brain-numbing occupation. They sat blithely chopping and slicing bits into gigantic steel basins.

Like the throngs of jute workers who streamed out of the mills, these women had the same problems, dreams and fears in life. They discussed the same topics, namely their families, money, houses and men in that order.

'Are you going to the pictures tonight, Maria?' asked one fat woman called Sadie, who was deftly clattering her knife against the surface of the table.

Maria was an attractive girl with a dark-haired, Italian look. She was in her early twenties and was as lazy as she was pretty. She pondered this loaded question while gazing languidly through eyes that were heavily mascaraed but lifeless and bored-looking.

'Eh expect so. Eh've got this new lad now. He works in Briggs on the Ferry Road. He's taking me out tonight but where we'll go, Eh don't know.' She made it sound like the chore of the week.

'Och, you've had too many lads, Maria. It's no right to carry on like that,' said Sadie, shaking her head. 'How many lads have you had this year?'

The popular Maria thought long and hard, her eyes suddenly taking on a hard calculating look. 'Eh think it's ten or eleven up to now.'

Her tone sounded like mine when Mum asked me to do the dishes twice in one day – fed up.

I did a quick mental count. We were now in the middle of October and if she had already gone through ten or maybe eleven boyfriends, she was either fickle or careless – or maybe they were.

Sadie sounded annoyed. 'Well, Eh only hope my Bert never meets you, "Miss Fickle Annie". He's spent three years fighting in Korea but after the armistice at Panmunjom, he's now home and wanting out of the army. Says he's seen some awfy sights among the Communists but what Eh'm trying to say is this – thank the Lord he wasn't writing to somebody like you, Maria.'

The papers and the Pathé News at the cinema had been full of the death and destruction in Korea. Also, a new word had entered our vocabulary: brainwashing. I hadn't a clue what it meant, but the Chinese government was accused of using this new method of torture on captured prisoners of war.

Maria, who hadn't taken offence at Sadie's remarks, was now lamenting. 'My mother has bought me another jumper, would you believe it? Ever since the clothes have come off the ration she's aye buying me something to wear. Eh've got two drawers in my dressing table that have ump-teen jumpers no even out of their bags.'

Although I didn't say anything, I wished I knew Maria's mum. She seemed to be a kind-hearted person in contrast to her grasping daughter. Maybe she would throw some of the unused jumpers in my direction.

Sadie shook her head in exasperation while jabbing her knife into another embryo-shaped ginger root. 'Heaven help poor fellows like my Bert who put their lives on the line for folk like you, Maria. Your mother must think you're very ungrateful.'

I felt sorry for Sadie and all her worry over her son. It was hard having to adjust back into Civvy Street and I knew Bella's son, John, was planning the same move as soon as his army service was up. It must have been a horrific war but, like World War II, all conflicts had their share of human misery.

Jean, who sat at the top of the table, turned to look at the clock. 'Thank heavens it's finishing time! Eh've got my messages to go before Eh get home. If it's no one thing it's another,' she sighed. I had the feeling I was back standing once more at the jute mill gate.

Sadie heaved herself out of her seat and gave me a big wink. 'What will you be doing the night, young Maureen? Will you be going out with a fella?'

I was furious with myself because I blushed scarlet, feeling the warmth spread from the back of my neck to my hairline. The question had been so unexpected that I didn't have time to appear cool and sophisticated, like world-weary Maria who now looked at me as if she had only just noticed my presence. She gave me a look as if to say this possibility was far beyond my capabilities. I shook my head. 'No.'

This statement wasn't altogether true but Maria had now turned her attention to her little case of mascara which she fished from her overall pocket. She added some spittle to the black oblong block, mixed it with the minuscule brush, and proceeded to add another heavy coat to the already overloaded eyelashes. She wiped away the tiny black specks that fell on to her cheeks. Clearly the eyelashes could hold no more weight and they were shedding the surplus mascara like apples in an autumn windfall.

By the time the bell went for finishing time, we were all ready to go and we made a hurried exit through the door and down the long corridors. I was almost hugging myself with pleasure. I felt a bit sorry that I hadn't told Sadie the truth about my plans for the evening but I was afraid that Maria might have poured cold water over my pleasure. Not only was I going out that night but Betty was coming with me. We were heading for Robbie's Dance Hall in Well Road, just off the Hawkhill.

It had all begun a week ago, one balmy autumn evening when Betty and I had been sitting on the close stairs, listening to the dance music from Mrs Ferrie's radiogram. She lived up the stairs from us and we often listened to the popular tunes that filtered down to us from her wonderful radiogram. Also, she owned what we thought was a great collection of records.

On that particular night, we decided to have our own private dance club. As we pranced up and down the length of the long close, we didn't notice John from the next close and his pal. We were dancing to the 'Golden Tango' when the two boys appeared beside us.

'Naw, naw, naw, naw, that's no the right way to tango!' said John's pal, who went by the name of Joe, 'Here, let us show you.'

With my feet going in different directions, he swept me along the close in a series of twists, turns and jerky movements. The only thing missing was a rose in my teeth. With John dancing with Betty, we spent a hilarious hour doing all the different dances. By now, the original music had stopped but we improvised with a mixture of whistling, singing and humming. In fact, we had such a good laugh that Joe suggested an evening out.

'Eh aye go to Robbie's Dance Hall. What about a night out there?'

Betty and I were over the moon and we talked about nothing else for days.

'What about your mum, Betty? Will she let you go to the dancing?' I asked, sure that the request would be turned down. But it wasn't.

'Mum says Eh can go with you but Eh have to be home early and no stay till the end.'

That was fine by me. The next few days were spent in a frenzy of wondering what to wear and, now that the magic night was here, we still didn't think our sparse wardrobes would yield anything chic and wonderful. As soon as I had my tea that night, I went through to see Betty.

I had cut off the arms of an old jumper and sewn a colourful floral edging around the arm-holes. 'What do think of this, Betty?' I asked, holding the vandalised garment aloft, 'Eh thought Eh would wear it with my dirndl skirt. Although it's two different floral patterns Eh don't think anybody will notice.'

Betty agreed. 'Eh've got to wear my slacks but Eh'll change into a skirt when Eh get there. My mum doesn't know about this so don't say a word. If Eh give you my skirt now, you can keep it for me because Eh'm sure my mum will be watching as Eh leave the house.'

She went to the wardrobe. 'Eh've got a surprise to show you. Shut your eyes.'

I did as I was told and when ordered to open them, Betty was holding a white, flimsy garment in her hand.

'What do think of my new bra?' she asked 'Eh made it out of two hankies, some ribbon and a bit of clastic.'

I thought it looked lovely and wished that I could have had one as well. Betty's home-sewn bra would never have given Messrs Gossard and Berlei any sleepless nights but it was functional and well made. Betty, with all the time she had on her hands as well as access to a Singer treadle sewing machine, could easily run things up.

'Oh, Eh wish you had made one for me!' I said, quite unhappy that I would be venturing forth to the glamorous Robbie's Dance Hall in my serviceable cotton vest while Betty was blossoming into exotic underwear.

'Eh'll make one another time. After all, my mum has a drawer just stuffed full with hankies.'

For one fleeting moment, Betty's two elderly aunties who lived on the Hilltown came to my mind and I could well imagine that they would also have well-stuffed hankie drawers.

One bone of contention in my mind was the fact that although I was now four months into my job I was still dressed like a schoolgirl. I would set off for work every morning in my old trench coat and, horror of horrors, my white ankle socks. Betty was the same but it now looked like she had the expertise to break free.

We were meeting John and Joe at the tram stop in Strathmartine Road but we knew this meeting was more of a business arrangement than a romantic date. This was just as well as we discovered John couldn't make it. No reason was given but we suspected he didn't have the admission money for the dance. We certainly couldn't help out because we had the bare minimum of money in our roomy but almost empty handbags.

'Never mind,' said Joe, cheerfully. 'We'll just go as planned.'

To give him his due, he was very gallant in escorting two giggling youngsters to their very first dance in a proper dancehall. We stood in a queue in Well Road, waiting for the hall to open, shivering in the early evening drizzle but almost bursting with excitement and anticipation. Once inside, we made straight for the cloakroom. Betty wanted to remove her horrible baggy trousers and woollen balaclava, which we added to our coats. The small woman in charge of the cloak-room was almost inundated with a flood of coats but she was obviously an expert in her job as she deftly wrapped each coat into a bundle and shoved it into a boxed contraption behind her.

We then stepped forth into the glamorous un-known and we were not disappointed. It was all we imagined it would be. There was a medium-sized dance floor and a gramophone was playing 'I Believe' by Frankie Laine, which, as with Mrs Ferrie, was one of our favourites.

A smaller room led off from the main dance floor and was furnished with a few tables and chairs. Quite a few people were sitting here and Betty and I stood on the fringe of this activity, soaking up the wonderful atmosphere. Perhaps because the room was small it had the appear-ance of being packed with dancers. The beat of the music, the dim lights and the blue haze from countless cigarettes which spiralled up to the ceiling all added to the magic.

Betty was wearing her bright-pink woollen jumper, the one that her auntie had knitted. It had a wide neckband that emphasised her white slender neck and she had on a floral skirt similar to my own. Meanwhile, I thought I looked like the bee's knees in my redesigned jumper with the matching trim that didn't really match. I knew Betty was annoyed that her jumper completely hid her pièce de résistance, namely her bra, and she said so. 'Eh wish Eh had one of those bonny see-through blouses. You know the ones Eh mean? Yon chiffon models.'

Personally, I was glad to have something to cover up my unlovely vest.

Joe arrived from somewhere and gave us a dance apiece before disappearing for the rest of the night. In fact, we never saw him again. Whether he still came to see John, we never knew or, quite honestly, cared. Betty and I were enchanted with this new dancing world and, even although we had to leave at nine-thirty because of Mrs Miller's curfew, we talked about nothing else on our way home, chattering animatedly as the tram wound its ponderous way along the dark, narrow streets.

'Do you think your mum will let you go next week?' I asked anxiously.

Betty nodded. 'As long as Eh'm back early.'

Now I was faced with a big, big problem – finance. I gave Mum my wages every week and she gave me some pocket money. This covered my tram fares to work and back as well as my dinner in the canteen. Once back in the house that night, I immediately began to work out ways of saving from this small amount in order to visit Robbie's every week. I put my savings plan into operation the following morning by ignoring the tramcar and launching myself like a rocket down the Hilltown and onwards to the factory. Savings were also made at dinnertime by eating the minimum of food. Mum would have been annoyed at this but I knew I could always fill up with a chocolate or six during the day. One small cloud settled over me that morning in the shape of Violet and her three chums. They were not as ecstatic as I was when describing my night out.

'We always go to the Palais de Dance in Tay Street,' said Violet. 'You should come with us on a Tuesday night. It's good fun.'

I made a mental note to mention this to Betty but, as things turned out, my time at Keillor's was fast running out. At the beginning of 1954, the entire place was abuzz with rumours of a big pay-off. Seemingly, due to the vagaries of the sweet export market, a big order had failed to materialise. I had told Mum about the gaffer and at first she warned me, 'Eh hope you're no giving him any cheek.'

When I shook my head, she said, 'Och well, maybe he doesn't like young folk working for him.'

Things were becoming worse. Before the rumours, everyone in the pool had been slotted into some sort of job in the complex but, now, quite a few of us were totally redundant every morning. The gaffer got round this by giving us cleaning jobs which I didn't mind but greatly annoyed the rest of the women.

'Bloody cheek putting us to mop floors when we were hired to make sweeties!' complained one irate woman, while the rest of her pals agreed.

Although I knew my days were numbered, I have to admit getting quite a shock when the pay-offs were announced and my name was on the list. Surprise, surprise! The works manager was a lovely, kind man, not like the gaffer. He had dark-brown eyes and a concerned, sympathetic manner which made me feel a bit better at losing my job. It was down to losing some lucrative order, he explained, but if things picked up then I

295

would be asked back to work. I almost said 'Over my dead body' but he was so nice that I buttoned my lippy lip, as Mum often called it. I met Sadie as I was leaving that last night and I told her all about the gaffer and how he seemed to hate me.

'Och, you must have been married to him in a previous life and given him a hard time,' she said.

I was appalled. Married to that old geezer!

She saw my face and laughed. 'Eh'm just joking, young Maureen. Cheer up!'

Cheer up? Well, that wasn't so easy. Mum and I were devastated by this grim news. George had started his first year at secondary school and was growing out of his clothes almost daily. And there was Miss Kemp. I just prayed I would never meet her on my way to the dole office. I couldn't help thinking how my bright new dawn was fast becoming the dark night.

CHAPTER 21

Ironically, I had noticed an advert for a waitress in Wallace's Restaurant while scanning the employment section of the paper a few days before losing my job. Mum had other ideas.

'You better sign on at the "buroo" just in case there's no jobs. After all, there was a lot of you paid off last night.'

With that pessimistic statement in my head, I set off towards Gellatly Street and the buroo, Scotland's name for the labour exchange. To my surprise I found the office empty of people and I was seen right away. Perhaps this was because it was a Saturday morning, or maybe I was just lucky. The girl behind the counter was very helpful so I decided to mention the advert. Did she still know if the job was still available? She went away to phone the restaurant in Castle Street and was back within minutes with good news.

'You've to go round right away for an interview with Mr Wallace.'

I looked at her in dismay. 'You mean right now?'

I was fully aware that I wasn't dressed for an interview. Although it was only May, the weather had turned warm and I had left the house in my faithful old cotton floral skirt, a thin blouse and bare legs, my feet thrust into summer sandals. The helpful woman nodded and I set off, wishing desperately that I had something fashionable and chic to wear. Still, with the confidence of youth, I was determined to bestow my limited talents on this new job.

When I reached the restaurant, my confidence was dented slightly when I saw the premises. I gazed at the brown-painted facade and the large window which was blocked off with hardboard. The warm bright sunshine seemed to emphasise the drabness and when I tried to peer through the door, my view was blocked by a high wooden screen. The place looked like a relic from the last century sitting quietly slumbering in the sun. To say I was unsure about this new venture would be an understatement and I hesitated on the pavement.

The shop next door, however, was a buzz of activity. Also owned by the Wallace family, it was doing great trade and the aroma coming out of the shop was mouth-watering. A large queue had formed and was now waiting patiently to be served with their paper bags of juicy meat pies and bridies. Taking a deep breath, I pushed the door open and marched in for my interview. I don't know what I was expecting in a restaurant but if I thought there would be lots of people sitting at the tables then I was wrong.

The room, with its dark-panelled walls, stretched out ahead of me and the tables were all set with white, pristine tablecloths and shiny cutlery. It was like entering the hushed atmosphere of a deserted church and I was quite apprehensive about it all. Mr Alf Wallace was sitting at one of the smaller tables, drinking tea from a china cup. I wondered if he was waiting for me to turn up. Although I didn't realise it then, I had arrived during the brief, halcyon, half-hour hiatus between the busy morning bridie trade and the frenetic lunchtime crowds. I liked him straight away and if he noticed my casual clothes then he never mentioned them.

The wage, however, was less than my previous one. 'We pay thirty shillings a week but you keep all your own tips, which can add up to a few shillings more,' he said.

While this piece of bad news was tempered by the anticipation of tips, I wasn't sure how Mum would react to the thought of ten shillings a week less. But it was a job and I was really pleased when he suggested a start on the following Monday. It now looked as if I wasn't going to be unemployed for even one day. I thought the interview was over when he stood up but he said, 'I think Miss Thomson will want to speak to you before you start. She is the manageress.'

He disappeared through the kitchen door while I sat on the edge of my seat. Within a few minutes he was back with a small woman dressed entirely in black. In her black dress and black sensible shoes she resembled a crow. She could have stepped straight out of a Jane Austen novel without so much as changing a curl. I almost gasped out loud in dismay when I realised she looked very old. Another thing was that while Mr Alf may not have noticed my clothes Miss Thomson certainly did. Behind her spectacles, her dark-eyed gaze swept over me. I realised she wasn't impressed by this young, gawky apparition standing in front of her, and with bare legs as well.

'When you start on Monday, you will need to wear a uniform which is a black skirt, black jumper and a white apron, cuffs and cap. Also stockings to be worn at all times,' she said, making sure I got the message.

Mr Alf must have sensed my dismay at this request because he started to say, 'Perhaps we can let the young lass have an advance on her pay to let her buy an outfit...'

Miss Thomson's frosty frown made him lapse into silence and he disappeared back into the kitchen.

You're frightened of her as well, I thought. Well, that makes two of us.

I could cheerfully have choked this manageress

who looked like a relic from a previous century, an age, no doubt, when everyone wore black and had oodles of aprons, caps and cuffs stuffed away in drawers similar to Mrs Miller's hankie drawer.

As I hurried back home, I did a mental journey around my wardrobe and had to concede that I didn't own anything with the remotest tinge of black. Mum, however, was delighted with my news and, like myself, felt that the anticipation of tips softened the harsh reality of the reduced wage.

She glanced at the clock in dismay when I mentioned the uniform. 'Eh wish we knew about this job earlier. Eh could have got a line from the Star Stores tickie man.'

Actually, I didn't want anything from the Star Stores because they never seemed to have anything that fitted me, or, more importantly, that I liked. Ever since that fruitless search for an outfit for Margaret and George's wedding, I had made a point of not going inside the shop. On that occasion, I had been saved by Mrs Knight's American frock but that was then and this was now and I couldn't see a uniform winging its way across the Atlantic Ocean.

What we did have was Vi, our old neighbour from the street who now lived a few hundred yards away in Marryat Street. She had worked in the hotel trade before getting married so I was dispatched at once to enlist her help. She came home with me, still wearing her tea apron and carrying a couple of stiffly starched white caps, very pretty little things edged with lace. 'This is all I could find from my hotel outfits but I think my friend Grace will be able to help out.'

Grace lived in Littlejohn Street and I arrived there via the Barrack Park, out of breath. She was out but her husband kindly had a rummage in a drawer and produced one small, white frilly apron. I was dubious about taking it in case his wife needed it but he waved away my hesitation, 'Naw, naw, just you take it. Eh'm sure Grace has loads of these but where they are, God knows.'

Back home, Mrs Miller had handed in an old black skirt that she had worn at some time in the long distant past. I was beginning to wish I had signed on the dole. 'It'll be far too big but if you unpick the seams and take it in, it should be fine,' she said. She also handed over a black knitted jumper and a cream blouse with frilly cuffs and collar. 'If Maureen wears this blouse under the jumper, it'll look like cuffs and a collar,' she said.

I knew everyone was being kind and I really did appreciate it but I tried to dismiss from my mind the vision I would present at work on the Monday morning with this array of borrowed bits and pieces.

Betty didn't help when she whispered, 'Eh haven't managed to make ... a you-know-what.'

She was obviously referring to the bra but that was the least of my problems. The uniform was taking shape but I hadn't mentioned the stockings in case Mum offered me her thick lisle ones.

'Eh don't suppose you've any stockings, Betty?' I asked, more in hope that anything. I wasn't surprised when she said no.

Mum always said I had what she referred to as a 'moochin face' but how Hannah, who lived in the next close, got to hear about the job I will never know. She appeared at the door on the Sunday with a pair of nylons in her hand.

'Eh've just worn these a couple of times but got a wee ladder in one of them. Eh've washed them and was going to repair them but if they're any good to you, you're welcome to them.'

Nylons! The magic stockings that came from the good old USA during the wartime shortages were like gold dust then. Even now in the 1950s, nothing was ever thrown out and nylons were no exception. Any ladder was immediately sealed with a dab of nail varnish before being repaired at home with matching thread or else invisibly mended at the Sixty Minute Cleaners. Most women clung on to their nylons like grim death and it wasn't uncommon to see some legs covered with tiny red or pink dots, almost as if the nylons had the measles.

On the Monday morning I viewed my *tout ensemble* with a jaded eye and reluctantly set off for Castle Street with the distinct impression of having jumped out of the fire into a volcano. I had just left behind one unimpressed gaffer and was now contemplating the disapproval of another, albeit female, one.

During the weekend, Mum had mentioned the long history of the Auld Dundee Pie Shop, as it was called. Grandad had been a regular customer when the shop was in the Vault, that warren of narrow streets behind the Town House, sadly now demolished along with a good part of medieval Dundee. As Mum said, demolishing the Town House was sacrilege and there was great protest at the time. Still, the Wallace family had made the successful venture into Castle Street as well as premises in Broughty Ferry and the Hilltown. Had I but known it, I was about to enter one of the happiest periods of my life. This was in the distant future and as I surveyed the restaurant in the early morning light, it still had that faded, neglected appearance as if time had passed it by.

I timidly knocked on the door. A woman's face appeared and she gesticulated with her hands. She looked like a demented refugee from the Punch and Judy show, waving her arms about and pointing towards the edge of the door. Faced with my incomprehension and totally blank expression, she mouthed, 'Go round the back. In the close.'

This close was beside the shop and I nervously entered it, quite sure there must be people about because of the babble of voices drifting out. The narrow entrance opened out into a paved court- yard. I soon traced the source of the voices which turned out to be a small, open-fronted shed full of bakers, having their break and early-morning smoke.

The woman who had pointed me towards the close was waiting and we walked through the hot, stuffy bakehouse which had a wonderful mixture of smells from the night's output of baking. We then went through a deserted and silent kitchen and into the dining room. The woman, who had red cheeks and lovely dark, curly hair introduced me to the other two waitresses who were laying the tables with crisply laundered tablecloths. 'Eh'm Nan and this is Margaret and Marian.

303

You'll soon learn what to do every morning.'

As I went around the vast room, laying out cruet sets and sugar bowls, I was relieved to see some of the staff were young. I really believed after my departure on the Saturday that the staff must be in the same age group as Miss Thomson. When the work was finished, we sat down to our breakfast which was hot rolls and cookies straight from the bakehouse. I found out that Nan was married with two children, Marian was engaged to a baker called Alex and Margaret, who was a very glamorous girl with golden blonde hair, was surprisingly single.

Miss Thomson made her appearance about eight-thirty and I was taken into the tiny back office to get a list of working conditions demanded by the indomitable manageress. She fixed me with a stern, beady eye which left me in no doubt who was the boss around the place. Then to make matters worse, she decided what she would call me. 'So you're not sixteen yet? Hmm, in that case I'll call you "The Bairn".' Like all unwanted nicknames, it stuck to me like glue and lasted for my duration at the restaurant.

Before twelve o'clock, she decided to put me on a station, which was what each collection of tables was known as. My two tables were right beside the kitchen door and were always the last to be occupied. Within a few minutes, the place was packed with people and I was amazed at the transformation from the empty, churchlike silence that had been my first impression to this clamouring jungle. The clatter of cutlery and crockery interspersed with the hypnotic babble of voices and the rhythmical swishing sound of the kitchen doors.

Miss Thomson approached with four customers, all working men by the looks of them. I had served a couple of customers before this quartet's arrival but they had come in singly and now here I was, faced with a positive mob.

'Four pehs and beans and four cups of tea, missus,' ordered one of the burly characters. 'Also tomato sauce and brown sauce and four plates of bread and butter.'

They were obviously hungry so I darted away to the bakehouse where racks of bridies and pies awaited any ravenous patron. I couldn't carry all the tea and bread and pies so I had to make three journeys. I hovered around the table, trying to put everything down but it wasn't easy. Dressed in my black and white I must have resembled an agitated penguin who had escaped from the zoo and the men were getting agitated as well.

'Just put everything on the table, missus, and we'll sort ourselves out.' said the burly man, while I glanced around the room in panic, frightened that Miss Thomson would overhear their loud voices.

Fortunately, a large queue had formed outside the door and she was too busy slotting people into seats like some gigantic jigsaw to notice my agitation. By now the kitchen was also a hive of activity and noise. Eric, the fish fryer, tossed his battered fillets into smoking hot fat where they violently sizzled and the chef pranced around serving huge portions of steak pie surrounded by a mound of boiled potatoes and vegetables.

The waitresses sped back and forth with trays laden with heavy plates, trying to keep out of the way of the bakers who regularly passed through on their way to replenish the shop's stock. I was mentally kicking myself for thinking the place was bypassed. In fact, it seemed as if the entire population of Dundee and district dined at Wallace's.

It was easy to see why the place was popular. Judging by the amounts of food on the plates, the menu had obviously been compiled for the ravenously hungry appetite that didn't know such words as calories or cholesterol.

When the four workmen left, I was delighted to see they had left me a sixpence tip. By the end of the day at six-fifteen, I had sore, tired legs and one and threepence in tips. Mum had said I could use some of the tip money for new clothes and I thought at this rate I would soon be the proud owner of the black, fashionable skirt in G.L. Wilson's window.

Mum was as good as her word and she got me a Provie cheque which I had to repay every week from my tips. Now that rationing was well and truly over, shop windows were once again filled with a large selection of goods.

Grafton's clothes shop in the Murraygate was one such shop with a tempting display. With the credit cheque almost hot from the press, I made a beeline to the shop during my time off one morning. As well as the mundane skirt and jumper I had to buy for work, I also chose a bright emerald-green coat with a fashionable wide flared hem and a wide belt.

306

Mum almost had a fit when she saw it. 'For heaven's sake! What made you pick such a bright colour? Folk will be able to see you from ten miles away.'

But I liked it, I was the one who had to wear it and I planned to show it off to Betty on our next trip to Robbie's which we still made once a week. Betty loved my coat. As regulars at the dance hall we were asked up to dance by the young men who also went every week. We still had our early curfew but what was very worrying was the fact that Betty seemed to get breathless more easily now.

And she was beginning to question this restriction with her mother. 'Why can Eh no stay on at the dancing till it's finished like other folk?' she stormed at her mother one night as we were about to set off.

'Well, Betty, if you don't come back early like Eh tell you, then you'll no be going.' Mrs Miller sounded adamant. She turned to me. 'Now, Eh'm making you responsible for Betty. Eh want her home by ten o'clock or else.'

Quite honestly, I was now beginning to worry about my pal's health. To start with, she hardly took a rest between dances and by the middle of the evening her lips seemed to take on a darker blue tinge which I hoped was down to the lights in the dance hall. At twenty past nine, I gathered our coats and bits and pieces from the cloakroom but she wouldn't come home.

'Eh'm staying here till it closes,' she said quite firmly.

'Well, you do that, Betty, but it'll be the last time

you ever get to the dancing,' I replied, equally firmly. 'Just you remember that.'

It was the nearest we had come to an argument since becoming friends all those years ago. She looked as if she would ignore me but the thought of being forbidden to come won the day and she stomped off to put on her trousers and coat. By the time we reached the house, I was alarmed to hear her gasping for breath. It was like that day when she had run after George and me.

The next day Mum said I had to go next door. Mrs Miller ushered me into the bedroom where Betty lay like a fragile doll. The doctor had been called out and he diagnosed a chest infection. Betty was to be confined to bed. Her mum sat beside us, clearly keeping an eye on her daughter and although Betty glared at her, she stayed firmly in her chair.

'What kind of day have you had, Maureen?' Mrs Miller asked. 'Have you had a lot of folk in the restaurant?'

As it was, we had experienced a very busy day because of the farmers. Once a week, on market day, hundreds of farmers arrived in the city. After their business was concluded, they arrived in droves, spilling into the dining room with their country conversations and thick, tweedy suits and bonnets which were always firmly attached to their heads.

'We get such a laugh at Nan – she's one of the waitresses,' I explained to my audience of two. 'Before the farmers come in, she puts on a dab of scent and she calls it "Coty de Coos". Then Chris, the cashier, who sits in her wee cubicle at

308

the door, says the farmers all look alike, a bit like the Chinese.'

Betty laughed and her mum looked amused.

'And another thing, they speak like this, *Fit like's yer tatties*, or *My grieve marks oot the dreels for the neeps*,' I said, trying to imitate one of the farmers but not getting the accent right. 'There's one farmer who wears a suit that Eh'm sure is made from binder twine. Every time he moves, long strings fall off his jacket. It's so funny.'

'You must get a lot of customers in the morning as well.'

'Oh we do, Mrs Miller. This morning Eh had two women who had me in a pickle when they asked for two "sair haids". I hadn't a clue what they were talking about but Margaret showed me the cakes with thick icing and wide paper bands around them. That's "sair haids", seemingly. The paper bands look like bandages.'

I could still recall my confusion that morning when the two women arrived. Quite snappy spoken, they bellowed, 'Two teas and two sair haids!'

One of them wore a bright headscarf with printed views of Vancouver splashed all over it while her pal wore a very chic lime-green chiffon scarf. They were obviously two women not to be messed with.

It was time to go but Betty looked upset when I stood up to leave. 'Eh'll no manage to go to Robbie's next week. Will you just go on your own?'

'Oh no, Betty, Eh'll just wait till you're better, so you'll have to hurry up and get out of bed.'

Mrs Miller came to the door with me and confirmed what I suspected, that it would be a long time before Betty went dancing again. Although I loved my night out, I couldn't bear the thought of going out without her. Mum said we could maybe go to the pictures once a week instead.

Mum and I had been regular picture fans before moving to Moncur Crescent. We often visited the Empire and Tivoli but our main haunt was the Plaza on the Hilltown. Now we could go to the Odeon on Strathmartine Road and although that seemed a good idea I just knew I was going to miss my dancing night.

Then, as fate intervened, I met Violet at the end of that week as I made my way towards work. She was still working at Keillor's as were Zena, Margaret and Mima.

'We're going to the Palais next Tuesday. Do you want to come with us?' she asked.

I mentioned Betty and her illness.

'Well, just come with us until she's better. Then you can both go back to Robbie's.'

I had to admit it was a great suggestion and I agreed to meet them at McGill's shop at the top of the Wellgate at seven o'clock the following Tuesday. I decided not to mention this new arr-angement to Betty because I didn't want to upset her. After all, it was only a temporary thing until she got better.

On the Tuesday night, I joined the four girls and we set off in high spirits at the thought of an evening out at the dancing. When we reached Tay Street, a long queue had formed, stretching snake-like almost to the Overgate. The minute I stepped into the interior, I was captivated. Whereas Robbie's was small, smoky and intimate, the Palais was light, roomy and very elegant.

The downstairs cloakroom was posh with large mirrors and comfy chairs. There was even a perfume machine on the wall which dispensed four different fragrances, Chanel No. 5 being one of them, I think. It cost sixpence a 'scoosh' and was the scene of many a misjudged aim, sometimes missing the paying recipient and hitting the person standing behind.

'For heaven's sake, Nancy! Will you watch what you're doing. You've just scooshed it over my new frock,' would be a typical anguished cry.

We never used this machine, preferring to carry our own little bottles of Evening in Paris for our evening at the Palais.

Upstairs, on a stage at the far end of the dance floor, waiting to begin an evening's dancing, was the Andy Lothian Band. As the band struck up, we made our way over to the line of squashy sofas that edged the floor. As we commandeered one, Zena gave me a pearl of wisdom. 'Mind now, if you're asked to dance, just say you're sorry but you can't.'

I had trouble digesting this morsel of contrary advice. Surely the reason we had come here was to dance? Then we saw the young man walking towards us. How he found the courage to walk across an acre of polished floor with five pairs of eyes staring at him I'll never know. I'm sure he must have thought it would have been easier walking into a German camp during the war. He asked me to dance and I leapt to my feet, completely forgetting the magic phrase. From the corner of my eye I saw Zena mouthing the words.

As my partner led me to the floor, I apologised for jumping up under false pretences. 'Eh'm awfy sorry but Eh'm no very good at dancing,' I told him – a fact that could hardly have escaped his notice when I tramped on his toes.

However, he was quite cheerful about it. 'That's OK, Eh'm no that great myself.'

With the polite preliminaries over, and the truth told, we began to move awkwardly around the floor. The large mirrored sphere rotated gently above us, sending hundreds of sparkling slivers of silver light cascading over the walls and floor like glittering sequins. With the tuneful strains of the band wafting over us, the effect was magical. It was like dancing in the middle of the universe, surrounded by exploding stars.

For me, the Palais was love at first sight and I was determined to visit this wonderful place again. I would wait until Betty was better to tell her about it and we would both come together. I just knew she would love it. Until then I half-hoped Violet and co. would ask me to go with them on the following Tuesday.

When the dance finished, my partner joined a group of young men. Their faces looked familiar and although I could have been wrong, I was sure some of them were bakers from Wallace's.

CHAPTER 22

Aggie was on her normal weekly visit and as usual was full of her own importance. To be quite honest, I could never understand why Mum put up with all the boasting. Tonight was no exception and she was over the moon with her news.

'Guess where meh man and Eh are going for our holiday during the Dundee holiday week?' she prompted, sitting back with her podgy hands folded together as if in prayer.

Mum, who knew it was hopeless to even venture a suggestion, looked suitably blank.

Aggie was ecstatic at this reaction. 'Well, Mr Robb and me are going to Butlin's Holiday Camp at Ayr. What do you say to that, Molly?'

I almost butted in to say I thought Mr Robb and her were spending the Dundee week at the Coup (the city rubbish dump) but I knew Mum would be wild at my bad manners. Still, I often thought Aggie deserved it, flaunting her good fortune in Mum's face when she knew how hard up we were.

Mum put on her impressed expression, again to Aggie's delight. 'That's smashing, Aggie. Eh hope you both have a good time.'

Aggie was both dumbfounded and ashamed-looking. 'Oh no, we're no going on our own. We're going with Babs and Ron and we've booked a four-bed chalet.'

'That was really good of Babs to think about taking you away for a holiday,' said Mum.

Aggie continued to look abashed. 'Well, Eh wouldn't say that, Molly, considering they were planning a week away together at the camp but meh man wasn't pleased about that arrangement at all.'

She stopped for a breath while Mum looked shocked. 'Don't tell me you've gate-crashed the couple's holiday plans?'

'That's just what we're doing,' said Aggie, self-righteously. 'Eh mean, we're no pushing our noses in where they're no wanted but meh man just said that he wasn't letting his lassie go off with a man for a week at a holiday camp. Heavens! Just imagine the hanky-panky that would go on. No, he put his foot down and we're going as well.'

Mum and I exchanged glances as we both visualised Mr Robb putting his enormous feet down. As Mum said later, it was a wonder he didn't go through the floor of the prefab, a house that was being ignored for once in the holiday conversation.

'Eh'll tell you about the holiday when Eh get back and Eh'll show you my photies,' Aggie said, while glancing around the living room. 'Eh see you haven't got a television set yet, Molly. You should just buy one on the never-never. Put down a deposit and pay five shillings a week.'

I was annoyed at her for continually harping on about a television. I knew Mum would love one and she regularly visited to watch at Nora and Charlie's house in Glamis Road if she saw something she liked in the radio and television

314

column in the paper. By this time they had five children and we hated to bother them, especially for something as trivial as a television programme.

Betty, however, was improving slowly. A course of penicillin had cured her chest infection but her asthma wasn't any better. Neither were her breathing difficulties. I felt I had to come clean about the Palais. It would have been all right if I had only planned that one night but I was now going with Violet and the girls every week. I thought it only fair to let her know.

She promised to come with me as soon as she was better. I gave her all the dance news, especially my budding friendship with the young man who had danced with me on my very first night. His name was Ally and he was an apprentice baker with a small bakery in Kirkton.

I loved the Tuesday crowd at the dancing. It was a young people's night and during the evening a score of balloons would be released from a net suspended from the ceiling. Some of these balloons contained a ticket which could be used to gain half-price admittance on the following week. This would be a big help to my budget should I be fortunate enough to find one. The drawback was that I had a phobia about balloons bursting and would always keep well away from all the good-natured horseplay that ensued when the net was released.

Ally, on the other hand, would gallantly leap into the frantic fray and present me with a balloon, and, if I was lucky, a half-price ticket. What joy!

Another pleasure was sitting with a soft drink in the Soda Fountain. This cool spot lay behind the bandstand, separated off by a glass partition. It was pleasant to sit and listen to Charlie Coates, the resident singer, or perhaps Jimmy Barton singing the latest hit, 'The Ballad of Davy Crockett', while wearing a raccoon hat. Overlooking the floor at the other end was a balcony for spectators which I thought was a terrible waste of dancing time. A glass display sign was suspended from this balcony which indicated the various dances.

We loved the quickstep, especially if it was an excuse-me dance or 'tip-off' dance as we called it. It was a universal girl's dream to be in the enviable position of having two men competing for the chance to dance with her. If it happened to any one of us it became the topic of the entire evening.

'Do you see yon guy over there? Well, can you imagine it? He's tipped me off twice tonight,' the fortunate one might say.

If some extremely pretty girl was always changing partners then a few catty whispers would emerge. 'Would you look at her getting tipped off again! Eh don't know what the fellas see in her, Eh really don't.'

Also, during the evening, Andy Lothian would announce any forthcoming engagements or marriages – 'The Palais Gazette', he called it.

One night, I spotted Maria, my mascara-clad former workmate from my factory days and I suddenly thought of Sadie. I managed to speak to Maria. 'How is Sadie keeping these days?'

Maria, as laconic as ever, gazed at me through her black-rimmed eyes. 'Oh, she's fine now but she had a terrible time with her son after he came back from Korea. His fiancée split up with him and he went a bit wild. Got charged with breach of the peace. It's a wonder you didn't read about it in the paper.'

I remembered Sadie's sudden spat with Maria and it all made sense now. 'What is he doing now?'

'Och, he's married now and got a kid. Sadie says he's a lot happier.'

Well, that was a blessing, I thought. Out of all the people I worked with, I always liked Sadie the best. Half an hour later I saw Maria again and she obviously hadn't changed one iota. She was busy dancing with one man while surveying the spare men who stood on the fringe of the dance floor through eyes still clarted with black gunge.

A most important part of going dancing was the ritual of getting dressed for the occasion. We all thought the fifties' fashion style was wonderful with our flared skirts worn over frothy, frou-frou petticoats and flat ballerina shoes, the whole ensemble set off with a jaunty scarf and a wide elastic belt called a waspie.

Mum had given me a lovely crisp nylon petticoat and a black taffeta skirt which was reversible and gave me two skirts for the price of one. I was really chuffed with my outfit. The skirt measured a magical 144 inches around the hem and swung out in delicious swirls with every move, while the petticoat rustled crisply with every step. I was like a cat with a bowl of cream. The petticoat, however, became a disaster when I washed it. It went as limp as a rag. Violet had the remedy.

'Eh aye wash mine in a mixture of sugar and water and when you iron it while it's wet, it goes all stiff again.'

I tried this method and it did work, but not only did it stiffen the fabric, the petticoat almost stood up by itself, like a pink and white jelly mould. Then there was my big problem, namely my straight hair. It was all right for Violet and her chums because they could hide their curlers under their white caps at work or put on a head-square on a Saturday. Girls who walked about the town with their dinkie curlers under a scarf were looked on as a bit common. 'Would you look at her, looking awfy orra!' would be the comment. But at least they had curls for the dancing at night.

I could well imagine Miss Thomson letting me run around the restaurant with curlers in my hair. She was a right stickler for work and always kept her beady eyes on us. Because of this situation, I reckoned that the sugar solution was ideal for me. Combing this sugary gunge through my hair certainly kept the curls in place but then concrete would have done the same job. And I had to pray that it wouldn't rain.

Mum owned an ancient pair of curling tongs that were heated on the gas cooker but because they looked like leftovers from the Spanish Inquisition I much preferred the sugar method. Mum, however, didn't like this practice at all. 'Your hair will fall out by the time you're thirty,' she warned.

This advice fell on deaf ears. As long as I had my curls, I didn't worry about the far distant future of being thirty. Anyway, when I reached that elderly age, I reckoned I wouldn't be going out much but would probably be spending my time knitting something grey and ghastly. So off I set for the Palais, as happy as Larry with sugary hair and sugary petticoat.

Worried about the prospect of having a bald daughter, Mum treated me to a perm. The DPM Dairy had a perm club and the members put a shilling or so into it every week. When there was enough money, they got their perms done in a hairdressing shop in Caldrum Street. This was an ordeal even worse than the curling tongs. The perm was called a 'Eugene Wave'. The hair was curled up over thick squares of rubber which lay flat against your scalp and then a machine was hurled into place. This machine had rows of heavy, heated clamps which were placed on the curls in a horrible, heart-stopping sizzle.

When they were all in place, it was more than you could do to hold your head upright with the weight of a Sherman tank resting on your neck. Meanwhile, bending to retrieve a dropped magazine needed at least two assistants to help you get up again. I was glad when the film star Audrey Hepburn became a household name because we all rushed out to copy her short, gamin hairstyle.

One of the surprises of the fifties was the emergence of the male fashion scene. For decades, young men had been miniature carbon copies of their fathers but now they erupted in an orgy of colour and style. It was as if some unknown creatures had emerged from a chrysalis. It was the age of the Teddy Boys with a plethora of drape suits with velvet collars, drainpipe trousers, bootlace ties and thick crêpe-soled shoes called brothel creepers. Also vastly popular was the slicked-back DA hairstyle. Very Tony Curtis.

We were also in the decade of Rock and Roll and all the beat music that went with it. We were also the first generation to live under the shadow of the atom bomb and after the destruction of Nagasaki and Hiroshima there was the general consensus that it could happen again. But I don't think we worried too much about it. We were having too much fun dancing the night away.

Because George was still at school, I didn't like to ask for more pocket money and I decided to go after a part-time job which I saw advertised for the Empress Ballroom, a single-storey building which lay in the shadow of the Royal Arch and Earl Grey Wharf.

This extra job was to help finance my dancing nights and it was a bit ironic that I took money from one dance hall to give back to another. The Empress held large dinner-dance events like the Firemen's Ball and the Woodchoppers' Ball on Tuesdays and Thursdays during the winter months and these were glittering occasions with the guests dressed in their evening finery.

The women, resplendent in elegant, long evening dresses, were a colourful kaleidoscope of taffeta, satin and silk while the men all wore smart suits. The tables were set out around the perimeter of the dance floor and, unfortunately for the waiting staff, there was no set time for dinner. The dancers could choose to eat when it suited them. If you were unlucky enough to have a table filled with dancing-mad patrons you could still be trailing around with plates of trifle at midnight.

The dance usually finished at one o'clock but the coat-clad company gathered in the foyer to await a small cup of consommé to warm them on their homeward journeys. By the time we retrieved the cups from behind plant containers and other hidey-holes and washed them, it was nearer two o'clock – time to pile into the owners' son's station wagon for the journey home. There was only one snag to this arrangement, the fact that the staff lived in different parts of the city. It was like an early morning mystery tour and I was the second-last passenger to disembark. It was usually almost three o'clock by then.

During my second night's stint, I met Avril who lived in Arklay Street and worked during the day at the Astral refrigerator factory. I thought this funny at the time and always silently referred to her as the three As. The following week, while I was lamenting about the long journey home, she said, 'Don't mention that jalopy run to me. Eh walk home now.'

As my house lay in the same direction, we decided to hoof it home together. It was fun to begin with as we marched briskly along the Murraygate. Under a canopy of glittering stars and a frosty moon, our clattering footsteps echoed loudly in the early morning silence of the deserted Wellgate steps.

When we reached the foot of Arklay Street, we paused to catch our breath, both of us steeling ourselves for the final furlong. Ahead of me lay the twin dark shapes of Dens Park football ground and the wall of the Bowbridge jute mill, both of which cast dark, sinister shadows across my path.

I had no idea what ghosties and ghoulies lay in Avril's path but with a quick cheerio we took to our heels, with me running up the middle of the road to keep well away from the black, looming mass on either side of me. In the distance, amongst a sea of darkened windows, one light shone out. It was our light and I knew Mum liked to keep the light on till I got home. I homed in on it and fair belted up the road. By the time I was inside the house, I felt I had run a ten-mile race.

Mum was annoyed as well. 'Eh'm fed up of this caper with you running up the road in the middle of the night, peching and panting. What will the neighbours think?'

As it turned out my days of this late-night working were coming to an end. Not because of Mum's disapproval but by the romantic fact that I was going out with my young man, as Jane Austen might say.

It all centred on the Empress Ballroom. Every month or so, the owners staged what was called the Big Band Sound and famous dance bands were hired to play at this. During this time, Dundee was fortunate to have the chance to see live such great names as Ted Heath, Johnny Dankworth with Cleo Laine, Ken Mackintosh and the zany Doctor Crock and his Crackpots, among many others.

Ally and I spent many a happy night listening

and dancing to these great bands that up till now had just been names on the wireless. For some reason, Violet and the girls didn't patronise these evenings and they stayed faithful to their night at the Palais.

During the day, the restaurant was a hive of activity from the moment it opened its doors until closing time. At nine o'clock in the morning, a throng of customers would surge through the door and descend on to the tables.

'The Bridie Brigade', we called them. Some mornings, especially after a late night's dancing, I would view this crowd through a half-asleep haze while keeping, at all times, a wary eye out for the manageress. She frowned on such behaviour but I don't think she had ever been in a dance hall in her entire life.

I stood at the side of a table, a small notepad in hand, to await the order, which was sometimes given very curtly. 'Two teas, two pehs and two cakes,' said two little no-nonsense women who were regulars and normally sat at the same table every week.

What a din they made if this table was occupied by someone else! 'Would you look at that!' the taller woman would bark in a sharp, yappy voice like a Skye terrier. 'You would think folk knew we always sit there.'

Her pal would nod glumly as they both deposited themselves at another table, looking as if they had been asked to go to live on another planet instead of a few feet away.

On the other hand, some customers took all day to make up their minds. 'An onion bridie, a plain bridie and a pie with beans. No, wait a minute, make that a bridie with beans and make sure it's the onion bridie and a plain bridie on its own. Forget about the pie but bring three teas and three sair haids efter our bridies.'

Working out this order took the mathematical genius of Einstein and, often, I would mix up the order, almost causing World War III. 'Oh look, the wifie's given us the wrong plates!'

It was comical to see the stushie this simple accident caused as plates and cups would be bandied around the table, sometimes ending in disaster and tears. 'Och, Bella, you've dropped your sair haid. Get the wifie to exchange it for another one.'

It was a standing joke with the staff that our customers nearly always had a sair haid after a Wallace's bridie or pie.

One pleasure was the arrival of some of the musicians from the big bands and there was always competition amongst the staff to serve them. Perhaps we all thought the odd talent scout would be with them and we would be whisked from obscurity to instant fame. In my daydreams, I would be instantly recognised as a new star of stage and screen but then that's what dreams are: total rubbish.

Marian was no longer with us as she was now married and expecting her first baby but Margaret and Nan were still there. Both were very popular with the customers, Nan because of her bubbly personality and Margaret because of her blonde hair and pretty face with its well-applied make-up. Her cosmetics, was how she referred to her bag of tricks with its various pots and tubes.

Pat, who worked in the office but took over the cash desk to let Chris away for her breaks, was a friend and we regularly chatted if time allowed. One day we were raving on about Ken Mackintosh and his wonderful band when one of the musicians overheard.

He came up to us and handed over some forms. 'I'm running the fan club for the band,' he said, ever so politely. 'Perhaps you two girls would like to join – and any of your friends as well.'

This was something completely novel for us and we took the forms with a squeal of delight. Later that night I got Ally and Betty to fill one in and we were now official members of our very first fan club. Betty was over the moon with this and within a few weeks we each got a large brown envelope containing a newsheet and details of the band's progress. We also got an invitation to come to different city venues to hear Ken Mackintosh free of charge.

The admission may well have been free but it didn't say how much it would cost to travel to such places as Glasgow, Edinburgh or, even further afield, Liverpool and Manchester. This small triviality was overlooked in the pleasure of the big brown envelope and Ally and I knew we could perhaps see the band again should it return to Dundee.

Whether Betty would manage was another story because her breathing seemed to be getting worse and her asthmatic attacks seemed to happen more often and last longer.

CHAPTER 23

The Butlin's holiday had been an outstanding success according to Aggie. She sat in the chair, twice as voluble as normal, with a huge pile of photographs in her hand. 'You've no idea what a lot of entertainment that's put on for the campers. That's what we were called. There was dancing and shows and competitions. You name it, it was put on.'

Mum and I sat in silence and looked at Aggie's black-and-white photographs while she provided the running commentary 'That's me in the singing talent contest.'

Mum looked surprised.

'Eh bet you didn't think your pal had any talent but Eh came tenth in the singing contest!' As if anticipating Mum's next question, she gushed on regardless, 'Well, maybe there was just twelve of us in it but Eh didn't come last, did Eh? Now this one is meh man winning the knobbly knees competition.'

She passed over a hilarious snapshot of Mr Robb with his trousers rolled up to expose the aforementioned knees, his huge feet encased in a pair of leather sandals that resembled miniature canoes. It took all our self-control to stop the laughter which threatened to explode and Mum had to go to the kitchen on the pretext of putting the kettle on for another cup of tea. She left me

326

alone with Aggie but I could hear the suppressed snuffles of laughter as she ran the cold water tap at full force in an effort to cover them up.

'Now this one, Maureen, is Ron. Taken as soon as he came out of the swimming pool. He looks really cold but it was an outdoor pool and the water was freezing but Ron managed to swim a couple of lengths which was a damn sight more than any of the other campers.'

This was the first time I had seen Ron the spiv and he looked innocuous enough, standing in a pair of baggy swimming trunks, his hair plastered wetly to his scalp like a skullcap. The goose pimples were clearly visible on his thin hairless arms and he looked so cold that I could almost hear his teeth chattering.

'Our chalet was pretty basic but it was comfy enough,' said Aggie, getting back to full throttle with her reminiscences. 'Every morning, the bell would sound for your breakfast and you would go to the dining hall and it was the same with the rest of your meals.'

Mum, who was a very slow eater, didn't like this arrangement at all. 'Oh, Eh wouldn't like to set my holiday around a bell, Aggie.'

Her friend pooh-poohed this scurrilous suggestion. 'Naw, naw, naw, Molly, you're getting the wrong idea. That was all part of the fun. All us campers together and the Redcoats saying, "Good morning, campers." Eh think you should consider a holiday there yourself. You can put down a deposit and pay a bittie every week at yon post office in Victoria Road. It's called Hunts and they're agents for Butlin's.'

She sat back in her chair with her second cup of tea and another ginger nut biscuit. She looked like a steam train that had finally ran out of power, her face taking on a crestfallen look.

'There's just the one thing that meh man and me are no happy about. Babs and Ron are getting married.'

Mum looked pleased. 'But surely that's good news, Aggie.'

'Well, it would be if they planned to have a big swanky wedding and reception but Ron's persuaded Babs to have a wee ceremony at the Registrar's Office and maybe a wee buffet at the prefab.' She pronounced 'buffet' as in buffeted by the wind.

'Ron says, what's the sense in spending money on a big wedding when there's more important things to spend your cash on? Well, the wedding's to be next month so Eh suppose Eh'll have to get cracking and write to Senga and Marvin. After all, Babs can hardly get married without having Senga as her matron of honour, can she?'

As Mum said later, there was no way poor Babs could have her special day without the royal presence lording it over the entire scene. No show without Punch.

Aggie was clearly unhappy about the marriage and she obviously didn't relish a son-in-law like Ron the spiv. In her opinion, he didn't measure up to Marvin the magnificent. Because of this unhappy end to the wonderful holiday, Mum almost forgot to produce her own trump card. I kept making faces at her and staring into the far corner of the living room where an object was standing, covered with a tablecloth.

'Oh, Eh almost forgot! Before you go, Aggie,' said Mum, trying to look innocent, as if she had just this minute stumbled over this mysterious object. 'Eh'd like you to be the first to see this.'

She swept the cloth away with a glorious flourish that would have done justice to a magician on a stage, to reveal our very own television set.

Aggie opened her mouth so wide that her National Health teeth almost fell out and, before she could recover her composure, Mum burst forth with her own financial journey around the new acquisition. 'As you know, George has left the school and got an apprenticeship with the DECS bakery in Clepington Road, so Maureen and him are going halfers with the seven-and-six weekly payment. We thought we would treat ourselves.'

Aggie looked quite put out but managed to say, faintly, 'Well, Eh always told you to get one, didn't Eh?'

'That's right, you did, Aggie. And do mind yon accident Eh had with my hand? Well, Eh got some compensation money for that so Eh put down a deposit and, as Eh said, the kids are paying it up for me.'

Then Mum, the horror that she was, even rubbed some salt in Aggie's gaping wound by switching the set on. *The Amos and Andy Show* appeared on screen, complete with guffaws of laughter from the audience, which in Aggie's case, was the last straw. Gathering up her handbag and photographs and calling for her fur coat, she left in a fit of pique which she tried hard to hide but which left a deep and smouldering atmosphere long after she left.

Mum was immediately contrite. 'Maybe Eh should have been less cock-a-hoop. Especially with Aggie worried about Babs and Ron. Eh only hope the lassie knows what she's letting herself in for.'

George, who had been sitting quietly while all the gossip was going on, got ready for his bed. He had an early morning start at the bakery, a job I suspected was becoming more like my time at Keillor's. His post may have been advertised as an apprentice baker but the job description should have read 'Chief Pot-scrubber' because this was his daily lot.

Ally, on the other hand, was learning all about the baking trade due to being in a small, family-run bakery in Kirkton. We had been going out together for over a year and it had been a fun-packed time of dancing, going to the pictures or just enjoying each other's company. He lived with his parents and a younger sister, Ann, who was still at school while two older sisters, Jessie and Betty, were married.

His mum was lovely and homely, forever cooking large meals for her family and baking huge mounds of pancakes and scones. His dad, Alick, was a police sergeant in the Dundee force and in the beginning I was a bit afraid of him. It all stemmed from my initial meeting with him. We had been at a late-night dance and were meandering along the High Street on our way home when this huge, burly looking policeman approached and literally towered over me. I thought he was as broad as he was tall.

'It's time you were home, lad. Get your skates on,' he said and, for a brief moment, I thought we were about to be arrested.

But Ally took it all calmly. 'Aye, Eh'm just on my way.' As we walked away, he said, 'That was my father.'

I almost fainted. 'You're joking!' But he wasn't.

Later on, when I got to know the family, he wasn't really frightening. In fact, he was a bit of a practical joker. One story he loved to tell concerned a tramp who would not stay away from the city coup at Riverside. He would regularly sleep in an old shed in the midst of all the rotting rubbish, which was not only dangerous to himself but was a serious health hazard. In spite of repeated warnings from the police and the council, the tramp wouldn't move away until Ally's dad gave it a try. Chipperfield's Circus was in town and the Big Top was erected at Riverside. One night, while the two policemen were patrolling the area, Ally's dad called out in a loud voice, 'My lion, my lion! Has anybody seen the escaped lion?'

Whereupon, the poor tramp leapt out of the shed and was last seen running towards Invergowrie. He obviously found a safer place to bunk down and everyone was happy.

Meanwhile, Mum was looking for a wedding gift for Babs and Ron. Now that rationing was well and truly over, it was proving to be a lot easier than during the wartime shortages. She decided on a pair of towels, marked with 'His' and 'Hers' on the borders. The assistant in McGill's store said they were the best-selling line that year.

Mum asked me to go with her to the Blackshade prefab and we set off a week before the wedding. Aggie had regained her good humour, mainly because Senga and Marvin were home. They were all in the house when we arrived, apart from the bridegroom, who was on one of his rounds, said Aggie. 'He's a commercial traveller as Eh told you in one of my letters, Senga, and his round takes him all over the place from Dundee to Aberdeen.'

Babs accepted the present with great pleasure and grace and set it beside a pile of other presents which were placed in her tiny bedroom. She lifted each card as she showed us the gifts and Mum made all the suitable noises that one makes on these occasions.

'Eh didn't know what to get you, Babs, but Eh aye say you can never have enough towels,' explained Mum as we admired the collection of toast racks, tea towels, ornaments and clocks, sheets and blankets and a beautiful dinner service which was the gift choice from her sister.

'Oh Babs, what a lovely looking dinner service!' said Mum, quite overcome with the grandeur of the gift which stood like a sore thumb amongst the more mundane items. 'You'll have to watch you don't break any of it.'

Back in the living room, Aggie was telling the assembled audience about the intended buffet. 'We're having a platter of boiled ham with lettuce, tomatoes and hard-boiled eggs, boiled tatties and peas. Then for pudding we're having trifle. Eh've also ordered a wee one-tier wedding cake from Rough and Fraser's bakery and some wee sausage rolls. That was Senga's suggestion. Then Eh thought at night, if folk were still hungry, Eh could make fish and chips and have a high tea with scones and bread and butter.'

'Over in the States, we call chips French fries,' said Senga, in a queer mixture of Dundee dialect and a transatlantic drawl. 'When people come around, we have a barbecue on the lawn. Isn't that so, Marvin?'

Marvin and Mr Robb were sitting together, discussing something masculine and were obviously fed up with all this talk of weddings and boiled ham platters. He looked up, surprised at hearing his name. 'Yes, honey, that's right,' he said, coming out with his standard phrase which clearly covered every situation. To everything Senga said, that was his stock reply, 'Yes honey, no honey, three pots full of honey, honey.'

Meanwhile, the bride-to-be sat quietly beside her father as if she didn't belong in this wedding scene, almost as if she were some outsider on the fringe of this important occasion.

Mum decided to bring her into the conversation. 'Have you got your wedding dress, Babs?'

Before she could answer, Aggie butted in. 'Aye, she has but what a job that was getting something to suit her colouring. It's no every colour that suits her,' said her mother, repeating herself in case Babs hadn't got the message about her difficult colouring.

When we arrived home, Mum commented on the evening. 'Eh think Aggie's getting worse! Eh just hope Babs is no getting married to get away from her mother.'

Then, two days before the wedding, the news broke and took us all by surprise. Aggie and Senga arrived at the door. Aggie looked terrible, her face all puffy and blotchy as if she had been crying, and Senga, in spite of her Californian sophistication, didn't look much better. Poor Babs had been jilted – or perhaps scuttled was a better description.

'Do you mind me telling you at the time that we wondered if he was married?' Aggie sobbed, wiping her eyes on a large handkerchief. 'Eh said that, didn't Eh, Molly?'

Mum, who wasn't sure what was going on, looked at Senga. 'What on earth's happened?'

Senga, who was upset but not so distraught as her mother, explained. 'Oh it was awfy. We were in the house last night when this stranger came to the door. A woman who had come all the way from Glasgow cornered Babs and told her she was stealing her husband. He wasn't divorced and now here he was, planning to get married again. And it was all Babs's fault. Of course, Ron was out but when he came in, he almost fainted. Eh'm telling you she fair wiped the smarmy smile off his face.'

I was agog at this news and fascinated by Senga's accent which seemed to keep slipping back to her Dundee roots the more upset she became.

Mum was really upset as well. 'Where is Babs now?'

'Dad and Marvin have taken her to my auntie's house in Strathmartine Road.'

Aggie was still sobbing and rubbing the hankie

viciously over her eyes.

'Aye, this woman from Glasgow said that Ron stayed at her house every month when he finished his rounds. The rest of the time she thought he was staying in hotels or guest houses. Mind you, the only good thing about this whole stramash is the fact that it was to be a quiet wedding so hardly anybody knows about it, thank goodness! Then there's poor Senga.' She stopped to view her daughter with a fond look. 'Well, Senga brought over a bonny frock from California to wear as matron of honour. A lovely coffee and cream, flocked nylon one with a ballerina skirt and a dinkie wee hat to match. It must have cost a bomb, Senga, and now it's wasted!'

There was a fresh burst of tears. Senga was genuinely fond of her sister and she waved this expense away with a wry smile. 'That's the least of our worries. We have to think about Babs now.'

I noticed the transatlantic drawl was back. Aggie then began to harp on about the wasted food and wasted expense. 'Eh've no idea what Eh'll do with my boiled ham and twa dozen sausage rolls and a one-tier wedding cake. If Eh had my way Eh'd push Ron's face into the ruddy icing, smarmy wee toerag that he is!'

'Well, Aggie, Senga, Eh don't really know what to say,' said Mum sympathetically.

Aggie produced a brown-paper parcel from her voluminous message bag and handed it to Mum. 'Eh've brought your present back, Molly. Now that the wedding is off, Babs said to give everybody their gifts back and say a big thank you as well.'

Mum was puzzled. 'Eh wonder how Ron's wife found out about the wedding. Still, Eh expect you'll never find out.'

'Oh, we know how,' said Senga. 'Seemingly, one of his contacts has a shop in Aberdeen. One day a customer was in this shop and overheard the owner congratulating Ron on his forthcoming wedding. He must have mentioned it to her and it seems this customer was a neighbour of Ron's wife's cousin and she thought she recognised him. It's a long story.'

Aggie and Senga stood up to leave and, at the door, Aggie turned to Mum. 'Eh always said he was a spiv.'

'At least the wedding was stopped in time,' said Senga. 'If it had gone ahead it would have been bigamy.'

Aggie was dumbfounded. 'Eh never thought of that. It was just that Eh was looking forward to the wedding. Meh man offered to buy me a new fur coat but thank heavens he only put a wee deposit down and the shop has offered to cancel the deal. He might lose his deposit of course.'

'You'll have to excuse Mom babbling on and on but she really is upset.' Senga was now in full control of herself, determined that the well-rehearsed American drawl wasn't going to slip again.

'Eh understand, Senga, and we are really sorry about Babs. And, as you say, it would be bigamy,' said Mum, helping Aggie on with her old fur coat. If Ron the spiv's wife hadn't intervened it would have soon been replaced with a brand new one.

Mum looked ruefully at the wedding present

still lying pristinely folded in the cellophane-wrapped box. 'Och well, Eh expect Eh'll find this will come in handy for another present.'

Then, this shock news was pushed out of our minds by our burglary. I discovered it on a Sunday, although the crime had taken place a few days earlier. I went to put the week's supply of shillings into the gas meter, which was situated on a high shelf in the kitchen and required one to stand on a chair to feed it with money. Because of this awkward position we only filled it once a week, and it was for the same reason that we never noticed that a thief had prised the padlock off and the money container was empty. To make matters worse, it was due to be emptied that week and had been almost full.

Mum was just in from her work at the dairy and she panicked at the thought of the burglar still lying low in the house. Then George mentioned nonchalantly that he had picked up a small padlock from the kitchen floor on the Friday afternoon but had not connected this with the meter.

I was sent to fetch a policeman from the police box at the top of the Hilltown and, within an hour, two policemen arrived to investigate the dastardly crime. I was glad that Ally's dad wasn't one of them, mainly because of the farce that had taken place while I was out of the house.

Faced with the empty money container, Mum ran through to Mrs Miller's house, clutching it in her hand. Up to this point, the box had only been handled by Mum, George and myself but it was now turning into a 'pass the gas box' situation.

Mrs Miller was aghast as she held the container.

'Heavens! It fair makes you afraid to leave your house,' she said, passing it on to her husband. Naturally Betty wanted to hold it, then Mrs Ferrie and Mrs Duff, our upstairs neighbours, who were coming along the close. They all wanted to be in on the action. They peered inside the container as if an odd shilling or two was perhaps still lurking in one corner.

Then Mum took control of it. That is, until Ally appeared on the scene, which was fast becoming a comical farce. Of course, Mum handed it to him and he had a good look inside it. I think George had another look followed by a second peep from Betty.

The police, when they arrived, stood in the middle of the kitchen and had a good look at the meter. 'There's an awfy lot of these kind of burglaries going about,' said one policeman, sagely.

'Aye, folk are having their gas meters broken into daily,' said policeman number two, shaking his head. 'There's no much we can do but take the box away for fingerprinting.'

On hearing this, Mum let out a loud wail. 'Eh've handled the thing and so have my children and there's Mr and Mrs Miller and Betty – then there was Mrs Ferrie and Mrs Duff and Ally.'

The policeman looked like he had been struck by lightning and his expression was priceless. 'Wait a minute, missus. Let me get this straight...' He held up his hand and counted all the names off. 'Eh make that nine folk who have handled this container. Do you mean to tell me you let

338

everybody handle the evidence?' He emphasised the word 'evidence' and we all gazed at the two policemen and nodded.

'Well, looking for a crook's fingerprints on this will be like looking for a needle in a haystack. Your best bet, missus, is to let the Corporation Office know about this and have them come up with a new padlock. Mind you, you will have to pay back all the missing money.'

Mum was furious. 'What do you mean, pay it back? Do Eh have to pay back everything the burglar stole? Surely that's no fair!'

'Well that's the way it is, missus. The Corporation think some of the meters are broken into by the tenants. You know, somebody in the house is hard up so they break open the meter and get some ready cash.'

'That's stupid! Would Eh send for the police and get half the ruddy close to handle the evidence if Eh had pinched my own money?' Mum was now wild at this suggestion of self-robbery.

He held up a large hairy hand. 'Now wait a minute, Eh never said that. Eh just said that a fraction of folk do it but the biggest majority are victims, just like yourself. You are just victims of the rising crime rate amongst meter raiders and, like most victims, you are the losers.'

This explanation, which was handled a bit more sympathetically than his earlier manner, pacified Mum a bit but she was still miffed. 'In my last house, which Eh lived in for years and years, we never had to lock our doors and windows. Never once did Eh get burgled, and here Eh am in a new house with a Yale lock on the door and snibs on the windows and Eh still get burgled.'

After the commotion died down and the policemen had disappeared back to their police box, Mum suddenly had a thought. 'Eh've just remembered. When Eh came home last week from seeing Nellie, Betty was standing with a young lad at her door. He was a stranger to me and he saw me open the door. Eh wonder if it was him that robbed the meter?'

It was a good thing the door had been open all the time the police had been in the house because they would have had a fit if they had seen our front-door key hanging behind the door on a long piece of string. We only had the one key and this was used by the three of us to get into the house. Mum's grand speech about Yale locks and snibs were no use against this easy access to the key.

Mum was suddenly serious. 'Now, you're no to mention this lad to the neighbours, especially the Millers. After all, Eh could be wrong and Eh wouldn't want to get Betty into trouble, especially now that she's getting out and about again.'

Betty was going to some sort of work course and although her breathing wasn't getting any better at least it wasn't worse. I was perplexed by the mention of this lad. Betty hadn't said anything but maybe she would on my next visit. Anyway, the key was taken down and Mum said she would get two other copies made and we had to be doubly sure that the house was to be locked up and well snibbed. Otherwise we could all be murdered in our beds, said Mum.

Mum had to pay just under two pounds for the missing money and seven and sixpence for a new padlock which greatly annoyed us all, even the neighbours. 'It looks like we have to subsidise the crooks now,' said Mum in disgust. 'It doesn't pay you to work hard for your money these days. You should just go out robbing meters.'

There were two bits of good news in the midst of this chaos. Babs and Aggie were going to California for a holiday. Seemingly, Senga and Marvin had paid for a return ticket for her unhappy sister while Aggie, instead of getting her new fur coat, got the chance of her fare being paid by Mr Robb. She jumped at this offer.

Another bit of mixed news was Ally and I had become engaged. Mum was thoroughly put out, as were my future in-laws. 'You're both far too young,' was the universal comment. 'And don't forget that Ally has to do his National Service when he finishes his time.'

The only person apart from ourselves who was thrilled was Betty, who being a young romantic said, 'Can Eh be your bridesmaid?'

'Of course you can, Betty, but the wedding's no to be for another two or three years. When Ally's National Service is over we'll plan it. Now what about yourself? Did Eh hear Mum say she saw you with a lad the other week?'

I knew Mum had said I wasn't to mention this but I wasn't caring about the robbery. I just wanted to hear if Betty had found herself a boyfriend.

'He's just someone who's in the same course as me. Eh've no idea where he lives or anything.

Sometimes he'll walk back with me and we have a great chat but it's nothing serious.' She sounded disappointed and I noticed her lips looked bluer.

Meanwhile, although my news didn't please Mum, she dug out the box with the His and Hers towels and handed them over. 'Well, Eh expect you'll be starting your bottom drawer and this can be your first item.'

I put the box in the dressing table drawer and wondered what had become of Ron the spiv. Was he back with his wife or was he still chatting up some unsuspecting girl on one of his rounds?

CHAPTER 24

Betty was dead. Her last illness was a short one but, unlike her previous attacks, it was an illness she would not recover from. Everyone was devastated by the tragedy of a life so young being so cruelly snuffed out. Mum and I sat in the neat living room of our neighbours and we cried along with her parents.

'This is something we've aye had at the back of our minds, ever since she was born, isn't it Dad?' said Mrs Miller quietly, her eyes red with tears.

Mr Miller, who was usually so easygoing and quiet, looked absolutely shattered and, to be quite honest, Mum and I felt the same. There was nothing we could say to help their grief. I couldn't understand why Betty hadn't got over this bout of illness.

'It was her heart,' explained Mrs Miller. 'It was damaged at birth and every time she caught a cold or an infection her lungs and heart just got that wee bit more damaged.' She stopped to wipe her eyes, taking deep gulps of breath as the emotion threatened to erupt in a surge of despair.

Mum, who was usually so good with other people's problems, didn't know what to say. 'Eh suppose there are words that folk say at a time like this, Mrs Miller, but there's no words that Maureen, George or myself can say that tell you how we all feel.'

I sat silent and miserable. A huge painful lump in my throat throbbed and made me think I was going to choke if I opened my mouth. I couldn't believe it. I had seen her just a couple of days before and she had chatted on about her work course and the possibility of getting back out into a social life.

The two aunties from the Hilltown arrived and we left, although Mrs Miller said there was no need to go. We didn't want to intrude on the family's grief.

Back in our own house, I told Mum about all the fun we had, growing up through our teenage years together, especially that wonderful night when we went to Robbie's Dance Hall for the first time. I suddenly saw her in my mind's eye, standing in her awful baggy trousers and ugly, knitted pink jumper that had made her look so tiny and fragile.

Mum laughed when I mentioned the home-made bra that I had been so envious of. Then there were the laughs we had while prancing up and down the close to the strains from Mrs Ferrie's radiogram. And there was that Saturday night when we had gone to the Regent picture house and two boys, who had got chatting to us in the queue, had followed us home. How important we felt when they chatted to us, only to have our hopes dashed when Betty's dad opened the door and chased them away. 'Honestly, Eh'm never going to get married at this rate,' Betty had complained, 'if my dad keeps chasing them away!'

'You know something, Mum,' I said, 'every Sunday night when you went to visit Nellie in Ogilvies Road, Betty and me would get dressed up and put on yon silly net gloves that we both loved so much, the ones that her mum found in a drawer. We would sit at the window and talk and talk about what we would be when we grew up. Betty had such grand plans. She was going to travel all over the world and see different countries. She knew it would never happen but it didn't stop her dreaming about it.'

Mum nodded sympathetically. 'Aye, life's certainly cruel to some folk. The poor wee lassie!'

'Then there was the times when we went to the carnival in Gussie Park,' I went on. 'Betty's mum would tell her, "Now you're no to go on the fast rides, Betty!" She aye got annoyed at this – said if her mum had her way she would only go on the kiddies' hobby horses and we would burst out laughing every time we passed them and saw the wee tots in their red buses. Betty said she would get into one but that Eh would get stuck! She really loved the Chair-o-planes and on one visit we spent all our money on them. The man must have thought we were daft.'

The next night Mrs Miller came to the door and asked me to go and say a last cheerio to Betty before the funeral. Never having seen a dead person before, I was reluctant but Mum said I should go and not hurt the woman's feelings. Betty looked so peaceful that my apprehension disappeared. She could just have been asleep. Her face was a waxy white, but then it always was, and her fragile features were as finely formed in death as they had been in life.

'You know something, Maureen? If her dad and Eh had our way, Betty would have been kept in the house and no allowed out to do the normal things bairns do. But we thought it was better for her to enjoy life, even if it meant this happening. Eh think the pair of you had a lot of fun together and Eh only hope she got some enjoyment in her short life.'

'Oh we did, Mrs Miller. We had such a lot of laughs and some of the things we got up to, well they were so funny.'

We loved the dancing and the 'Monkey Parade' every Sunday night. We walked up and down the Overgate along with hundreds of people, just looking and speaking to folk. It was stupid really but we loved it.

I took one last look at my pal and she looked like the very first time I ever saw her. The only thing missing was the twin red patches on her cheeks.

After the sad funeral, Mum and I would

regularly pop in to see the Millers. To start with, I didn't like mentioning her name because her mum looked so grief-stricken, often sitting quietly in her chair but giving a deep sigh every few minutes as if trying to overcome her overwhelming sense of loss. But, encouraged by Mum who felt Mrs Miller wanted to hear the stories, I would sit and tell them all about our exploits. Mrs Miller laughed out loud when I mentioned the homemade bra.

'The wee devil! Eh often wondered what had happened to those hankies. She could have used a couple of old ones instead of the two best ones!' she said before suddenly bursting into tears.

One evening, she asked me to help with Betty's bedroom. All the old memories came flooding back as I helped to fold the fluffy eiderdown and put the nighties and pyjamas away into a box. I thought of the many hours I had sat with Betty in this bedroom during one illness or another and how we had planned our outings so carefully. At that moment, I hoped with all my heart that, in her all-too-brief life, Betty had known some enjoyment. I hoped she had managed to get her see-through chiffon blouse, the one she so longed for that first night at Robbie's. But most of all, I really hoped that she had managed her trip to the City Square to see in the New Year.

My late Grandad said we should always cherish the good years and somehow store them in our memory, to tide us over the bad years and the bad times. This was good advice because, in my memory, I can only recall Betty when she was laughing.

CHAPTER 25

It was to be the wedding of the decade. Grace Kelly, that golden goddess of the movie screen, was marrying her fairytale prince, Rainier of Monaco.

This was to be followed a day later by another wedding, namely ours. Ally's five-year apprenticeship had come to an end and now the spectre of two years' National Service was looming. I could see only a grey, dismal void in my life due to this enforced parting but Mum said, 'Two years will soon go in. Heavens! We've been in this house six years now and the time has fair flown by. No, you mark my words, two years will be over as quick as a wink.'

Ally was hearing the same words at home. This may have been true for older people but to a pair of youngsters it was the end of the world. Because of this, we suddenly made up our minds to get married before he left, no matter where his final destination might be. This was a decision that was met with horror on both sides of the family.

'Now, what did you tell me?' said Mum. 'That you were both going to wait for two or three years at least? You're only seventeen and that's no age to settle down to married life, especially with a husband in another part of the country.'

'But that's no a problem, Mum,' I tried to explain. 'We've worked it out. We'll wait and see where Ally gets a posting and then Eh'll go down and get a job nearby.'

Mum just shook her head. Then Ally's mum, Peggy, came to see us and she voiced her misgivings. Mum agreed with her. 'Eh know what you mean. They've no house or money and they're both far too young.'

I couldn't see what all the fuss was about. After all, getting married now was just as convenient as later on and I wondered if Grace Kelly was having all this bother. Faced with this determination, Mum relented but added, 'Well, if that's what you both want then there's nothing we can say, but don't come howling to me when the novelty wears off!'

With this dire warning in mind and the call-up papers due any day, Ally went to see the minister of Clepington Church, the Revd David Reid. A few years before, Ally had been a member of the Boys' Brigade and had attended this church regularly.

We didn't know how long it took to arrange a marriage but the minister said that three weeks was the earliest because the banns had to be read out. He also offered to marry us in the manse in Albany Terrace on Saturday 21 April.

Mum said thankfully, 'Well, we'll no be rattling around in a big church so that's a blessing.'

I don't know what the Kelly household were forking out for their nuptials but ours was to be a low-key, low-cost affair. Not so much a penny wedding, more like a thirty-bob occasion. I asked Pat from work if she would be my bridesmaid and she agreed to supply the necessary support on this big step to the altar. I told her, 'Now, Pat, you're not to spend money on buying a new outfit. Just wear what you have because Eh don't want you going to a lot of expense for a quiet wedding.'

Pat promised to do that, 'I can wear my new brown costume, brown shoes and handbag and my cream hat.'

'That sounds fine,' I said. 'Then afterwards it'll just be a meal in the house. Eh've no idea what Eh'll make but Eh'll think of that later.'

The next few days were a frenzy of planning. Ally asked his pal Davie Gray to be best man and it was decided it would just be the four of us, plus Mum and George and Ally's family. On my way to work every morning, I passed Paige's fashion shop in the High Street and I had seen the ideal outfit. It was a dress and bolero in thick cream moiré with self-coloured embroidery around the neckline which made it very dressy. I thought it was really swish looking and of course the assistant, who was probably on commission, agreed.

My headgear was a cream-coloured half-hat which was all the rage at the time. This style gripped your head in a vice-like claw but it was fashionable and that was the selling point. Like Pat, I also had brown shoes and a handbag like a small shoebox. In all, it looked like it was going to be a 'brown do'.

Mum decided on a menu of home-made soup, steak pie and trifle for the wedding meal and it was agreed that I would buy the food and she would make it. Ally had baked a lovely two-tiered wedding cake with a bride and groom on the top.

A few days before the big event I decided to undergo the ordeal of another Eugene Permanent Wave in order to have some fetching curls under the vice-like grip of the half hat. Unknown to me, the girls at work were planning a surprise. After work on my last day, Mr Alf made a lovely speech as he presented me with a pile of gifts – blankets, a clock and other useful presents. I was quite overcome.

Margaret, Nan and Pat then approached with a voluminous tablecloth which they quickly wrapped round me and a baby's potty was thrust into my hand. With Pat dressed as the minister and carrying a bible in her hand, we all set off for Moncur Crescent via half the city's streets and byways which were full of pedestrians. They gazed at this motley band of noisily singing women with amusement and I was grateful for the camouflaging, all-enveloping tablecloth. Bringing up the rear, with one of Wallace's silver-plated trays in her hands, was Nan. She kept banging a soup ladle against the metal surface and the noise was deafening. By the time we reached my house, we could hear the tuneful strains of Guy Mitchell singing about his 'Truly, Truly Fair' from Mrs Ferrie's radiogram.

Nan managed to pick up the beat of the song with her ladle and tray and we were soon belting out the words along with Mr Mitchell. It was hard to guess who was the loudest but I reckoned Nan won the contest by more than a few decibels. In fact, Mum said she heard us a good fifteen minutes before we put in an appearance.

Once inside the house I was overcome again when I saw the spread of sandwiches and savoury titbits. As well as helping to organise the party, Margaret and some of the girls had spent their time off that morning helping Mum with the food. Later on, when the party was in full swing, Ally and his pals arrived from their stag night. As usual, the talk got round to Miss Kelly's wedding and the fact that she was having two ceremonies on two different days.

Mum put her thoughts in a nutshell: 'Two ceremonies! Thank the Lord we just have the one – what with the cost of everything.'

As for me, well, being young and daft, I was really quite chuffed that my wedding was to be the day after this exotic film star's one, even though we were miles apart in everything, including money, looks and the glamorous location of Monaco and Monte Carlo.

On the penultimate day, I did a quick check on the plans and everything seemed to be going well. I had my curls, frock and cake in that order and the food was in the kitchen waiting to be cooked. The buttonholes were due to be picked up the following morning and I gave myself a mental pat on the back for the seemingly smooth end to three weeks' planning.

Looking back, I think it was this smug complacency that brought down the wrath of the gods on the entire day. As it was, I should have recognised the signs which had been evident all week. Mum had been complaining of toothache for a few days but she said it was just a twinge.

Neighbours had been coming to the door all

week with small, paper-wrapped parcels. 'This is just a wee minder for your wedding,' they said as they sat down to a cup of tea and a sandwich. Before joining the company, Mum had to take a couple of aspirins or an Askit powder to help with this small 'twinge' of hers.

Aggie called, fresh from her Californian jaunt, with her suntan and blue-rinsed hair. On that occasion Mum was so speechless that she almost forgot to take her painkillers. Aggie took two minutes to hand over the present and two hours to gabble on about the joys of her holiday. 'Eh'm telling you, Molly, if you ever get the chance to go to America then you should make the effort,' she said, touching her blue curls. 'And this rinse is all the rage over there. Nobody's got grey hair in the USA. It's got to have a tint through it and maybe you should try one yourself.'

Mum, who would sooner have faced an executioner's axe than have blue hair, had her mind on other things, namely her teeth.

'Did Babs come back with you?' she asked, hoping to make a quick dash to the kitchen and the bottle of oil of cloves.

'No, she's staying on for a wee while longer. In fact, she's thinking of applying for a work permit so maybe she'll no come back. Senga and Marvin are so good to her.'

This small toothache twinge, as Mum put it, was obviously just biding its time to blossom forth into a full-scale issue and it happened the day before the wedding. Mum came home from work, almost passing out from the pain, and her jaw looked swollen and painful. We made a quick journey down to Doctor Jacob's surgery and waited while a multitude of ailments passed through his door.

When it was our turn, his diagnosis was clear. 'You've got a large abscess on your gum.'

He handed over a prescription for penicillin and warned her, 'When this infection dies down I want you to go to the dentist to get that bad tooth out.'

Mum, who at that moment would have agreed to anything, nodded glumly. She had an obsession, bordering on a phobia, about dentists. In fact, I could remember an incident years before when, during my childminding days with Cathie, she had paid a visit to the Dental School in Roseangle to have a tooth removed. Cathie and I had been quietly sitting in the waiting room when a brown blur darted past and rocketed out the door. Mum had taken one look at the equipment and the drill in particular before taking to her heels.

The doctor said the penicillin would take a day or two to work, which wasn't good news. She was almost banging her head against the wall with the pain and she went to bed with a cold wet towel pressed against her painful jaw. I decided to make the soup that night to save time the next morning and, fortunately, we had bought a ready-made steak pie from the butcher's. The trifle didn't take long to prepare and I went to bed with the hope that Mum's face would be less painful the next day.

It wasn't and she said she felt worse. I didn't know what to do but, feeling I had to carry on regardless, I set off for the florist's shop in the City Arcade. The girl behind the counter gave me an odd look when I mentioned the four button-holes.

She picked up a large jotter and scanned the pencilled list. She gave me another look and slowly ran her finger down the page.

'Your name's down here but it's been cancelled.'

I was annoyed.

'What do you mean, cancelled? Eh ordered them last week and Eh certainly didn't cancel them. In fact, the wedding is this afternoon.'

She drew her finger down the list again and shook her head, 'Well, Eh'm sorry but your name's been scored out which means you've been cancelled.'

By this time I was beginning to think being scored out might not be such a bad thing if it would remove me from this stalemate. Then I had a brainwave. 'Can Eh speak to someone in charge, please?'

She gave this request some thought before disappearing around a high-shelved unit full of flowers. I could hear her whispered conversation with some invisible person.

'She says she never cancelled them but her name's been scored out.'

I thought if I heard the words 'cancelled' and 'scored out' again, I would scream. The stage whispers were still going on. 'Well, Eh don't know who scored out her name but the button-holes aren't done.'

The girl suddenly appeared with an older

354

woman who was obviously unhappy. She approached with an apologetic smile. 'Eh'm awfy sorry but there seems to be some mix up with your flowers. Somebody must have rung up to cancel and your name got scored out by mistake.'

I was sorry too – and a bit angry as well. 'Eh need them now and Eh can't come back.'

'The problem is,' said the older woman, 'that we have a big wedding order to do – lots of elaborate bouquets – and we don't have time to do yours.'

Full of disappointment, my face fell at this dire news and on seeing this, the woman wrote down a message on a paper bag and sent me to a warehouse that lay alongside the docks.

'Take this to a woman there and maybe she can help you.'

By now the morning was going in so fast that I practically ran to the warehouse and handed over my piece of paper. The woman scanned it and shook her head. 'We've got this big wedding order to finish but Eh'll do my best.'

There was a small chair wedged in between a high stack of Fyffes banana boxes and I waited for a miserable hour while the big bouquets were expertly entwined. Someone was obviously having a grand big wedding in Dundee that day. Three cheers for them, I thought. I waited impatiently for my four paltry buttonholes, thinking darkly that Grace Kelly wouldn't have had this problem.

I was back home for twelve-thirty to find Mum bravely trying to get going in the kitchen but George and I made her sit in the living room with a cup of tea. The potatoes needed to be peeled, the table set and the kitchen floor washed.

Then Uncle Charlie arrived in the middle of the chaos, clutching an electric iron as a wedding gift. At that moment I would have given anything to see Auntie Nora and get her expert help at our moment of crisis but Charlie explained that the present wasn't supposed to be delivered until after the wedding but he happened to be passing. Also appearing on the scene was Pat, all ready to do her bridesmaid's duties. By then the kitchen floor was washed.

During the weeks leading up to my big day, I had been browsing through a magazine that contained 'A Bride's Countdown to the Altar'. This article had never mentioned being down on your knees washing the kitchen floor amongst the manicures, facials and hairdos. Also, everyone appeared to be relaxed and elegant amidst the champagne glasses and I didn't recall one bride surrounded by pots of steaming potatoes or trying to seat eight people around a table designed for four.

Fortunately, although I did try hard to persuade Uncle Charlie to stay, he said he had to be home which meant I had the luxury of an empty space at the table. To be quite honest, I almost called the whole thing off but didn't know how to cancel a wedding. Where do you start?

Ally's mum arrived and when she saw how ill Mum looked she said she would stay at home with her and let the four of us go to the manse. As Pat and I piled into the taxi beside the groom and best man I felt I had spent the morning at the 'steamie' because of my red, flustered face. So much for elegance and beauty and calm radiance!

Still, by the time we reached Albany Terrace I felt a bit better. And the sun was shining at least. The wedding ceremony was held in a room with a high ceiling and book-lined walls. Although it was a simple service it was very moving.

When we stepped down the path, we were delighted to see some of our friends waiting on the pavement to congratulate us. We made a quick stop at the photographer's studio in Lindsay Street for a few photos. I would have loved the photographer to have come to the house but it was too expensive and we settled for a few conventional and stilted photos plus some amateur snapshots back at the house.

Because we had no flashbulb attachment, it meant all the snaps had to be taken outdoors and we streamed out into the back green. The cake had to have this alfresco treatment as well, so we carefully carried it out on its small table and all took turns to pose beside it, trying to look cool and relaxed but still managing to appear as nonchalant as a group of Eskimos in a heatwave.

As usual, Mum thought about the neighbours. 'Everyone will be wondering what we're doing standing around a cake,' she said, no doubt desperately hoping that no one was peeping from behind the long sweeping wall of curtained windows. Someone, I can't remember who, joked that if we had known about this mass movement of people and cake, we would have hired Pickford's removal van.

In spite of the morning's hassle, the meal went down well, I think, with a good deal of laughing and jostling around the small table. The cake was then cut and a small slice passed around with cups of tea. Mum, who now felt the edge taken off her pain by the antibiotics, said, 'What a big cake for just the seven of us! We could each get a quarter.'

Actually, I think the meal was substantial with home-made scotch broth made with a marrow-bone, followed by the steak pie with the famous potatoes. We were all stuffed.

It was now time to leave for our trip to Butter-stone, a tiny hamlet situated between Dunkeld and Blairgowrie. Ally's sister Jessie and her husband Dave lived there and we had planned to spend a few days with them. Because we were unhappy at the thought of leaving Mum with her toothache problems, we offered to stay.

'No, it's all right,' she said, 'Eh'm feeling a wee bit better and it's no like last night when Eh thought my head was going to explode.'

Ally's mum, Peggy, nodded in sympathy and she said she would pop down to see her during the week. With that final problem settled and Pat and Davie in attendance, we made our way by tramcar to the bus station in Lindsay Street to await our transport to Blairgowrie.

When it arrived, we almost burst out laughing because the bus looked so ancient and dilapidated with its spartan wooden seats. The passengers were obviously old friends because they called out to one another and chatted in a close intimate way, calling each other by their first names and asking after all the families and close relations up to and including second cousins last removed.

One woman, who had obviously been on a massive shopping spree, tried to board the bus with her multitude of parcels and paper bags. She had two shoeboxes from Birrells, three large, paper-wrapped parcels from G.L. Wilson's department store and other innumerable bags. Because she was finding it difficult to squeeze everything through the doorway, one old man with a red-veined, weather-beaten face and a thick tweed suit with a flat bonnet sticking out from one pocket, strolled down the passage to help her. 'Give me yon two parcels, Ina – and the shoeboxes. Heavens! You've been buying up the entire town by the looks of it!'

While this was going on, a voice called from the back of the long queue, 'Will you get a move on, Ina, or else we'll be here all night! Heavens, woman! You need a whole bus to yourself!'

As we stepped on board amongst these cheery rural passengers, Pat and Davie emptied two boxes of confetti over us. It blew around our heads in a whirling, multicoloured cloud and swirled up the length of the bus to finally settle on Ina's purchases.

'Now, mind and behave yourselves,' said Pat and Davie in unison and, as thirty heads swivelled round to gaze at us, we made our way to the back of the bus with our small suitcases in tow.

'Look, it's a bride and groom!' whooped Ina, as we squeezed past. 'All the best of luck to you both!'

With faces like beetroots, we sat down beside the red-faced man but he seemed more interested in his shiny brown boots than a pair of newlyweds, a preoccupation that didn't go unnoticed by Ina. 'Is that a new pair of boots, Tam?' she shouted, peering across the passageway.

'Aye, it is, and they cost me twenty-nine and eleven. A damn disgrace if you ask me. My last pair just cost me ten bob,' he grumbled.

'Och, aye, and how long ago was that?' asked the spender of the year.

This rickety bus wound its way along the narrow country road, slowly dropping its passengers off at the ends of farm tracks. Ina got off at one such road end, a road that didn't appear to have any habitation for miles and she slowly waddled along the dirt track as if she had all the time in the world.

It was gloaming when we reached Blairgowrie and we discovered that our connection to Dunkeld would be in two hours' time. By now, the sunshine had disappeared and a sharp, chilly wind was blowing the daffodils in the Wellmeadow Garden. They shone like a golden beacon in the fading light and I had to smile when I recalled the prophecy from last year. All the girls in the restaurant loved going to 'spooky' nights and we would all congregate in someone's house with the fortune-teller in attendance.

On one such night, this teller of the future turned out to be a man, which was most unusual as it was normally the domain of women. I quickly forgot most of his prophecies but one thing did stick in my mind. He said my wedding

360

would be when daffodils were blowing in a spring breeze.

A breeze wasn't what I would have called this cold wind and we were both shivering. I would have loved a hot cup of tea but the only shop open appeared to sell only ice cream and sweeties. We settled for two ice-cream cones and sat on a bench to eat them.

The Dunkeld bus was a replica of the previous one and we joined another host of farm workers and their families who had clearly been in the town for the day. Jessie and Dave lived in a lovely picturesque cottage on the hill above the hamlet. Better still, by the time we arrived to its cosy warmth, the tempting smell of supper wafted out of the kitchen.

Our days were spent walking and exploring the sparkling lochs that lay like glittering gemstones on the fringes of this road but we did make one excursion to Pitlochry. Once again we boarded the little bus which sat for a while in the square in Dunkeld. The small white houses had a neglected look and were empty and I was disappointed because it was a lovely little square. However, I found out a few years later that they were being renovated for the National Trust and they are now cosy and attractive houses.

We trundled along the Great North Road, which surprised me by its narrowness. Perhaps because of its grand title I expected a wide, sweeping thoroughfare, instead of this glorified lane. Ally said Pitlochry was a town full of hotels and guest houses and he wasn't wrong.

I was surprised by all the wooden boards which

advertised holiday accommodation but, looking at its lovely setting, I could well believe the holidaymakers would love coming here every year. It was raining as we stepped down from the bus, a fine drizzle that fell from a grey sky, and the mountains were shrouded in a mist that lay in wispy strands across the spring foliage.

After our dinner in the Tower restaurant, we decided to be adventurous, at least as far as I was concerned, and we hired a small boat on Loch Faskally. The old man in charge of the boating station was quite chatty 'This used to be just a river until the dam was built by the hydroelectric scheme. Now it's a man-made loch.'

We took our little boat almost to the edge of the great white dam that, according to our informant, had been opened in 1951, just five years previously. The falling raindrops made soft plopping sounds on the surface of the water and flocks of colourful little birds darted out from the trees that edged the calm water. There was a deep silence broken only by their high-pitched chirping, the soothing splash of the oars and our own echoing voices that sounded unnaturally loud in this lovely green and quiet place.

I didn't know where Grace Kelly and her prince were at this moment but it couldn't have been any better than here.

CHAPTER 26

The ominous-looking letter was waiting for us when we returned home. Mum said, 'It looks like your call-up papers, Ally.'

I stood with bated breath while he read the contents aloud: '"Please report to Blenheim Barracks at Aldershot on Thursday 10th May, 1956." They've also sent a travel warrant for the overnight train to London and one for transport to the camp.'

So that was that, I thought. For a while I had harboured the small secret hope that his name might have got lost in the midst of the thousands of young men but this hope was now dashed. We had decided to stay with Mum for the time being and it now looked as if this time would be brief.

We both went back to work on the Monday. I mentioned the move down south again but Mum voiced her usual cautious concern. 'Do you no think you should wait a while before making plans like that? After all, he can get posted to a different part of the country from where he does his training.'

'One of the waitresses at Wallace's knows somebody that has spent his whole two years at Aldershot so it'll probably be around there where Eh find a job.'

Faced with this supreme confidence of youth, Mum just shook her head.

Ally was going into the RASC as a baker and on the evening of 9 May we all set off for Taybridge station and the overnight train. It looked as if quite a few young lads were heading off for the army as well and the platform was crowded with families in tight little groups all huddled up against each other.

As with all farewells, there was the usual mixture of emotions, from the suppressed sobbing of one young woman with a tiny baby, to wet-eyed mothers, back-slapping pals who would soon be servicemen themselves. We arrived late on purpose because it would have been terrible to have a long-drawn-out farewell. Ally's mum, Peggy, and Mum were standing quietly on the fringe of our group. As for me, I had experienced ten days of conflicting emotions and I was now pale-faced and almost drained of feelings.

The one thing that kept me going was the thought of our wonderful plans which we hoped would bear fruit in six weeks' time after his training and when he got his permanent posting.

'Eh'll maybe get some leave after my square-bashing,' he'd said, referring to his initial training.

The train steamed slowly into the station and there was a scurry as men jumped aboard with their bags. There was a final slamming of doors and all the onlookers with platform tickets clutched in their hands watched as our loved ones were whisked away to do their duty for Queen and Country.

Bella arrived unexpectedly when we reached the house. I was glad to see her because it took my mind away from my self-pity which was threatening to erupt at any minute. Peggy had gone straight home as her husband was due to finish his shift. Bella was her usual cheerful self. 'Och, look on the bright side, Maureen. It'll soon go in,' she said, heaving herself into a chair. 'Still, it's a shame about this awfy National Service. Eh've had three laddies in the army and according to them it was terrible with all the senseless kit inspections and the "bull".'

'Aye, you're right, Bella,' I said, not really in the mood for expressing or analysing my feelings. In fact, I was truly down in the dumps.

Bella was still on her high horse over John, her son. 'That was a terrible time he had in Korea, fighting the Chinese Communists. Aye, young laddies go away for two years and they never know where they'll end up. It could be any place in the world.'

On seeing my face, Bella said, 'Och, it's different now. After all, it's peacetime and they'll no need so many soldiers in the overseas postings.'

As I handed Bella another cup of tea, I sincerely hoped not.

A couple of days later I got a letter from Ally. He had settled in at the barracks but it wasn't a happy place. The sergeants shouted at the young conscripts and a few of the lads had run away in the vain hope of reaching home. This understandable foolishness earned them the wrath of the army and added to their misery. A second letter was the news from Ken Mackintosh Fan Club and contained its usual list of forthcoming appearances. There was also a bulky, brown-wrapped parcel tied firmly with string. I couldn't think who would be sending a parcel to me but on opening it, Ally's blazer and the rest of his clothes spilled out. I panicked at this sight, not understanding the meaning of the returned clothes, and I called out to Mum who was in the kitchen.

She rushed through and I wordlessly handed her the parcel. 'What in heaven's name is this?' she said, taking the parcel and viewing the pile of clothes.

'Something must have happened!' I cried. 'Eh mean, why would they send his clothes home?' Memories of the awful stories Bella had narrated over the years about her sons' army days came flooding back and I couldn't help but worry.

Fortunately, Mum found the single sheet of notepaper that was tucked in beside the folded clothes in the parcel. 'You daft gowk!' she said, after reading the note. 'Ally's sent these back because it's army regulations.'

I sat down in relief and gathered the things together. The navy blazer was his pride and joy and now he wouldn't be wearing it for two whole years. I didn't know if servicemen were allowed to wear their civvy clothes when they were off the camp but I made a mental note to take them with me when I eventually went down south.

The dance band fan club letter was also lying on the floor and I was suddenly filled with sadness, not only for Ally being so far away but also for that lost and bygone part of my life. The happy, teenage dancing years with Betty and Violet and the girls were now in another world that was a thousand light years removed from my life now.

Mum said that, if you keep busy, the time passes much quicker and she was right. The weeks were going in and before long I was filled with anticipation of the forthcoming weekend leave. Ally arrived home with a rough-looking khaki uniform and full of the stories of the six weeks' training.

'Oh, it's all right once you get the hang of it,' he told his mum and dad when we went to visit them that first evening, 'We have to shave in cold water every morning and if you don't shave the sergeant bawls at you and you get a swearing if your hair isn't short enough. Then there's the kit inspection. It has to be laid out on the bed with everything folded up the right way or else the sergeant will throw it on the floor and make you do it again.'

Peggy was annoyed, as any mother would be at this cavalier treatment of a son. 'That's terrible! Some folk shouldn't be put in charge of young lads.'

Ally was philosophical. 'Well, Eh have to say that my time in the Boys' Brigade has been a help during the earliest days.' That and also the fact that he had regularly gone camping with his pals to the Sidlaw Hills as a youngster. They had learned to rough it then and this was good training for the sadistic harping on about ablutions and spit and polish.

'There's one lad in the billet who's having a terrible time with his kit. In fact, some of the lads made it up for him one night and he had to sleep

367

on the floor so he didn't disturb it.'

'Are you managing the Blanco on your webbing and the Brasso for your buttons and badge?' his dad asked.

'Aye, Eh am. It's a hard job but no so hard as trying to get a shine on my boots. It's almost impossible,' he said ruefully. 'Some of the older recruits burn their boots with a match and then polish them but you have to be careful you don't burn the boots through.'

I told them of my stupid panic at receiving his clothes and Peggy said she would have reacted in the same way.

'You know, it's a funny feeling posting off your clothes like that,' he said, 'almost as if you're giving up your last link with life before the army.'

Back in the house, Mum was eager to hear all the news of army life and before I could blink the weekend was over and I was saying cheerio at the station again. Ally didn't know when he would get another leave but promised to let me know the minute he got his posting.

'Nobody tells you anything in the army but surely Eh'll hear in the next couple of weeks.' Then he suddenly added, 'Oh, by the way, don't send me any money every week when you get your allowance. Just put it in the savings.'

This had been Mum's idea. 'Eh don't think conscripts get a very big allowance in the army, especially if they have to buy Blanco and Brasso and other things. You should send him a pound a week and include it in one of your letters.'

I had taken this advice and I had dutifully sent off the pound note every week but, if he wanted me to save it, then I would.

I had left the restaurant a week before. I regretted it almost at once but I was in a restless frame of mind and didn't know what to do. I felt I was in limbo, waiting between a job in Dundee and a move to the south. I just hoped and prayed that he would get a permanent posting soon and then we could fulfil all our plans.

At the end of the week I debated about including the pound note. I didn't want to hurt his feelings but, after a good deal of thought, I sent it anyway. If it was returned, then I would save it. After all, as Mum pointed out, a married conscript didn't get such a big allowance because most of it was paid to his wife. Years later he confessed to waiting in a sweat in case I did what he wanted and didn't send it. After a week of the army's gourmet meals he was always glad to escape to the NAAFI and one of Lyons' apple pies.

By now he was billeted at Number 3 Training Battalion in Farnborough, learning all the intricacies of a field bakery. There was seemingly a strange situation going on and no one knew where they were being posted. Because of this and also because I needed to get another job quickly, I answered an advert for a post in the Vidor factory on the new industrial estate. I reckoned I could work there until the elusive posting came through and I only had to give one week's notice if I wanted to leave.

The factory was a vast impersonal place and I was put on a machine which resembled the one in Keillor's, except the small boxes were filled with batteries instead of sweets. Keillor's, however, had been a clean job, unlike this place. My machine was right beside the Dolly Shop, a name that conjured up visions of sweet-faced dolls dressed in frilly frocks but was in fact one of the dirtiest places I had ever seen.

I think men were the only people employed in this section and they worked in a cloud of black dust all the time. At the end of the shift these men would appear with black faces glistening with perspiration and looking like refugees from the *Black and White Minstrel Show*. I almost expected a rendition of 'Sonny Boy'.

On arriving home every night, the first thing was to have a bath and wash my hair but even with this daily routine I still felt my hands were grubby with ingrained dirt. The woman on the next machine to me showed me the bucket of Rosalax, a barrier cream that was supposed to protect the skin against constant grime. I wondered if the men in the Dolly Shop had to smear it all over their faces as well.

I also hoped and prayed that my next letter would bring the joyful news from Farnborough but there seemed to be a clampdown on information.

Then, a week before my eighteenth birthday in July, the news broke that the President of Egypt, Colonel Nasser, had seized control of the Suez Canal, much to the fury of the British and the French governments. Nasser in his speech that day said these governments could 'choke to death on their fury' and that he would use the canal's revenues to finance the Aswan Dam. The Prime Minister, Anthony Eden, retaliated by saying that 'Nasser could not hold a thumb to our windpipe.'

The rest of the world just held its breath.

There was also trouble in Cyprus between the Turkish and Greek Cypriots and the exiled Archbishop Makarios was in favour of using armed action to regain the island's unity with Greece. An army of terrorists, EOKA, was responsible for the shooting of several British servicemen as well as the usual tactics of an insurgent band.

In September, Ally suddenly appeared home on two weeks' embarkation leave. He didn't know where he was going but it was overseas. To say I was alarmed would be an understatement, especially with all these alarm bells sounding in various countries. His weeks of training at Farnborough had been an intensive training course for an overseas field bakery and the rumour was that something big was about to happen.

To make matters worse, the son of Peggy's neighbour had been posted to Leuchars with the RAF. This branch of the services was known as 'The Brylcreem Boys' and it seemed to be a more cushy number than the rough and tumble of the army.

Uncle Davie, Peggy's brother, was a lovely man who worked on the railways. He stayed in lodgings in Perth all week but spent his weekends in Dundee. The neighbour was always chatting on about her son's National Service. 'He gets paid danger money, you know,' she told Peggy one day.

On hearing this, Uncle Davie quipped, 'Well, it must be from the sparks from the fireplace!', a

371

statement that rang true because he was home every weekend. This fact filled me with deep envy.

By now, all hopes of moving south had gone west and we had no idea how long this overseas posting would last. All we knew was that it was too long.

Aggie arrived one night as we were leaving to go to the pictures. We got the normal three-minute synopsis in the lobby. 'So you're home, Ally,' she said stupidly, because he was standing beside me. 'Babs has got a job in California as an office secretary. It's in the same firm as Marvin and she's awfy happy. Meh man was just saying what a blessing she met Ron the spiv because if she hadn't met him, she would still be working in the tattie merchant's office. No that there's any-thing wrong with that,' she added hastily. Maybe she thought we had a hundred tattie merchants hiding in the lobby cupboard. 'No, it's just that her world's been widened if you know what Eh mean. It's a different life over there, in California. Apart from the sunshine Eh mean. Naw, folk seem to enjoy themselves more. Go out to dinner parties and barbecues and the like.'

Mum, who had been listening to this outburst, shouted out to her friend, 'Aggie! For heaven's sake, will you let folk get off to the pictures in peace?'

Aggie, who was never embarrassed in her life, looked surprised at the thought of anyone fancy-ing a film instead of life as lived in California.

We made our escape. It was good to get away from the house now and again and, although the arrangement suited us at the time, it was a bit of a squash with four of us in two rooms.

I had taken time off work but the days just flew in and it was time for leaving again. I was beginning to think the interior of the Taybridge station was my bête noire but on this particular evening the platform was packed with khaki-clad servicemen. The situation in Suez and Cyprus was tense and the Territorial Army and reservists had all been called up.

The men sat on benches or lounged over their kitbags. I wondered if some of these men had seen service in Korea because they had the stern, lined faces of men who had seen death and destruction. They also had the look of men who knew that another conflict was looming and I felt sick as I watched the motley crowd.

'Why do you think these soldiers have been called up?' I asked but Ally didn't know. All he knew was he was being sent to some field bakery in order to feed all the extra troops.

The station had the bleak atmosphere of a transit camp that night and while we stood there the soldiers lit up their Players' Full Strength, the Woodbines and the Gold Flakes, cupping their hands over the blazing matches. A mini-whirl-wind swept along the bleak platform, catching all the discarded debris and shoving it between the pillars. The pigeons, normally so noisy and pre-datory, watched quietly from the roof, their beady eyes taking in all the activity below.

We stood beside a pillar, mostly to escape the chilly wind but also to escape the mass of people. Ally was speaking above the noisy hubbub.

'Maybe Eh'll no be that long abroad. Sometimes overseas postings can last just a few months.'

But we knew that wasn't to be. Not with all this military presence around. A voice crackled over the Tannoy above our heads but most of the words were disjointed and echoed in the vast cavern of the station. The voice stopped and within a few minutes, a train pulled into the station. It appeared to be fully occupied, again by uniformed servicemen and to my worried eye it seemed as if the entire British Army was on the move.

There was a rush to get aboard and the men hauled their kitbags on to their shoulders as they waited in the large snake-like queues that had formed at the doors. Ally was one of the last to get on board and he managed to squeeze in beside a small portion of the window which was wound down. The train jerked noisily forward, emitting a great whoosh of steam while the guard closed all the doors before raising his flag and blowing his whistle.

It then steamed slowly away, carrying Ally and all the other soldiers off to perhaps another war in some far-flung corner of the world. He waved and called out but his words were snatched away by the wind while I stood motionless watching the small white blur of his face as he slowly disappeared into the night. Then even the bright tail light was no more.

The station was now deserted and the only sound was the strange echoing from the departed train and the rustle of discarded wrappers and cigarette packets. A score of cigarette stubs lay scattered on the stone platform, ground under the heels of army boots and bearing sole witness to the military presence a few moments ago. The wind caught the golden fragments and added them to its haul of debris. My lone footsteps resounded in the cathedral-like cavern and I walked slowly towards the entrance with a pile of rubbish following me along the platform.

The pub on the corner of Union Street was brightly lit and I heard the noisy babble of voices drifting out through steamed-up windows that had been opened to allow the chill autumn air into the smoke-filled interior. How strange, I thought, how everyone's life seemed to be going on while mine appeared to be in limbo.

Because I half-expected Aggie to be at the house, I decided to walk along the deserted Esplanade. The water lapped gently against the stone wall, just as it had done all the years before when Mum and I and George had walked along it on summer days.

The lights of Newport and Wormit flickered across the watery expanse of the river, glittering on the surface like falling stars that had suddenly found a friendly planet. There was no moon that night and the darkness closed around me like a warm, comforting quilt. I was grateful for the black anonymity of it.

The rain, that had hung over the city like a grey tantrum all day, finally started to fall in a thin drizzle, casting circled rainbows around the gas street lamps of Perth Road. Like some peeping Tom I gazed through the windows into the cosy scenes of domestic family life. People moved around their living rooms, secure in the knowledge of the warmth of their own four walls.

A man walked towards me, his overcoat buttoned tightly at the neck and a newspaper tucked under one arm. He glanced at me for a few seconds before opening the gate of a house with golden lights. The click of the gate was followed by the thud of a door and then all was quiet again. The circles around the lamps grew more intense and although I blamed the raindrops I knew it was unshed tears.

I caught a tramcar in Tay Street and by the time I reached home, the rain was falling in sheets that literally bounced off the pavements. Mum looked up as I entered and if she had shown a sympathetic face then I think I would have burst into tears. Instead, she made a great fuss about my wet clothes and went to make some tea. 'Eh'm waiting for a film to come on the television,' she said, appearing with the teapot and a pile of buttered toast. 'It's called *The Reluctant Heroes* and it's a comedy with Brian Rix.'

This film turned out to be a comic version of your everyday National Servicemen and it was so funny that by the end of it we both had tears in our eyes.

I got a postcard a few days later from Malta. Ally was en route for Cyprus, Episkopi in fact, and he was joining the 99th Field Bakery. At the end of October, British and French troops landed in the Suez Canal area and seized it back in a military coup. This didn't last long when the Americans protested. Very soon it was handed back to Egypt and Colonel Nasser.

A few days later, we witnessed the Hungarian

Uprising on the television and all the brave people standing up to their Russian overlords. Sadly, it was cruelly crushed when the tanks arrived and Mum and I followed the story every night as it unfolded. Bella said there was going to be another war and I could well believe it. Ally and all the young National Service conscripts would be once again in the middle of it.

CHAPTER 27

I just knew that 1957 was going to be a bad year almost before it was a week old. Ally still had 500 days to go in the army while Mum, who had never got around to seeing the dentist after her painful abscess, was now suffering toothache on a daily basis.

Dr Jacob wasn't sympathetic. 'What did I tell you last April when your abscess cleared up?' he said, giving her a severe look over the top of his glasses. 'Do you remember I told you to go to the dentist?'

Mum looked abashed. 'Well, Eh was going to go, Doctor, but Eh've got this awfy fear of dentists. Eh mean, it's no just an ordinary fear but more a terrified feeling.'

'Right then, I'll write a prescription for one tablet and I want you to take it before going to the dentist. It will calm your fears,' he said, writing on the prescription pad. His illegible handwriting resembled a spider that had somehow fallen into an ink pot before strolling over a pristine sheet of paper. 'Now remember what I've said. Make an appointment with a dentist right away.' He gave her a reproving look and his terrified patient got out of her chair.

Mum would have liked to ignore this ultimatum but she knew the situation couldn't go much longer, not with the amount of pain she was suffering every day. In fact, she was forever pushing little wads of cotton wool impregnated with oil of cloves into her tooth.

Her colleague, Nellie, offered to go with her to the dentist at the top of the Hilltown and that support plus the magical tablet swayed her. However, when I came back from the factory that night, I discovered the dentist had taken all her teeth out and had ordered a set of dentures for her. She looked really ill but it was hard to determine at this point if this was caused by the painful gums or the effect of the gas anaesthetic. Nellie was sitting beside her and she was still dressed in her white works overall and white turban.

'We went to the dentist right after work,' said Nellie. 'Your mum said she was feeling fine and she said she felt she was walking on air.'

Well, she certainly wasn't walking on air now, I thought. The tranquilliser had now worn off and her face was very sore, just like it was on my wedding day.

'Mum just needed to get the one tooth out, Nellie. Why did the dentist take them all out?'

'He said that it was only a matter of time before they would need to be taken out so your mum said just to go ahead,' said Nellie, who was obviously upset although it wasn't her fault.

It was more the fault of the tablet that had given Mum her Dutch courage. Perhaps if she had been in her usual terrified way, then she may have stuck to the one tooth. By now she was awake and dying for a cup of tea. She looked pleased to see me and said to Nellie, 'Now, you're no to worry, Nellie, Eh'll be fine by the morning. It was just that Eh felt really sick.'

Nellie looked relieved. 'Oh that's fine, Molly. Eh was worried about you but it's been the effects of the gas.'

'Aye, that's what it was – the gas,' Mum said, trying to convince herself that this discomfort was a temporary thing and that come the morning she would be bouncing back to work, albeit minus her teeth.

As it turned out, it was seven days later before she felt better and able to return to the dairy Trying to provide a tempting selection of soft cooked food was a trial. Never a big eater at the best of times, she now seemed content to eat a few mouthfuls now and again, interspersed with her cups of tea.

I made eggs in every form – scrambled, boiled, poached and lightly fried – and fish in milk and ice cream till she was sick of the sight of it all. 'Don't make me another egg because Eh'm really scunnered with them, and Eh don't like fish in milk. Just give it a wee fry but keep it soft and Eh should manage it. Eh really fancy some mince and a doughball as well,' she said, while gazing at the piece of haddock lying in a pool of white sauce.

George was now in the second year of his apprenticeship but was still in the land of the pot-scrubbing, a fact that annoyed Mum intensely. 'What a cheek that bakery has in making a laddie wash pots all day long! You would think now that he's in his second year he would be getting shown how to do some baking. After all, he's supposed to be a baker.' She turned to me. 'Was Ally washing pots as long as this?'

'No, Mum, he wasn't but he was in a small family-run bakery and Eh think you learn a lot more there than in a big concern like the Sosh. Also, Ally went to night school in Cleghorn Street.'

George was also attending this night school but he wasn't getting the daily training, always being fobbed off with excuses and promises of learning the trade at a later date. As Mum said, 'Aye, when he's sixty.'

Meanwhile, hundreds of miles away, Ally had too much to do. The 99th Field Bakery were turning out 25,000 loaves a day, all hand-made in a long trough then fired in diesel ovens that were portable and set on wheels.

Because of the terrorists, the island was under a strict curfew and the troops had a guideline of no-go areas which had to be adhered to. In order to avoid any ambushes from the EOKA fighters, the bread was delivered to the surrounding camps at night. It was transported to Nicosia and other places by an armed guard.

Fortunately, the beach wasn't out of bounds to the soldiers and they spent all their spare time getting a lovely suntan and swimming in the

Mediterranean Sea. I now had a lovely collection of postcards and snapshots from the island and it seemed a shame that such a lovely place was at war with itself and the British government.

Aggie put in an appearance during the week of Mum's illness. Our front door, as I have mentioned earlier, had a bell that was worked by twisting the handle. This action sent shrill squeaks into the rooms but for some unknown reason the sound was different under Aggie's hand. Perhaps she twisted it too hard, but it always sounded like a cat being half-strangled and in the final throes of its ninth life. Anyway, Mum said weakly when she heard it, 'Heavens! It's Aggie and here's me with no teeth yet.'

'Could we no pretend to be out?' I suggested, more in hope than anything. I wasn't in the mood for Aggie's chatter this night because I had just received a letter from Cyprus describing the dangerous night convoys and I was worried.

Mum was mortified. 'She'll know we're in because she'll have heard the television. No, you better let her in.'

By the time I reached the lobby, the half-strangled sound echoed loudly. As I hung up the musquash coat, the new version, I warned her, 'Mum's no feeling awfy well. She's off her work.'

This was a mistake. I had forgotten that Aggie loved a good illness to chew over. Putting on her serious po-face, her 'coffin expression', as Mum called it, she approached the living room. 'Oh, Molly, Eh've just heard you're no well...' She suddenly stopped, with her mouth open, 'Heavens! Where's your teeth?'

Mum was annoyed. 'Where do you think they are? Eh got them out at the dentist's, didn't Eh?'

'Oh, you don't look well and you've got a right yellow look! Almost as if you've got the jaundice,' said Aggie in her usual tactful manner.

'That's probably because of all the eggs Eh've had. Eh'm getting fed up with them. Forty different ways of cooking them as well and that's enough to make anyone yellow.'

Aggie, who caught the exasperation in Mum's voice, turned to me. 'Well, how's married life treating you?'

I almost said that since the April of the previous year, I had seen my husband for a total of thirty days and he was now away to a spot where mean-looking, gun-shooting Dead-eye Dicks and terrorists seemed to lurking under every bush; that servicemen were being shot in the street and death lurked around every corner. But I didn't. Instead, I just smiled and said, 'It's fine, Aggie.'

I caught Mum's eye and she was about to say something about my innocuous reply but I glared at her. 'How's your family, Aggie?' she said instead.

Every time Aggie was on the point of boasting, she always gave a deep sigh and visibly swelled, her entire body filling with maternal pride. 'Wait till Eh tell you my news!' she said, glancing at us both, her head swivelling with each glance. 'Babs has met a man!'

'What do you mean, "met a man"? Surely they have around sixty million men in America, give or take a million or two, and most of them will be staying in California. You've said so yourself

Aggie,' said Mum.

'Naw, naw, Molly, Eh mean *met a man!*' she emphasised, stressing the last three words.

'Oh, Eh see. She's met one romantically?'

'Aye, that's what Eh do mean and no only has she met him but he's asked her out for a date.'

She sat back in her chair, looking really pleased with herself. I caught Mum's eye once more. I could have been wrong but I was sure she was about to say something about a palm tree and dates. I gave her another warning look and she blew her nose to cover up her expression.

Aggie asked if she had a cold. 'You have to be very careful of getting a cold, especially when you get your teeth out. It can affect your nerves and give you terrible pains in the head.' She stopped briefly and looked a bit confused. 'Now where was Eh? Oh aye, Babs has been asked out by the wonderful man who works beside her in the same company. Marvin also works for this company. Well, he asked her out for a date. That's an American term for going out to the movies or to a dance.'

When she stopped for breath, I almost added that it wasn't only the cold that gave you a pain in the head. There was a certain person who had the same effect and she owned a musquash coat.

'Now, Maureen,' she said, taking me completely by surprise, 'when do you think your man will get his next leave?'

'He'll no get one, Aggie. The next time Eh see him will be when his National Service is finished.'

She looked flabbergasted. 'What? Do you mean

383

in May 1958? In over fifteen months' time?'

Or 460 days, I thought, which made it seem less. 'That's right. Cyprus is packed with troops now and the bakers have to make all this bread to feed them. Nobody seems to know what the position is.'

'Well, Eh really thought we were going to have another war when Suez was invaded but it seems to have fizzled out now. Then there's that awfy carry-on in Hungary. The Russians are a mean-looking lot. Did you see the massacres on the television news? It fair makes you shudder,' she said, shaking her head at the thought of the black-and-white, grainy images on the television. 'Meh man was saying that a young chap who works beside him is dead keen to go out to Hungary to fight with the freedom fighters. But the Red Army have tanks and machine guns and bombs and everything, so how can a wee chap who drives a tramcar help over there?'

It was certainly a worrying time. One girl I worked beside in the factory was, like me, waiting patiently for the return of her National Service-man husband. His service was over but he still hadn't been discharged. With every extra day that passed, she convinced herself that something was wrong, almost as if the big Western powers had something up their sleeve.

By now I had a headache and I shuddered to think how Mum was feeling but Aggie was still in full flow. 'Senga and Marvin have got another car and it's a Cadillac. It's about as long as this room and it does ten miles to the gallon.'

Mum wasn't going to let her off with this

elaboration. 'You can't have a car as long as that. Heavens! The roads wouldn't be wide enough for them all.'

'Eh'm telling you, Senga says it's as long as her lounge and her lounge is about the same size as this room,' She glanced around the walls as if mentally measuring them. 'But Senga's house is differently decorated. Of course, she's younger than you, Molly, so her tastes are far more modern and up to date.'

As usual she was on her feet a good ten minutes before she asked for her coat, her hand on the door handle. 'Well, Eh better be hitting the road or meh man will wonder where Eh am. He's aye telling me no to leave him on his own but Eh tell him no to be so daft.'

After she had gone, Mum said wearily that Mr Robb must be nuts not to treasure this short time on his own, spent in peaceful contemplation. I felt a vague feeling of dissatisfaction, one that I had been experiencing over the past few months. Perhaps it was something to do with the amount of days Ally still had to do in the army. Or maybe it was my job. There was nothing I could do about the army but maybe I could change my job. That at least was an option.

Then I found out that how strange life can be at times. Sometimes a decision is made for you overnight and so it was over the Vidor factory job. There had been a rumour going around the factory floor over the past few weeks but these whisperings now turned into a deafening roar. A big pay-off was expected, due to the same old hoary story of a thwarted export order. It was also rumoured that the company ran a policy in regard to their workforce of 'last in, first out'. If this was true then my particular role in the complex lay at the end of the line.

Because of this situation, I decided to look for another job and this turned out to be as a waitress in the restaurant of Draffen's department store. The vacancy was in the Cottage Room, which lay right under the eaves and was decorated in a mock-Tudor style with brown Windsor chairs and dark wooden tables. This restaurant catered for shoppers and business trade and offered a table d'hôte menu which I think was priced about three and sixpence for a three-course meal. On the floor below us were three other restaurants, the Blue Room, the Dining Room and the Coffee Lounge, which catered for all tastes and purses.

Mum couldn't understand why I hadn't asked for my old job back in Wallace's but I had been in a few times and most of the old faces had moved on to pastures new and strangers had filled the gap. Anyway, I never liked returning to a job, feeling it was a backward step. I liked meeting new faces and had already become friendly with Hannah, Pat and a few others in Draffen's.

Getting to work every morning was a problem because of the four flights of stairs which rose like Everest from the staff side entrance. One morning, to avoid this trek, I made my way to the lift which was situated at the back of the ground floor of the store. Unfortunately, the man who operated the lift got wise to my antics. The next morning, he barred my way. 'Eh ken you. You work upstairs and workers are no allowed to use the lifts,' said the operator, who was disabled. The rumour was that he had been shell-shocked during the war, which was terrible if it was true.

'Oh, come on! It's a long climb up all the stairs and it doesn't take you a minute to run me up,' I said, trying to look fragile and incapable of such a strenuous exercise.

But he was adamant. 'No, you're supposed to use the stairs. This lift is for the use of customers only.'

I was furious as I raced up the stairs, wild at him and wild at myself for wasting precious time on the stupid lift instead of getting myself clocked in. This was the only restaurant I knew where the workers had a time clock, and heaven help you if you were habitually late.

By the time I reached the staffroom I was red-faced and mad. Hannah was still there. 'Eh've no time to waste, Hannah. Eh'm late already,' I said, lurching towards the small clock.

'Don't bother with that,' Hannah said, 'Eh've clocked you in. I saw you having an argument with the lift operator and Eh knew you wouldn't win.'

That's what you think, Hannah, I thought. The next morning, wearing my best coat and shoes and a long scarf draped across my face, I swanned to the lift. 'Take me to the Cottage Room, young man,' I requested in my best pan-loafy voice. 'Now, Eh'll be going to the Cottage Room every day during my long holiday in Dundee so Eh'll see you tomorrow and thank you.'

He almost fell over in his haste to press the

buttons. I got away with this act for about a week until he twigged and rounded on me angrily, 'Eh'm no taking you up again! You have to use the stairs.'

'Eh don't know how he found out it was me,' I moaned to Hannah as we stood in front of the staffroom mirror.

Hannah laughed. 'Eh'm surprised you got away with it for even one day because you looked just like yourself. Even your voice.'

I was amazed. 'Is that right?' I said, seeing fame and fortune as an actress on a stage slowly evaporating before my eyes.

Meanwhile, back at home, Mum had taken possession of her new dentures but she didn't like them and was forever complaining. 'Eh just can't eat anything with them. Eh think Eh'll take the bottom set out.'

'Look Mum, the dentist said you had to persevere with them and no take them out to eat anything. Otherwise you'll never get used to them.'

Faced with this situation, she began to eat less and less and was beginning to look ill again. I told her to do what she thought suited her best, but still her appetite didn't return. She managed to go to work every day but she was so tired that she went to bed the minute the tea was over. I was really worried. Even Nellie noticed it and urged her to see the doctor but Mum was adamant that the trouble lay with her new dentures. 'Eh can't eat with them, Nellie. By the time Eh've managed a few mouthfuls, the food is cold.'

I tried getting round this problem by serving a

very small amount and keeping the rest hot in the oven but, the minute she finished her portion, she would view the rest as a second helping. 'Eh'll eat it for my supper,' she said.

Then one day the mass X-ray van came to the dairy Mum joined her fellow workers in the queue to be X-rayed without a worry in the world. Even when she was recalled, she told Nellie, 'It'll be my old pleurisy scar showing up. Eh've been X-rayed before and Eh got recalled then. What a worry Eh had until they told me it was just the scarring due to the pleurisy Eh had in 1947.'

'Oh Eh do hope so,' said Nellie, with a worried frown, 'because Eh've been recalled as well although they did say it could be because Eh didn't remove everything with metal in it.'

Mum laughed. 'You're no wearing a bullet-proof vest, are you?'

This cheered Nellie up and she remarked, 'It's easy to see what kind of pictures you like to go and see. Is it the gangster ones with Edward G. Robertson and Peter Lorre?'

The two women, along with all the folk who had been recalled, went back for another X-ray and, as it turned out, Nellie got the all-clear but Mum was told the shattering news that there was a shadow on her lung that wasn't anything to do with the old scar. We were devastated by this grim news, especially Mum. Doctor Jacob said it meant hospital treatment and he added, 'This will mean a stay in Ashludie Hospital and it will be for months rather than weeks. It all depends on how fast the shadow responds to treatment.'

As far as Mum was concerned, this was a death sentence. Wasn't it a well-known fact that tuberculosis patients were sent to sanatoriums like Ashludie to be wheeled out into the fresh air every day, whether in rain, hail, snow or wind, in the vain hope that the elements would provide the cure? But as we all knew, a cure wasn't always on the cards.

She was so upset the week before her admission to hospital that Nellie, Bella and Aggie, who for once didn't mention her family, all tried to cheer her up. But Mum had made up her mind she was being sent away to die. The manageress of the restaurant gave me the morning off to take Mum to the hospital. She had been fretting about her old dressing gown, one minute saying how tatty it was, then the next saying it didn't matter, she wouldn't be wearing it for long.

George and I decided to buy her a lovely red, velvet, full-length housecoat that she had spied in Marks & Spencers and had fallen in love with. We also added a fluffy, winceyette nightdress and cosy slippers.

'There now Mum, you'll look like a real toff,' we said, as I packed a small suitcase that Mrs Miller had lent her.

Mrs Miller was full of sympathy as she stood and watched us leave the close. She shoved a small bag of sweets into my hand as we passed. 'Put these barley sugars in her bag in case your mum is feeling sick on the bus.'

With Mum giving the house and Mrs Miller a last backward glance, almost to say she wouldn't be seeing it ever again, we set off for the bus station at Lindsay Street. Special buses ran from there right to the hospital, which was very convenient. It was possible to catch an ordinary service bus to Monifieth but that meant a long walk to the hospital which sat in its own extensive grounds above the village.

We arrived just before dinnertime on one of the coldest, wettest days of the autumn and, as we walked through the grounds towards the main door, leaves were cascading down on to the driveway before being whisked away by a fierce wind that swirled around our ankles. I recalled the night at the railway station when Ally had left for Cyprus. The wind had blown the debris around that night and now it was the turn of the leaves and dead flowers. For a brief moment I wondered if all the sad upheavals and partings in my life were to be heralded by nasty, cold winds.

The nurse took Mum away, holding her by the elbow while carrying her small case in her other hand. She turned as they set off along the corridor. 'You can wait till your mother gets settled and then you can say cheerio.'

Although this was meant in a light sense, as in 'Cheerio, I'll see you tomorrow', Mum turned with a stricken look on her face and I felt terrible. I gave her little wave and said I would wait.

I later found her lying in bed in a small, glassed veranda with a lovely view over the parklands to the sea beyond. Although the water wasn't visible, you just knew it was there. There were five other beds in this ward but they were all vacant. I was allowed to sit for a wee while until the doctor arrived. Mum was upset but tried to hide it by chatting about the household arrangements. 'Now you should manage all right. George usually makes his own tea so you won't have to rush home from work for that.'

This was fine because, with George having his early morning start, he was normally home by early afternoon, while I didn't get finished at Draffen's until after six o'clock at night.

'Another thing,' she said, 'if you have any trouble with the insurance money just go to the office in Tay Street.'

My mind was on this terribly silent ward and I hoped she wasn't going to be left on her own all the time. If she was, her imagination would be working in treble time.

'Aye, Mum, you're not to worry about us. We'll be fine. Now, promise me you'll eat your meals in here and no just pick at your food.'

She nodded, giving me a look that suggested the cook wouldn't be needed for long in her case. When the nurse came back, Mum jumped out of bed and began to put on her lovely red housecoat. The nurse started to object but Mum dismissed this.

'Eh'm just going to wave to my lassie from the window.'

'Eh'll be back at visiting time tonight,' I promised as I left the ward.

As I walked down the drive towards the bus, I could see her red-coated figure at the window and I kept looking back and waving until she was a mere coloured dot at the far end of the wild and windswept grounds. I almost ran back to tell her to pack her small suitcase and come home with

392

me. After all, if she was going to die then it should be at home but I didn't.

Back in Draffen's, Hannah was waiting with a sympathetic ear, which was nice of her because she had her own problems. She was a divorced mother with two teenage sons to support. As usual, money was the universal problem or, rather, the lack of it. 'Eh think there's so much can be done with TB now. You know, new drugs,' she said.

'Oh, Eh hope you're right, Hannah!' was all I could say. After all, she hadn't witnessed the thin, ill figure standing at the window.

After work, I caught the bus to the hospital and was surprised to find Nellie and Bella waiting. 'We thought we would pay a wee visit to your mum,' they said simply and this gesture touched me immensely. Mum may not have enjoyed good health or money but she was blessed with good friends.

'How was she when you left?' asked Nellie. I shrugged in a noncommittal way. I felt I didn't want to describe the sad figure in the red coat.

Mum was lying in bed, dressed in her pale, winceyette nightie and looking frail and ill, her face almost the same colour as the pillowcase. However, one thing I was pleased to see was that the five other beds were now occupied. 'Did these folk come in after you, Mum?' I asked, glancing around the now-busy veranda with its patients and visitors.

'No, they were in a day room, Eh think,' she said. 'They all appeared in a bunch at teatime.'

Nellie was looking sad. 'Are you feeling any

393

better, Molly? Did they mention what treatment you're getting?'

'Aye, Eh'm getting dosed up with something called Streptomycin,' she said wearily. 'And here was me thinking all my problems were caused by my teeth. Do you mind me saying that was what caused my tired, washed-out feeling, Nellie?'

Nellie nodded. As usual, it was left to Bella to cheer up the conversation. 'Och, you'll be out of here in no time. Just you wait and see.'

CHAPTER 28

Of all the wonder drugs in the antibiotic range, Streptomycin, which was discovered in 1944, was the magic cure for tuberculosis. Until the 1950s, TB was still a big killer, a sword of Damocles that hung over and wiped out entire families. There was no cure except for the fresh-air treatment, which saw long rows of beds being wheeled out in all kinds of weather, including snow showers which landed like a white quilt on the patients' beds.

But now that Mum knew she wasn't facing a death sentence, she cheered up considerably. Of course, she wasn't as ill as some of the patients in the hospital, mainly because the X-ray had picked up the shadow on her lung in time to be helped by the new drug. Sadly, for people with the disease now far advanced in their lungs, the initial treatment was an operation to remove the damaged tissue. One such patient was a young girl who was at the far end of Mum's ward.

'There's a lassie in here who says she knows you,' said Mum, on my third visit. She lowered her voice. 'She's due to have an operation this week because her lung is damaged.' She sounded sad.

When I approached the girl's bed, I was astounded to see Janie, my old school friend from the Rosebank Primary days. I hadn't seen her in years because by the time we reached Primary Six her family moved to a new house. This took her away from the school and the terrible house they occupied in Rose Lane. The war had just ended and with houses difficult to come by most people took what they could get. Sometimes these dwellings were pretty bad and run down. I could still recall the day they got the key for a brand new house. Janie's dad was telling us all about it and he was very excited. Her mum was busy making the family meal but she was as excited as the rest.

We sat and chatted about the old days but I didn't like to mention the forthcoming operation. I waited to see if she would bring the subject up but she didn't. Afterwards, I wondered if she had wanted me to say something about it, but that's life, isn't it? You hesitate and then you lose the moment. That's what happened with Janie and me. The final bell went for the end of visiting and I was on my way home.

As I travelled home on the bus, I sincerely hoped everything would turn out well for her. Although she didn't go back to Mum's ward, I still visited her a few times and she seemed to be recovering. I never saw her again after she was discharged and I only hope she has had a long and happy life.

Because we were contacts of a TB patient, George and I had to have regular check-ups at the Chest Clinic in Constitution Road, a building that lay right across the road from the old cemetery. During Mum's many years in the jute mill, we had passed this brick-built building many times on our trips to Little Eddy's but never knew what lay behind the facade. We certainly knew now. On our first visit, we were both given an X-ray but, because they were negative, we were told to report back in six months' time.

This was a blessing for me because I was on the hunt for a house. This chore was like searching for gold. Although I had our name down with the Corporation, we were well down on the points list. Even people with two or three children often didn't have enough qualifying points so I reckoned my only chance lay with the private factors who rented out flats in the older types of tenements. Every day, on my time off, I did the round of these factors, mainly in Union Street and Commercial Street. The answer was always the same: 'Nothing today, sorry.' Some days I had to steel myself to enter the offices because the girls who were manning the typewriters always looked at me in exasperation.

As Christmas approached, I was glad that this year was almost over. Ally still had 134 days to go and it was time to make up his festive parcel, which was sent at a cheap rate because it was going to a BFPO address. Peggy and I clubbed together to fill a large box with cake and short-bread, jam, marmalade and chocolate as well as mundane items like razor blades. Mum gave me a couple of pounds to add a wee luxury to cheer up the austere conditions of army life.

George decided he would bake a cake for Mum. He iced it and then spent a few nights painstakingly decorating it. Piping on the 'Merry Xmas', he patiently formed the letters and if they went a bit askew he scraped them off and started again. I wasn't looking forward to the festive season as this was my second Christmas alone since being married. At least Mum had been at home last year and it hadn't felt so lonely. Fortunately, the restaurant was to be closed only for one day at Christmas and one day at Hogmanay and that didn't leave time to mope.

We took the finished cake to the hospital on Christmas Eve. The place was looking bright and cheerful with a decorated tree and colourful garlands hanging from the ward walls. Ashludie also had a lovely café which was used by the patients and visitors alike. Mum would meet us there as it took away the hospital atmosphere, for a short while at least. She was delighted with her cake. George apologised for the untidy lettering but she waved this aside.

'Och, you're still learning, which is no thanks to the beggars at the Sosh,' she said, holding the cake up so it could be admired by all and sundry. 'Now, what have you got organised for tomorrow?'

Ally's mum and dad had asked us for the day to

their house but I felt it was too much work for Peggy, what with Anne, who was still at school, and Peggy's two brothers Davie and Robbie. I had said we would see them later in the week. Mum was looking at George.

'Are you going anywhere tomorrow?'

George had planned to go dancing in the evening but apart from that we had nothing planned. Like me, George loved his dancing but he wanted to learn the steps properly, like a ballroom dancer, while I had been content with the music and the company. George was to go on to take part in amateur dancing competitions with his dancing partner, Jean. They always looked so glamorous together – especially at one competition which was held at the Albert Hall in London.

When we got back home, we had a visit from Nellie. She handed over an envelope containing three pound notes. 'Molly was in the "menage" at work,' she said. 'You know, the Christmas Club. We've all added a wee thing to make sure you have a bit extra at this time of year.'

I was quite overcome with this unexpected kindness. 'Oh, Nellie, Eh don't know what to say! It's really good of all the workers to think of us. Tell them we said thank you very much.'

We knew what we would buy with this windfall. Now that Mum was spending some time in the day room and the café with her fellow patients, we decided to treat her to a new skirt and blouse from G.L. Wilson's department store. I would have liked to have gone to Draffen's but it was too expensive and well out of our price range.

By now, I was working in the Dining Room, which catered for a more middle-class clientele. Unlike the Cottage Room, this part of the restaurant had an à la carte menu which meant you could choose anything from the list as everything was priced individually.

One bugbear was the table stations. Wallace's had one of the fairest ways of dealing with the thorny issue of tips, a system in which everyone moved around the room like a giant clock and each got their fair share of good and bad tables. Draffen's, however, had static stations which had the same waitress all the time, week in and week out. This may have seemed a trivial situation to the customers but the tips were meant to top up a low wage. Some people earned a great wage with their tips while some others were on the hardship line.

Hannah was such a person and I often felt sorry for her as we both had rotten stations, tables tucked away in corners that were always the last to be filled. On the afternoon before Hogmanay, some of the girls decided to have a small celebration. 'Let's club together and buy a bottle of something,' suggested Millie, who was a proper devil. Not only did she have the very best station in the room but she wasn't averse to pinching the best customers if she could.

We were all non-drinkers but as we felt we all needed cheering up we chipped in with two shillings each. Port and lemonade must have been Millie's tipple because she arrived back with a bottle of each. The dining room was an attractive place with its large corner bay windows

(Millie's station) but another pleasant place was the pantry. This also had a large window which opened inwards like a door and overlooked the busy Nethergate and Tally Street. We all sat with our tiny drinks and voicing our hopes for the coming year.

'It'll no be long before your man's back,' said Hannah, clutching a small tumbler in her plump, pink hand.

'Eh know but it doesn't look as if Eh'll ever find a house. The office girls are getting tired of seeing me. Eh'm sure they dread it when Eh appear,' I said, a feeling of despair hanging over me like a grey, wet cloud.

'You'll never get a house by going in every day,' said Millie, butting in. 'You have to know if someone's giving up a house then you go and ask for the key.'

So it was as simple as that, I thought. No wonder I was making no headway. All I had to do was camp outside some tenements and watch for a flitting van. I didn't say anything because she was probably being helpful, which, according to the cynics, didn't happen often.

I went to see Mum on Hogmanay and George went dancing at night. I stayed in. I was working on New Year's Day because of the annual sale and, anyway, I didn't feel festive.

'Guess who Eh saw tonight on my way to the dancing?' said George, when he arrived back later. With no answer forthcoming from my direction, he said, 'Auntie Evelyn and Uncle Jack.'

'Where was this?' I asked, feeling guilty over the fact that we never paid them a visit now, not like

400

when we were children.

Evelyn was our dad's sister but, as he was no longer in our lives since going off to Grimsby all those years ago, we hadn't kept up with his family like we should have. Evelyn and Jack had been very good to us and we should have treated them better.

'It was beside Well Road. Just across from Isles Lane where they stay with Granny Macdonald.'

'Did you tell them Mum was in Ashludie? Or that Eh was married?' I asked, only to be amazed when he shook his head to both questions.

'No, Eh just said hello in the passing. Maybe they didn't know it was me. In fact, Eh wish now that Eh had asked after Granny but Eh was sure they wouldn't remember me.'

'Don't be daft! Of course they would have remembered you. You should have introduced yourself,' I said.

Obviously this piece of advice was too late and, over all the years since that incident, I've always regretted not getting in touch. I've told myself that life was too busy with all our worries but that's just an excuse. I feel like saying, 'You were so good to us, Evelyn and Jack, and I'm sorry.'

One consolation at this time was the fact that the calendar for 1958 showed the five months leading up to Ally's homecoming, not like last year when it seemed like an eternity until his discharge. I was glad to get back to work and Draffen's sale generated a great deal of business. The store was thronged with bargain hunters and most of them found their way eventually up in the lift to the restaurants. The tables were full of weary-eyed women who sat down with loud sighs and piles of parcels around their feet.

'Two Russian teas and two macaroons, please,' said one elderly woman who looked like some royal personage. Perhaps she was a Grand Duchess of all the Russias, but her friend kept referring to her as 'Jean'. The Russian teas were served in tall glasses encased in a silver filigree holder and they always looked elegant with their slices of lemon floating on the top. The macaroons were a speciality of the restaurant. A limited number were made every day by an elderly baker who seemed to bake this item and nothing else.

Occasionally, the clothes department would put on a fashion show. Two or three very slim and pretty models would swan around the tables, weaving sinuously between the piles of parcels, their expensive dresses swishing seductively as they floated around. Every now and then, they would stop to let the customers admire the merchandise and the lovely designer hats, their heads tilted to show them off to the best advantage. Sometimes a fur coat would be draped around a shoulder and these coats were from a different world to Aggie's musquash.

'What is the price of the ocelot coat?' asked one customer, lifting her spectacles to her eyes to get a better look at the garments while the model paused to discreetly tell her the price. Should the customer's voice be loud, the waitresses, who normally kept out of the way of the haughty models, would overhear.

'A thousand pounds!' we would say in awe. 'In that case, we'll have two each!'

For us workers, with our paltry wage of under four pounds a week, these desirable clothes were but a dream. I didn't mind that, mostly because I didn't fancy any of the fashions on show. One thing that did annoy us was the fact that this wage would have been larger if we didn't have the three shillings and sixpence a day meal allowance deducted from it. This would have reasonable if the food was decent but, to be honest, it was barely eatable.

Most days we got spiced ham with potatoes and vegetables. The ham had clearly been cut for a couple of days because it was showing signs of old age. Each slice had a dehydrated, curled-up look with an inch of dark red around the rim. This wonderful gourmet meal was followed by reheated two- or three-day-old steamed puddings which had been left over from a previous lunchtime's menu.

As well as this daylight robbery, another annoyance was the ashtray farce. These were made from porcelain and had the store logo printed on them. They cost twelve shillings and sixpence to make. Should you be careless enough to break one, then the twelve and six was deducted from your pay. One day I did drop one and it broke cleanly in half. The manageress said to take it to the restaurant manager and chef, who ran the place like an omnipotent little god. He pursed his lips as he surveyed the two halves, an expression which annoyed me so much that before he could open his mouth, I waded in. 'Eh'm really sorry for the breakage but it was an accident and Eh'm no paying for it. It's a terrible job if you can't have a breakage without having to fork out twelve and six from a measly wage, a wage that has to have tips to supplement it, and if Eh have to pay, then Eh'm going to see Mr Draffen himself.'

I sat back, fully expecting to be given a week's notice but I didn't care. I had watched Mum struggling for years trying to earn a decent wage and I was now in a similar situation. Perhaps if she hadn't worked herself so hard in her job she wouldn't now be a patient in Ashludie Hospital.

'I expect the two halves can be glued together so I'll say no more about it,' he said, while I sat in stunned silence.

Later, the manageress approached and warned me. 'You have a real streak of aggression in you that isn't very attractive,' she said, before heading off in the direction of Millie the Minx, who as usual looked so angelic that the only thing missing was her halo.

I gazed after her in amazement. As far as I was concerned, I was only sticking up for myself and if that was unattractive aggression then so be it.

Later that night I met Bella and Aggie at the hospital. Strangely enough, they both had good news to relate. Bella arrived first and this gave her the chance to get a word in before Aggie monopolised the conversation with her garbled stories. 'What do you think of this, Molly?' said Bella, handing over a letter. 'We've got the key to a new house!'

Mum was pleased for her. 'Where about is it?'

'It's in St Mary's Woods and it's a semi-detached house with three bedrooms and a big garden in the front and a drying green at the back. We're all pleased and it'll be such a difference to Norrie's Pend.'

'Eh'll have to come and visit you when Eh get out of here, which should be in four months' time. Eh'm making good progress,' Mum said, which was the truth because she had put on a bit of weight and her colour looked quite pink and healthy. 'The only thing Eh can say is thank goodness for Streptomycin.'

I remembered Janie. Mum said she was also making progress. 'There's so much can be done now for TB,' said Mum. 'It's no like in the bad old days.'

Aggie then appeared and Bella stood up to say cheerio. 'Eh'll be back in to see you and give you all the gen about my new house.'

She passed Aggie in the doorway and gave her a big wave before she took her ample frame towards the homewards bus. It wasn't that she disliked Aggie but, like the rest of us, she sometimes found her a bit overpowering with her chatter. Aggie was talking even before she reached the bed. The café was only open for the afternoon, which meant the evening visiting was done in the ward.

'Wait till Eh tell you my good news!' she shouted out, while the woman three beds away looked at her in surprise, thinking Aggie was heading towards her as a visitor. The expression on her face was a picture. You could almost see her brain searching desperately to identify this stranger.

'Eh'm saying, wait till you hear this!' Aggie repeated while a mere few yards away and much to the other patient's relief.

'Heavens! This is the second bit of good news Eh've had tonight,' said Mum in amazement.

Aggie's face fell at the thought of coming second in the good-news stakes.

'Well, Aggie, what is it?'

Aggie, who had recovered quickly from the ignominy of not having the monopoly on glad tidings, puffed herself up in readiness to launch forth. 'It's Babs, isn't it? She's just gone and got married to her man! You know the one – him that took her out for a date and the one that works beside her and Marvin.'

As with Bella's house news, Mum was really glad to hear this wedding news. 'Oh, Eh'm pleased for her and Eh hope she has a long and happy life.'

'Well, meh man and Eh were a bit put out by the suddenness of it but Senga has written to say that was what Babs wanted and maybe after the last time it's for the better. We've promised Senga and Babs and Marvin and Ritchie – that's his name, by the way – that we'll go out and visit them. Mr Robb said that he was going to work lots of overtime and save up as hard he can just to pay for the return tickets.'

I had been telling Mum about my search for a house and, after Aggie departed, she asked me how I was getting on. Alas, I didn't have good news like Bella and Aggie.

Then a week later I met Millie on the stairs as we both did the four-minute-mile dash to clock in.

'Eh've heard about a house key that's being

handed back today,' she told me. 'Shepherd, the factor in Commercial Street, is the one dealing with it and the house is in Victoria Road. My pal's sister had a look at it but she doesn't want it.'

I couldn't believe my ears. Was this someone who had the key to a precious house and was refusing it? I was suddenly suspicious. 'Is there something wrong with the house? Why is she handing the key back?'

Millie was honest about it. 'The house needs an awful lot done to it and quite a bit of money spent on it. That's why she's turned it down.'

I could barely wait until my lunch hour and, deciding to forgo the mummified Spam, I made a beeline for the factor's office. The girl behind the typewriter gazed at me as I burst in. Her hands were coolly poised over the keyboard while I was all red-faced and perspiring. Here was another unattractive facet to match the aggression, this sweating.

'I was wondering if you have a key for a house to rent?' I said, aware that I resembled something the cat had brought home while this delicate creature with her prim, grey twinset, neat tweed skirt and double row of pearls around her neck sat in cool contemplation.

'No, I'm sorry we don't,' she said, looking down at her fingers on the keyboard.

For a terrible minute I thought I was too late. 'Have you handed a key to someone this morning?' I almost bellowed at this ethereal creature but she shook her head. So far so good, I thought. 'We haven't had a key to give out for weeks

407

now,' she said.

As far as she was concerned the matter was closed but I knew this wasn't true – not if Millie had got her facts right. I decided to give it one last shot. 'Eh heard that a key was going to be handed back this morning. My colleague told me.'

I gazed wide-eyed at her but she gave no sign that this was true. I pushed on regardless. 'This house is in Victoria Road and this person doesn't want it so Eh was told to come down here and see you because she doesn't want it.' I stopped, aware I was repeating myself, which wasn't giving out the right image. After all, who wanted a tenant who was daft?

'The house is in Victoria Road,' I said again. I couldn't help all this gabbling.

The woman looked blankly at me for a full minute while I thought I had suddenly sprouted a beard. She then went over to another typist who sat at the other end of this office. After a quiet word with her, she went over to a cabinet and took out an enormous key with a cardboard label tied with blue string. She placed it on the counter before my amazed eyes.

'This is the key for 63 Victoria Road. You can have a look at it but we need to know right away if you want to take it.'

I almost leapt ten feet in the air with delight but instead I grabbed the key with a shout of grateful thanks and rushed up the road to see it.

The flat was directly above Jessie Bell's tiny newsagent's shop and was reached by a long sloping close and a circular stair which led on to a plettie. At first I though it was the flat at the top of the stairs because it looked vacant but the key wouldn't fit. I then noticed another curtainless window which overlooked the plettie and the clock tower of St Andrew's church. My delight soon turned to utter dismay. The last tenant had removed the fireplace and taken it away with them. In fact, the entire wall looked like it was in danger of imminent collapse. Apart from that, the rest of the house just needed decorating but it was obviously the partly demolished wall that had frightened off the previous key holder, luckily for me.

I stepped over the grey debris that had landed almost in the middle of the room and had been ground into the floorboards. The sun was shining through the dusty, smeared windows. I then looked at the two bedrooms which were darker and sunless because they faced the road and the bleak stone wall of the jute mill. Before I left to return to work, I knocked at the door across the tiny lobby. It was opened by a chubby, cheery-looking woman who had grey, curly hair and friendly eyes. Dressed in a floral overall, her name was Mrs Ririe and I liked her immediately.

'Excuse me,' I said, 'Eh'd like to introduce myself. Eh'm going to be moving in next door – at least Eh will when Eh get it done up.'

'You'll find it's in an awfy state because him that was in the house took the fireplace out to sell it,' she said. 'He was hammering and banging at it for ages. Wait and Eh'll show you the toilet.'

She returned with another big key and opened the door that was on the plettie. 'We're lucky because it's just the two houses here that share the toilet. We take turns to clean it as well as our turn at cleaning the stairs.'

After leaving Mrs Ririe, I was left with just enough time to visit the factor's office to accept the house. This was noted in a large ledger and I was told to return to the office the next day to sign the tenancy form and pay a quarter's rent. By the time I reached Draffen's, I was over the moon. I felt really lucky because if it hadn't been for Millie I would never have had the nerve to keep badgering the girl in the office and would have taken at face value her denials of having any vacant houses.

I did feel a bit sorry for Pat, one of my colleagues who was also married and searching desperately for a house, like the entire married population of Dundee. I hoped she would land lucky and I couldn't wait to tell Mum and Peggy about it. With just over a hundred days to Ally's release from the army, I hoped to do a bit of cosmetic work to the flat as well as installing a new tiled fireplace. Apart from that, we could spend time decorating it and buying the furniture after his enforced military training was over. Then Mum would have her bedroom back when she returned from the hospital.

CHAPTER 29

Peggy almost had a purple fit when she saw the house. It was the wall with the removed fireplace that was giving everyone the wrong impression of the place. For that I was grateful because it had been this gaping hole that had put off other would-be tenants. If it hadn't been for this, I would not be standing amid a pile of rubble with my mother-in-law, trying to show the flat's potential to her.

'You have to imagine the room with a new tiled fireplace in it and the wall cemented over. Then when it's papered and newly painted it'll be looking great.'

She stood transfixed in the middle of the debris and gazed at the wall and ceiling. 'You know something,' she said, 'it's a wonder when this fireplace was removed that the entire building didn't collapse as well.'

Mrs Ririe, who had come in with us on our arrival, voiced the same concern. 'And, to make matters worse,' she said, 'He did it himself and didn't get any expert help.'

'Well, that's no a problem because Eh've bought a fireplace from a shop in Ann Street and they're coming next week to install it. Then you'll see such a big difference,' I said with pride.

Mum, who hadn't seen the wanton destruction, was pleased that I had found a small place of our own. I told her about the fireplace without going into details. 'Another thing Eh'll need is a gas cooker. Eh suppose Eh'll have to buy one.'

Mum said she had heard of gas cookers being hired from the gas showroom in Commercial Street. 'You should go and ask them. It'll cost a lot less than laying out the money for a new one.'

The following two weeks were spent running around the various shops. I managed to hire a new cooker from the showroom and the rental charges were indeed a lot less than buying it outright. I also spent a lot of time in the paint and wallpaper shops and the furniture stores. Although I initially thought that decisions about furniture and decorating should be made jointly, I just got carried away and, by the time Ally was demobbed, the flat was fully furnished and decorated.

The fireplace men spent a whole day just plastering the wall before installing the fireplace, such was the damage that had to be repaired, and I was told this would have to be added to the bill. In fact, the men said they had never seen anything like it. I held up my hands and said, 'Not guilty. It wasn't me.'

Every Wednesday, I went to see my in-laws after visiting Mum at the hospital and it was lovely to arrive and sit down to a great, hot, home-cooked meal. Peggy was also counting the days to her son's homecoming but, unlike me, she would score the days off the calendar until the end of May. She said one night after my weekly visit, 'If you need a help with papering or painting, just give me a shout and Eh'll help.'

By the middle of February, the fireplace and cooker were installed and, just as predicted, the room took on a different aspect. One night Peggy, Ally's sister Ann and I set about stripping the old wallpaper from the kitchen walls and she couldn't believe her eyes when she now saw the neat room with its creamy-coloured tiled fireplace with the brown trim. The gleaming white cooker stood beside the newly scrubbed kitchen cupboard and everything looked shipshape.

'Eh never thought this room would ever look like this,' she said in a surprised voice.

I tried hard to suppress a slightly smug feeling, knowing full well how smugness always led to some catastrophe in my life. I just looked pleased. We set to work with wallpaper scrapers and, although we didn't know it at the time, this job would take a whole week. There was layer after layer of different wallpapers on the walls, each one showing elusive snatches of the various tastes over the past hundred years by the look of it. Ann was busy scraping and suddenly uncovered a sheet of newspaper showing the death of Marie Lloyd. The room had obviously been papered with newspapers in 1922.

We eventually reached the virgin plaster and it had been painted in a dark green which must have made the room appear like the inside of a bottle. Then I heard through the grapevine that the small ads in the paper were full of handymen who papered rooms for thirty shillings a room, with the owner supplying the wallpaper of course.

The man arrived on a Sunday and I left him

with the six rolls of lovely cream-coloured paper which had a gold leaf spray printed on it. When I returned in the early afternoon with sandwiches and tea, he was almost finished. It was very well done and I was delighted. However, when Peggy arrived later, she said, 'Should the spray no be sitting up the way instead of drooping downwards?'

'Eh don't think so. Eh think it's been put up the right way,' I said emphatically.

Right up to the time we left the house in the early 1960s, I was never sure who was right – Peggy or me.

By now it was approaching D-Day, as in Demob Day. Determined that one room in the house should be perfect, I spent a Saturday afternoon in Grant's furniture shop in the Murraygate. I chose a dining-room suite in dark oak. The salesman showed me the latest in a sideboard, namely a cocktail cabinet. Apparently this innovation was extremely popular and highly sought after by the good folk of Dundee. Why this should be was a mystery. I doubted if a tiny minority in the city had ever tasted a cocktail, let alone have the expertise to mix one, but I was impressed and planned to put fancy tumblers in it.

I also bought twelve yards of red linoleum (which was fitted by a workman from the shop), two red, uncut moquette fireside chairs and a large grey rug. I can recall how thrilled I was when everything in place, including the wedding presents and the small radio and Dansette record player which we bought before Ally went into the army, paying it up at a few shillings a week.

It was now twenty days and counting and I think his parents were more worked up than I was. It also looked like Mum would be coming home not long after Ally so events were moving fast. There was still trouble in Cyprus between the Turks and the Greeks and I hoped that this wouldn't flare up again like Suez. George and I had another six-monthly check-up but once again this proved negative. It would appear that Mum's infection hadn't spread to her family.

At work, Hannah was my confidante and she listened to all my fears regarding Ally's return. I was so sure that something would happen to prevent this.

'Of course it'll no,' said Hannah. 'There's conscripts being demobbed every day. In fact, there's been three in my street in the last couple of weeks.'

'Eh expect Eh'm worrying over nothing,' I admitted.

Hannah was annoyed at Millie for palming her off with three well-known non-tippers while keeping her table for a party of good tippers. It has to be said that people couldn't always leave a tip and I often thought it very unfair of the management to expect the public to finance our wages.

'Did you see madam showing folk to my table?' said Hannah, looking cross. 'That's no her job but the manageress never seems to notice it. Eh need my tips as much as her. Eh've a family to feed as well.'

Although I agreed wholeheartedly with Hannah, ever since the episode of the house I tried to forget Millie's manipulative behaviour. I still couldn't understand why she had given me the information about the returned key but she had, and I would be ever grateful to her.

Ally was due home about the end of May and, although I didn't know the exact date, I was aiming to have the house finished for around the 23rd of the month. Suddenly, on 14 May he appeared at the door early in the morning. George, who was getting ready for work, answered the door in such a nonchalant, laid-back way that I had to laugh.

'Oh, it's you, Ally. Come in,' was his response to someone who had been away for almost two years, which to me seemed more like a lifetime.

We went to see Mum in hospital and she teased him over his super suntan. 'Eh'll have to join up in the army if it gives me a great colour like you!' she laughed.

The entire week was spent visiting relations and friends. Then we spent time at the house, papering the two bedrooms. To begin with, I decided to help with this job but as I approached a section of wall with a strip of pasted paper, an enormous spider scuttled up the wall in an effort to escape possible death by decoration. In a panic, I dropped the long strip of paper all over the floor, my feet and the entire front of my frock, leaving a sticky gunge that took ages to clean off. After that little disaster, I stuck to painting rather than being stuck to the wall.

Within a couple of weeks of Ally returning to work, Mum was discharged from the hospital as fit and cured. This was a far cry from her first day there. She wasn't allowed to go back to work until her all-clear X-ray which would be in a month's time. She really missed the company of the hospital and as they had all been long-stay patients, friendships had been formed.

Nellie was a constant visitor and Bella made the journey every fortnight from her new house in St Mary's Woods. It was also at this time that I heard of a job in the DECS (the Dundee Eastern Co-operative Society – part of the Sosh) shop at the corner of South George Street. The wage was far in excess of the one paid by Draffen's and I was thrilled to get it.

It was as if I had been transferred back to my childhood days with Cathie and her daughter, Sylvia. During those days, we paid many a trip to the Sosh in the Hawkhill and I was now working in a branch of this great institution. I noticed that the procedure hadn't changed over the years. The customers still placed their books in the narrow wooden compartment on the counter and an assistant would pull the bottom book through. They would then call out the name loudly in the direction of the crowd of waiting women who stood patiently with their shopping bags.

It was like a time capsule from Cathie's era except that the shelves were now stacked high with grocery items while huge mounds of butter sat on the marble slab and gigots of ham hung from hooks. The bacon slicer was still in the expert hands of one person, namely a Mr Allen, who was also the under-manager. I loved this job with its variety of tasks and the customers who

417

always had time for a chat over the purchases of their bacon, eggs and butter.

One morning I was watching Mr Allen slicing his bacon when I suddenly felt unwell and had to hurry out to the back green which lay behind the back door. I felt better after a few minutes in the fresh air but couldn't bear to think about any fatty foods like the butter, margarine and the cooking fats. A week later, I was at Mum's house doing the washing. We had treated her to a washing machine, which was a great boon to her. I also got to use it, which was a great boon to me.

Aggie appeared in her usual good form. 'How are you keeping, Molly?' she asked. Then, without waiting for an answer, she immediately leapt in with her chatter, her face beaming, 'Wait till Eh tell you the latest news. Eh'm to be a granny! Babs and Ritchie are expecting their first bairn. What do you think of that? It's due in August next year.'

Mum just looked at her over the top of her glasses. 'That's good news, Aggie. Do you want to hear mine? Eh'm to be a granny as well – in July next year.'

Aggie gave me a look as if to suggest I should have waited till Babs had announced her condition before spoiling her mother's big announcement.

'Well, imagine that,' she said without feeling. 'Still, maybe Babs will be early and Maureen will be late and we'll have our grandchildren at the same time.'

The woman was impossible, I thought, as I turned back to the week's pile of dirty clothes.

What Mum and I hadn't told Aggie was the fact that this was my second pregnancy. The first had resulted in a miscarriage six months earlier. I can still recall the smell and atmosphere of the ward in Maryfield Hospital and the different symptoms of the various women who were in for one ailment or another in their pregnancies. All were as worried as I was.

Afterwards, the nurse, who was obviously trying to be sympathetic, said the baby had been perfectly formed. I've never forgotten that distressing news and wished I hadn't been told. I thought what I had lost was a bunch of cells and now it hit me hard when I realised I had lost another human being. I mentally gave the baby a name, Charlie, after Uncle Charlie, a name I thought would have suited either a boy or a girl.

But I was now expecting again and the sick spells were becoming worse. I was finding it very difficult to hide these from the manager, who normally sat in his glass-fronted office every day. I sometimes had to leave a customer standing in mid-order while I rushed outside. After a couple of minutes I would return as if nothing had happened. Although I can laugh at this behaviour now, at the time it wasn't so funny. The strange thing was that not one customer ever complained or even mentioned their runaway assistant – this Houdini of the Sosh.

Then the sickness passed as suddenly as it began. I was now feeling great, which made the manager's conversation all the more annoying. I knew my overall was getting tighter every week but I didn't think it was that bad until he asked me into his office to ask if I was expecting.

I had to tell the truth: 'Yes I am.'

He looked quite apologetic. 'Eh'm afraid you'll have to put your notice in. The company has a strict rule that once a pregnant woman starts to show, she has to leave. We think it offends the customers, and, another thing, this job can be very heavy with lifting boxes and that would be a worry for us.'

The strange thing about this sex discrimination was the fact that I accepted it, just as thousands of women had done before me and would do for a few more years to come. In fact, I was lucky because, if I had been employed in any of the professions like nursing, I would have had to give up work when I was married, let alone on becoming pregnant.

I went to Doctor Jacob Junior, who was now in practice with his father and he put me on the insurance until the birth, which was five-and-a-half months away. It was just my hard luck that my bump had been noticed.

Aggie arrived for tea one afternoon. She had been harping on about never being invited to the house. We had furnished the big bedroom with a suite taken on hire purchase but the small bedroom was still unfurnished, except for the pram. This was a situation that bothered Mum because she was superstitious about the pram being in the house before the baby was born. But I had no other place to put it. I could hardly ask Mrs Ririe and her son David to store it in their tiny flat and Mum didn't have the room either.

The reason the pram was there early was

because it was secondhand. I saw an advert in the *Evening Telegraph* newspaper and I hurried to see it at an address in Dura Street. It was nothing special, just an ordinary grey Tansad pram, but it was almost new and selling for six pounds. I snapped it up right away, much to Mum's dismay.

Of course Aggie spotted it. 'Oh, Eh see you've got your pram. Should it be in the house before the baby's born?' she wondered, giving me a quizzical look.

I pretended I hadn't heard her. Mum just nodded her head as if to say, it's not just me that thinks it's unlucky.

'Our Babs has picked her baby carriage,' Aggie informed us, 'that's what they're called in California. Well, she's picked it and she says she's got her cot with the bumper pads around it.'

Mum stopped her. 'What on earth are bumper pads?'

'They're fancy padded bits that go round the sides of the cot to stop the bairns banging their heads off the bars, Eh suppose,' she said lamely. 'Well, that's the pram and cot sorted out. Babs had her baby shower the other night and she was inundated with baby things.'

She stopped when she saw our puzzled faces. 'A baby shower is just a get-together with your friends and work colleagues and neighbours and they all bring presents with them for the baby.'

'There you go, Maureen,' said Mum, 'just organise a baby shower and maybe you'll get soaked!'

Although we laughed, poor Aggie didn't get the joke. 'Well, Eh haven't seen a picture of the baby carriage but Ritchie was saying that it's really big and roomy.'

'What, as long as Senga's Cadillac?' said Mum with a cheeky smile.

'No, Molly, it's no as long as that. Eh told you Senga's car was as long as your room.'

Mum was penitent; 'Aye so you did Aggie.'

Aggie then turned her attention to our kitchen. 'Eh see you've just got linoleum. Do you no think you should get a carpet for the wee one to crawl around on? We got our carpet square from Henderson's and it was just a wee deposit and ten shillings a week.'

'No, Aggie, we can't afford a carpet with all the baby things we need,' I said through gritted teeth.

'Well, meh man was saying that we should go out to California in time to see our first grandchild and Eh think that's what we're going to do.'

Suddenly, Mum felt so sorry for her, being so far away from her two daughters. 'Aggie, that's what you both should do. Have a good holiday and see your family and the new bairn.'

I saw the two women out and walked down the stairs with them, these two soon-to-be-grandmothers.

We were in the middle of a heatwave when the baby decided to put in an appearance. Ally had an early morning start in the bakery but Mum had warned me to get in touch the minute I felt the slightest pain and I did, at seven-thirty one morning. I caught the bus across the road from the house and landed at her door. Mum went into a slight panic and said we should make our way to Maryfield Hospital right away. Because I didn't know any better, I agreed.

Needless to say, I was far too early and could have put off my admission until that evening but I made a mental note for a future time – if there was going to be another time. This decision was reached mainly because of the castor oil. The young nurse was quite matter of fact about it. 'We'll get you ready for bed then give you a dose of castor oil,' she said, vanishing into a room and appearing with a large glass of the obnoxious oily liquid. 'Now, swallow this and get into bed.'

I gazed in horror at the almost-full tumbler and reckoned it must have held a bottle and a half at least. The nurse arrived back and looked at the still full glass. 'Hurry up and swallow it. It's taste-less.'

I felt I had to be honest with this bright-eyed, bushy-tailed young woman who had obviously never tasted castor oil in her life.

'Eh'm sorry, nurse, but Eh don't think Eh can drink this. Eh'll be sick.'

'Oh, I see. Well, let me put some orange juice in it to make it taste better.'

She added an inch of orange liquid to the oil where it floated on top of the surface. By now, the orange-layered drink looked repulsive and I thought about heading to the bathroom where I could maybe pretend to swallow it as I tipped it down the sink.

Almost as if she had read my mind, she said, 'I'll come with you in case you throw it away.'

I gave her a hurt look as if to say, would I do that? I was at the bathroom door with my mentor following close behind me when she was called

423

away. I was almost rubbing my hands in glee when she returned with one of the cleaners. What was this nurse – a clairvoyant? The cleaner was a small, elderly woman who was stuffing her duster in her overall pocket.

'You better hurry up and drink it, lass, because if you don't they'll just give you another glass.'

I was seriously thinking I had entered the Spanish Inquisition by mistake when the cleaning woman said, 'Hold on a minute. Eh'll give you something to help.'

What, I thought, apart from a general anaesthetic, could possibly help? I was on the verge of tipping it away when she appeared with a slice of bread in her hand.

'Well, the old trick that my granny used to do is this – just hold your nose and drink it, then quickly eat this slice of bread. As you swallow it, it takes all the oiliness away.'

Because there was no escape for me, I did as I was told. It was touch and go whether the bread could be swallowed in time because I felt this terrible retching in my throat. Fortunately, the bread did the trick and the moment passed.

The day stretched into night and it got hotter and hotter. Ally arrived in the evening but was only allowed a few minutes to visit, the rule of husbands being present at the birth being still a thousand light years in the future. I was left alone with my thoughts and the gas and air machine, which I was seemingly using wrongly. I had somehow managed to make myself semi-conscious – a state that annoyed the night nurse.

'No, no, you're using it all wrong! You just put

the mask on your face when you feel a pain coming on. You don't leave it on all the time.'

I felt like telling her to go raffle herself but I was too stupefied because of the gas. Then after hours and hours that seemed like a lifetime and after hearing countless other babies being born, it was all over – albeit with forceps.

Meanwhile, Mum, who could never get the hang of a public phone, never mastering the intricacies of button A and button B, got Norah, one of her workmates, to phone for her. She received the news that a son had been delivered, if not by divine angels then by the divine help of the gas and air machine.

'Oh, thank goodness it's all over!' said Mum. 'Especially on the hottest night of the year.'

Ally arrived early in the morning, straight from his work, but I could barely keep my eyes open. The baby, named Alick after his father and grandfather, had weighed in at a massive nine pounds ten ounces, making him the heaviest baby in a ward full of tiny babies. In fact, the woman in the next bed pretended to become quite shirty when her little four-pound son was brought to her. 'Nurse, will you keep that big laddie out of sight when my wee lad gets brought in!'

A week later we went home. Ally had baked a cake with pink and blue icing – blue for the baby and pink because it was my twenty-first birthday.

Every morning, after the nappies were washed and hung out to dry in the downstairs courtyard, I would put the baby in his pram and we would set off on our adventures around the town.

Strangers and friends would stop and peer into the pram, remarking what a wonderful baby he was. I had to agree.

By coincidence, Violet and Margaret, my old dancing chums, had also had a son each and we would meet up with our prams and exchange notes about our little geniuses' habits. Mostly, however, I liked to go to see Mum every lunchtime, picking up her shopping on the way up the steep incline of the Hilltown, then staying for a quick snack with her before she went back to work. Then I did a quick hour of housework for her, as she wasn't that long out of Ashludie, before setting off back to my own house, holding on tight to the pram as we headed back down the hill.

One day Mum mentioned an old friend. 'Do you mind Katie who married and went off to Kuala Lumpur? Eh've often wondered how she was.'

How could I ever forget the wedding, the film-star looks of Ricky and the meal at the Val D'Or restaurant?

'It's just that Eh saw her the other day but she wasn't with Ricky. She was with this wee lad. But maybe it wasn't Katie,' said Mum, shaking her head.

But it had been Katie and we bumped into her on the Hilltown the following week. 'Eh was going to come up and see you, Molly,' she said, while a small man stood beside her. 'This is Gerry.'

Gerry said a cheerful hello and Mum gave Katie a look as if to say, where is Ricky? Katie got the message and said, 'Eh don't live in Kuala

Lumpur now. Eh got a divorce from Ricky. It was the jungle that got me – nothing to do week in or week out and nothing but heat and bushes and bugs and strange animals. Gerry and me have got a house in Lochee Road.' She gazed at the man with a tender, motherly look that I had never seen on her face before.

Mum was looking at Gerry and she said, 'Eh hope you don't think Eh'm cheeky but you're awfy like a lad called Jeemie that used to be a bookie's runner around the Hilltown years ago.'

Gerry's face brightened. 'Aye, that's my brother. He works in a bookie's shop now. Eh've never liked the horses but Jeemie loved them. Eh'm an electrician.'

As they set off arm in arm down the Hilltown, Mum remarked, 'Eh wonder how long that will last.'

I didn't say anything but, judging from the motherly look she gave her new love, I thought perhaps it would last a lot longer than her previous marriage.

One person I did feel sorry for was Mrs Miller. She would pop into Mum's house every lunchtime and she loved holding the baby.

'You know, you're really lucky to have such a healthy son. Poor Betty never looked like this, God rest her soul.'

'I know, Mrs Miller. I often wish Betty was still here. What a lot has happened over the past ten years!' I said sadly.

With the decade fast drawing to a close, I recalled how eventful it had been. Aggie's daughter had given birth to a girl and the proud

427

grandparents were now in California. No doubt Mum would see the clutch of photos at a later date and hear the detailed description of Aggie's now-extended family.

As for our family, it had been a decade of ups and downs, happiness and sadness, meetings and partings, illness and recovery. And although there had been death, there was also life – life in the shape of the four-month-old baby who was now asleep in his pram.

The publishers hope that this book has given you enjoyable reading. Large Print Books are especially designed to be as easy to see and hold as possible. If you wish a complete list of our books please ask at your local library or write directly to:

Magna Large Print Books
Magna House, Long Preston,
Skipton, North Yorkshire.
BD23 4ND

This Large Print Book for the partially sighted, who cannot read normal print, is published under the auspices of

THE ULVERSCROFT FOUNDATION

THE ULVERSCROFT FOUNDATION

... we hope that you have enjoyed this Large Print Book. Please think for a moment about those people who have worse eyesight problems than you ... and are unable to even read or enjoy Large Print, without great difficulty.

You can help them by sending a donation, large or small to:

**The Ulverscroft Foundation,
1, The Green, Bradgate Road,
Anstey, Leicestershire, LE7 7FU,
England.**
or request a copy of our brochure for more details.

The Foundation will use all your help to assist those people who are handicapped by various sight problems and need special attention.

Thank you very much for your help.